(1)

270.4 W16

Carnegie Library of Pittsburgh

4400 Forbes Ave.   Tel. MA 1-7300

FINES: One cent a day on juvenile cards and two cents a day on adult cards for each book kept overtime.

A borrower is responsible for books damaged while charged on his card.

See folder INFORMATION FOR BORROWERS for full details.

OEMCO

The Advance of Christianity Through the Centuries, Vol. II

General Editor: PROFESSOR F. F. BRUCE, M.A., D.D.

THE GROWING STORM

THE GROWING STORM

Sketches of Church History from A.D. 600 *to* A.D. 1350

by

G. S. M. WALKER

M.A.(*Oxon.*), B.D., Ph.D.(*St. Andrews*)
Lecturer in Church History and Doctrine in the
University of Leeds

Wm. B. Eerdmans Publishing Company
Grand Rapids 3, Michigan

Circ

This American Edition
is published by arrangement with
The Paternoster Press
London

CONTENTS

PREFACE

THE RISE AND FALL OF THE MEDIEVAL PAPACY IS, BROADLY speaking, the subject of these pages. Although it became a laughing-stock and was treated as a scandal, at the outset the Papacy had sought to embody a great idea—the same idea as that for which Scottish Covenanters were later to contend and suffer—that the spiritual is superior to the temporal, morality to politics, and Christ to the kingdoms of mankind. In the Middle Ages men grappled with problems not unlike our own; but the rôles were so surprisingly reversed that it is often hard for a modern mind to decide which was the angels' side. Monks were busy preaching puritan sermons, scholars were almost all fundamentalists, early "Protestants" were devoted to the Virgin, and there was a sort of evangelical revival which won warmer sympathy from the reigning Pontiff than would have been shown by an English Bishop of the eighteenth century. The various convictions, catholic and evangelical and liberal, were well and widely represented, sometimes fermenting together in the same brain; then, as tension mounted and the storm-clouds gathered, distinct parties drew apart in a struggle that was to lead on to the Reformation.

I have tried to illustrate this complex period by telling the story of a few characteristic lives. Enough background has been provided to make the narrative coherent, but some important matters have had to be omitted. I have given more space to the later part than to the earlier, and paid more attention to Western Europe than to the East. Footnotes have been deliberately excluded because, in attempting to cover seven and a half centuries, their length would have become prohibitive. However, the Bibliography should provide some guidance for further study of the facts; to the authorities there listed I owe almost all of what I may have gleaned.

My warm thanks are due to Professor F. F. Bruce and Mr. Howard Mudditt for suggesting this book; to The Paternoster Press and their printers for their speed and diligence; to Mrs. J. A. Hortox of Leeds for typing my untidy manuscript; and to my wife and daughter for prolonged forbearance.

G. S. M. WALKER

Department of Theology,
The University of Leeds
October 1961

7

CHAPTER I

GREGORY THE GREAT

AT WHAT POINT DID THE MIDDLE AGES BEGIN? THE ANSWER may vary according to the type of institution in which we happen to be interested, and it will depend in the last resort on how we define what is typically medieval; none the less, it is worth while attempting an answer to the query, if only to clarify the definition. The conversion of Constantine, and the foundation of the Christian Roman Empire in the fourth century, were events of momentous import for both the Church and the civilization of Europe. It may well be said that then there occurred the decisive break with antiquity; and from then onwards, in the East, there flows a continuous stream of Byzantine culture, radiating from that new capital beside the Bosporus, which bears the name of an Emperor revered by Eastern Christians as the "thirteenth Apostle." Yet the tolerance granted to Christianity by the fourth-century State did not at once make all things new. The fabric of imperial administration was unchanged, the conservative aristocracy remained stubborn in its paganism, and although official support began to make it fashionable to profess Christianity, yet the new faith continued for some time a minority religion. The education, the intellectual climate of the period was still classical, and Western Europe had to wait for the barbarian invasions of the fifth century before the old order completely disappeared. Indeed, in the West, it was the fusion of Teutonic and Roman elements which produced the medieval synthesis. By now, the orthodox faith had been defined in the first four ecumenical councils; the papacy, ruling in a Rome that had been deserted by the Emperor, now acquired a status that was genuinely international; in the general decline of culture, Western clergy began more and more to monopolize the administration of public affairs and the education of mankind; and the Roman heritage of ordered society was quickened by the impulse of a fresh vigour from the barbarian invaders. To Christianity, already interpreted in terms of Hellenistic thought, was added a mass of popular pagan superstition, above which even the best minds of the age were scarcely able to rise. And while the imperial fortunes were restored by Justinian in Italy and Africa, a

9

period of germination during the sixth century blended the many
seeds of history into the variegated pattern of the Middle Ages.
The men of the time were essentially backward-looking, humble
before past grandeur, transmitters of gathered wisdom. Cassio-
dorus the scholar salvaged much of classical and patristic literature; Benedict of Nursia codified the monastic discipline of the
West, thereby furnishing the Church with what was to be her
chief agency for mission; and Gregory the First, who reigned as
Pope from 590 to 604, not only made the papacy a moral force in
politics, but also systematized a body of doctrine that was to
endure for centuries to come. It is not unreasonable to begin a
study of medieval Church History with the life of a man who,
almost alone among Popes, has been accorded the titles of both
sainthood and greatness.

Born about 540 of a noble and wealthy Roman house, Gregory
was the great-great-grandson of Pope Felix III, who had been left
a widower with children before his ordination to the priesthood.
Gregory's father Gordian held an administrative office connected
with the Church, and occupied a magnificent mansion on the
Caelian hill; his mother Silvia was canonized as a saint, from
which it is evident that the boy grew up in a pious as well as
wealthy home. Two of his aunts also died in the odour of sanctity,
leaving behind a younger sister, who had taken the veil along with
them; she now returned lightheartedly to the world, eloped and
married the bailiff of her family estates; and contemplating the
double scandal of apostasy and misalliance, Gregory remarked
sadly that many are called but few chosen. He followed the usual
course of grammatical studies in his youth, and his biographer
tells us that his attainments were well above the average; but
neither then nor later did he show much interest in literature as
such, though he was ready to welcome the service of both art and
music to religion; and some legal training must inevitably have
been included in his early studies. When he was about five years
old, Rome, already depopulated and partly ruinous, was besieged
by Totila the Gothic king; suffering and starvation were acute;
and four years later, young Gregory saw a repetition of the siege.
It was obvious that in such times a youth of his position would be
early called to leadership; in fact, when barely thirty, he was
appointed to the high office of urban prefect. Something of the
Roman senator clung to him till the end, and in his epitaph he was
to be described as "God's consul;" but for the moment, he soon
turned his back on both wealth and honours, resigning his office,
founding six monasteries on his Sicilian estates, and making the
family mansion on the Caelian hill into an establishment of monks,

which he himself entered, not as abbot, but as a simple brother.

It was a dramatic but paradoxical renunciation. For Gregory was deeply concerned to alleviate distress; he later returned, albeit unwillingly, to the direction of affairs; and it must have seemed his clear vocation to rescue what he called the "rotten old ship" of Rome. His flight from the world was due in part to his religious nature, to a desire for solitude and peace with God. The years that he spent as a monk were the happiest period of his life, though he practised such severe austerities that his health was permanently impaired. In his sermons on Ezekiel he tells us; "When I was in the monastery, I could refrain my tongue from idle words and hold my mind almost constantly in an attitude of prayer." And looking back on those peaceful days, he writes in the preface to his Dialogues:

> With sorrow I recall how, when once I was a monk, I rose in contemplation above all transitory and mortal things, and thought only of the things of heaven, how my soul, though pent in the body, soared beyond its carnal prison, and gazed with ardour upon death itself as the way of entrance into life. But now, because of my pastoral duties, I have to endure secular business, and after so splendid a vision of peace, I am spattered with the world's dust. . . . Now I am tossed by the billows of a mighty sea, and the ship of my soul is dashed by the storms of a great tempest; and when I remember the state of my old life, I sigh as one who looking back beholds the haven he has left.

But there was an even deeper cause which drove him to the monastery. Gregory believed firmly that the end of the world was near. The theme of impending judgment is continually repeated in his letters, of which some eight hundred and fifty have survived. He thought that volcanoes were the gates of hell, and that their mouths were growing larger to take in the increasing number of damned souls. At such a time, something might indeed be done to palliate suffering and to still the turmoil; but the main business of life must be to prepare for heaven.

The Caelian monastery was named after St. Andrew. Its inspiration was Benedictine, for Gregory admired the founder of Monte Cassino and did much to encourage the spread of his institution; and although it is not certain that Benedict's rule in every detail was observed at St. Andrew's from the start, the sack of Monte Cassino by the Lombards about 585 sent its monks to Rome, where they were able to teach the full observance. Gregory, like Luther after him, was an exemplary monk, fasting beyond the limits of his strength, and on one occasion being enabled to complete the fast only through the prayers of a brother monk. The

house was well endowed from Gregory's inheritance, so that
there was no need for manual labour and time was available for
books and meditation. Not only did Gregory learn the discipline
of prayer and sacred study, he also felt the call to mission; and
although the evidence is not conclusive, it was possibly at this
date that he saw some angelic Angles in the slave-market, and set
off to convert the English. In Bede's familiar tale, the budding
missionary makes several puns on the young slaves' country and
kingdom. But the habit checked the punster, for as he set out he
stopped to read, and a locust settled on the open book, and the
word *locusta* sounded like *loco sta*—"stay put;" so, while Gregory
waited, messengers overtook him from the Pope, commanding
his return to Rome. But England was not forgotten. A few years
after his accession to the papacy, Gregory was ordering the pur-
chase of English slave-boys to be trained at Rome as missionaries,
and in 596 he sent Augustine, one of his own monks, to Canterbury. The result was decisive for the future of Christianity in
Britain; despite a lingering opposition from the native churches,
the country was now provided at least in outline with a regular
scheme for the diocesan hierarchy, and its religious ties were
firmly bound to Rome. Moreover, the monastery of St. Peter and
St. Paul, which Augustine established at Canterbury, was the first
Benedictine house outside of Italy, and from it, among other
sources, came the inspiration of the Northumbrian schools in the
time of Bede and Alcuin.

Meanwhile, Gregory was appointed one of the seven deacons
who acted as the Pope's personal aides in governing the Roman
Church. The city was then troubled by plague and floods, menaced by a Lombard attack. Pope Pelagius II decided that he must
send as nuncio to Constantinople an experienced and able man,
and in the spring of 579 Gregory was despatched to fill the post.
During the six years which he spent in the capital, he never learnt
Greek, and can hardly have made many friends; indeed, his attitude
seems to have been somewhat critical, for he controverted a
theory of the patriarch that the resurrection body would not be
material, and did so with such vigour that after the dispute he had
to take to his bed from exhaustion. But there was one, like himself
a visitor from the West, to whom he wrote in later years "the
image of your face is ever impressed upon my inmost heart."
This was Leander, soon to be made Bishop of Seville, and already
distinguished for having converted the Spanish Prince Hermenegild from Arianism to the orthodox faith. Leander suggested
that Gregory should write a commentary on the Book of Job,
and the work, though begun at Constantinople, grew into so

enormous a treatise that it was not finally published until 595.

It is not merely a commentary in the usual sense, but much more a vast corpus of moral and ascetical theology, the longest, though not perhaps the best, of Gregory's works, and destined to provide a fruitful mine for subsequent expositors of the Bible. His attitude to Scripture is completely fundamentalist. After a short discussion as to whether Moses wrote the Book of Job, he breaks off with the words: "It is very pointless to ask who composed this volume, since we believe loyally that its author was the Holy Ghost. He it was therefore who wrote these words when He dictated them for writing and inspired the scribe's workmanship, transmitting through the latter a history for our imitation." Gregory goes on to inquire whether, on receiving a letter from some earthly prince, we would trouble to ask what pen had been used to write it. Augustine of Hippo had already called the sacred writers hands that noted down what Christ dictated; Gregory goes even farther in the direction of verbal inspiration; the human agents are not so much as hands, but mere mechanical pens in the grasp of God. But Gregory is not a pure literalist; to him, the Bible is a book "written within and without," so that allegory lurks behind history, and beneath the letter we must search for the spiritual sense. He is deeply concerned to find a practical and contemporary relevance in Scripture, extolling it above all other writings because "in one and the same passage, while it narrates the text, it declares a mystery, and it knows how to recount the past in such a way that, in the very act, it can prophesy the future. . . . Job, while speaking of his own case, preaches ours . . ." Gregory understands that the historical meaning must control the allegorical interpretation, for he says: "I embrace both together, as it is indeed necessary to do, so that allegory may sow spiritual fruits, which none the less are borne by truth from the root of history." In this method of exegesis, he was but following the programme of Jerome, to "erect on the foundation of history a spiritual edifice;" but the length to which interpretation could go may be judged if we turn to his comment on Job 9 : 9, where Arcturus is said to signify the Church, with its seven stars, placed near the pole so that it never sets, while Orion, that portent of stormy weather, means the martyrs, and the Pleiads, harbingers of spring rain, are the doctors and teachers of the Church. That the Book of Job is a poem, Gregory seems never to have realized. He treats it as an elaborate play of symbolism, with the *dramatis personae* cast as follows: Job himself is Christ, his wife represents worldly-minded Christians, his friends the heretics who are converted, and Elihu is the arrogant type of orthodox believer. Three aspects or interpretations of the book are in fact distinguished—the plain historical; the allegorical or typical, which refers to Christ and the Church; and the moral—and Gregory runs three parallel commentaries to correspond. Thus, Job's sacrifice on the eighth day (in 1 : 5) historically prefigures the resurrection; allegorically it refers to Christ purifying the hearts of His preachers; morally, it urges us to cleanse our good intentions by the sacrifice of prayer. Though it became one of the most popular books of the Middle Ages, the whole ethos of Gregory's *Moralia in Job* is foreign to the modern mind. But the burning pastoral concern of the work should not be forgotten: "Holy Scripture is set before our mind's eye like a mirror, to show us our own inward visage, for in it we recognize our faults and graces."

At Constantinople, Gregory accomplished nothing in the political sphere. The Lombards controlled North Italy, and Pope Pelagius wrote imploring help, but the Emperor Maurice had other concerns which prevented him from heeding the nuncio's entreaties. Gregory had learnt enough to realize that Rome must fend for herself—a knowledge which was later to influence his own conduct in the papacy—and when he returned in 585 or 586, all that he brought was an arm of St. Andrew and a head of St. Luke, as relics for his Caelian monastery, of which he now became the abbot. Here his rule was zealous to the point of severity. One of the monks, a medical man by profession, who had faithfully attended Gregory himself in illness, confided when dying to a brother that he had three pieces of gold, professional fees, hidden in his cell. Gregory ordered that the delinquent be left to die alone, then had his body thrown on a dunghill with the gold, while the monks cried: "Thy money perish with thee." But after thirty days the stern abbot relented so far as to hold requiem masses for the soul of his late doctor, which may have originated, or at least popularized, the practice of celebrating mass as a "month's mind" thirty days from death. The unseen world, beautiful yet frightening, seemed very close within the monastery walls; meditation on heavenly themes was cultivated, of which Gregory wrote that "when the mind tastes that inward sweetness it is on fire with love;" and he tells us that his hero Benedict once had a mystical vision of the entire universe gathered under a single sunbeam, a vision which Bernard of Clairvaux considered equal to the intuitive knowledge of the angels. If one may quote a modern statement of the Benedictine ideal, from the *Declarations* of the English Congregation, "our primary function is to do on earth what the angels do in heaven."

But Gregory was not left long in enjoyment of his peaceful re-

treat. Pelagius died of the plague in 590, and the unanimous voice
of the Romans insisted that the former prefect and present abbot
should mount the papal throne. He was desperately anxious to
refuse, resorting to subterfuge and flight in an effort to escape
promotion, but when he saw that acceptance was inevitable, he at
once and characteristically took the lead. Plague was sweeping
through the insanitary city, and Gregory, one of the greatest of
medieval preachers, delivered to the crowds in face of death a
celebrated sermon, which was recorded from the lips of the
speaker by his namesake, Gregory of Tours. More than that, he
organized a penitential procession in seven streams to pass
through the infested streets with chant of litany; as the march proceeded eighty persons fell dead, but at last the Archangel Michael
was seen to sheathe his destroying sword above Hadrian's Mauso-
leum, that fortress tomb which since the tenth century has been
called the Castle of Sant' Angelo. Whether the legend be late or
early, each feature in it is typical: the penitential exercise, the
liturgical ceremonies, the expectation of miracle, the threat of
doom. And, more practically, the new Pope made generous
arrangements to relieve the poor.

Several portraits have been drawn of Gregory as Pope. In one
he is shown with his parents, all three of the figures wearing what
might be described as albs and chasubles; for these garments, the
formal dress of a Roman citizen, were not yet distinctively sacer-
dotal, and the sole priestly vestment worn by Gregory is the
pallium, a narrow strip of white material, wrapped round the
neck, decorated with crosses, and in the Western Church used
only by the Pope and those archbishops to whom he granted the
privilege of wearing it. John the Deacon, in the ninth century,
describes a portrait which he considered to have been a contemporary likeness: a well-formed figure, a long face with slender nose
and prominent chin, a small tawny beard and a fine forehead
adorned with two neat little curls, the complexion dark but fresh
—though in later life it acquired an unhealthy tinge—the expression mild, and the hands graceful with the slender, tapering fingers
of a writer, the one bearing a book of the gospels while the other
makes the sign of the cross.

More important is the picture of his own mind which Gregory
has left us in the *Pastoral Rule*, a book intended to set forth his
high ideal of the ministerial office, and thus also to explain his
reluctance in accepting it. In a letter to the Emperor's sister, he
complained that he had been divorced from Rachel, his beloved
life of contemplation, and by a judgment wedded in the night to
Leah, the active life; but, having accepted the engagement, he

threw himself into pastoral work with energy. Borrowing a phrase from Gregory of Nazianzus, he defines the cure of souls as the supreme art; therefore the pastor must lead an exemplary life, speaking plainly or keeping silence as circumstances direct, adapting his sermon to the different needs of his hearers, with humility and sympathy, serving rather than commanding, loving truth more than praise, meditating daily on the Word of God, and finally examining how he himself practises what he tries to preach. A profound knowledge of human nature is displayed in Gregory's own sermons; he was the first preacher to make systematic use of anecdote and illustration, popularizing the more severe models of patristic oratory. For the theory which lay behind his practice, we may quote a few sentences from the *Pastoral Rule*. The good pastor "should not only be close to all by compassion, but also above all by contemplation;" "dead to carnal passions, he already lives in the spirit, renouncing the world's delights, fearing no adversity, desiring inward gifts alone." Isaiah (52 : 11) had bidden those that bear the vessels of the Lord to be clean; "and the Lord's vessels are borne by those who, in faithfulness of character, undertake to lead their neighbours' souls to the eternal treasury." "The spiritual guide must know that often vices clothe themselves as virtues, avarice describing itself as thrift and extravagance as generosity;" but "the pastor will deal with all cases aright if, filled with the spirit of holy fear and love, he studies carefully each day the precepts of the sacred writers." Various classes of men require a variety of spiritual advice: "slaves should be warned to remember their lowly lot, masters must not forget the common humanity in which they are equal to their servants." This *Regula Pastoralis*, written at the start of Gregory's pontificate, can still be read with profit; it did for the secular clergy what the Benedictine Rule had already done for monks; it was prescribed as compulsory reading for the medieval episcopate, translated into Greek during Gregory's lifetime, and later turned into Old English by King Alfred.

At Rome his first care was to dismiss the throng of lay favourites who had frequented his predecessor's court. A strict, almost ascetic, and exclusively clerical régime was instituted, in which, John the Deacon tells us, the Pope figured as the "paterfamilias of Christ;" twelve strangers were entertained daily at his table, and these were believed to have included angels unawares; cooked meals were sent to the sick and infirm, a long register was kept of the regular beneficiaries of his bounty, and his generosity became so proverbial that, according to legend, when his successor Sabinian sold corn from the papal granaries instead of giving it away, Gregory's ghost appeared and struck the avaricious pontiff a mortal blow upon the head. The papacy was then the largest landowner in Italy, holding estates also in Southern France, Africa and the Mediterranean islands; these were administered by rectors whom Gregory employed as agents for a general supervision of Church affairs. Throughout the West he kept a watchful eye to prevent oppression and injustice; and though he urged the State to persecute heretics and pagans, he was careful to protect the rights of Jews, using no more pressure for their conversion than the offer of a partial remission of rent. He paid sufficient attention to detail to regulate the order of precedence among the deacons at Cagliari in Sardinia; when the bishop of that place ploughed up his neighbour's field before mass one Sunday, only the extreme old age of the culprit saved him from degradation by the wrathful Pope. Other prelates were less fortunate: the Bishop of Naples was deposed for criminal conduct, the Bishop of Taranto, suspected of keeping a concubine, was advised to abdicate. Jealous of the prestige of Ravenna in North Italy, Gregory forbade its Archbishop to wear the pallium, except when officiating in church or on solemn processions. In his dealings with the West, Gregory always acted on the assumption, sometimes tactfully veiled, that all the churches were subject to the jurisdiction of the Roman See. A Roman Synod in 595 enacted general canons against simony, fees offered for ordination, payment for the privilege of being buried in a church, and the superstitious use of vestments which had been placed on the Popes' coffins at a funeral. But there was also a gentler side to Gregory's administration. While ready to remedy abuses, he regarded good bishops as his brethren. The see of Ravenna was later occupied by an old friend, a monk from St. Andrew's called Marinian; when he fell ill in 601, the Pope sent him the best medical advice that he could find in Rome, urged him to come there for treatment, and excused him from keeping fast and vigil. A Bishop of Chiusi, prevented by sickness from attending the annual synod, received the present of an excellent horse. And near his own death we find Gregory sending a thick cloak to a bishop who suffered from the cold of winter.

In Africa he had to deal with a resurgence of Donatism. "God," he wrote to the prefect, "will require at your hand the souls that may be lost;" and by his sheer insistence he made the imperial officials listen. In Spain he was able to watch over the spread of Catholicism after the martyrdom of Prince Hermenegild, receiving from Leander, to whom he sent the pallium, triumphant reports of the orthodox conduct of the martyr's brother Recared. In France the chief scandal was simony and immorality among the

B

higher clergy, who were to a great extent subservient to the
Merovingian kings. By grants of the pallium and by frequent
letters, Gregory was able to exercise some influence over the
French Church. More important, he corresponded with the monarchs, thus laying the foundations for that personal contact between the French court and the papacy, which was to bear fruit in
the coronation of Charlemagne. An Irish monk wrote to him
from the forests of the Vosges, asking help against simoniacal
prelates from "the holy Lord and Father in Christ, the fairest
ornament of the Roman Church." This correspondent was
Columban of Luxeuil, a fiery preacher of repentance, who had
found himself in trouble with the hierarchy, on the pretext that
his Celtic calculation of the Easter date differed from that observed
in France. At this period, the French observance itself differed
from the Roman, and there can be little doubt that the real complaint against Columban was his unbending stand for righteousness. However, he launched into a vigorous defence of the Celtic
Easter, mingling expressions of deference with outspoken criticism of Rome; he asked for advice in dealing with clerical immorality; he praised Gregory's *Regula Pastoralis*, and requested
copies of several commentaries by the Pope. That Columban
should have appealed to Rome is a fact of great significance, for it
shows how Gregory was regarded as a champion of the oppressed.
The Pope must have recognized a kindred spirit in the Irish
monk, but the situation in France was highly complex, and it
seems that he did not reply.

When dealing with the East, he was careful to remember the
status of its four patriarchs, at Antioch, Alexandria, Jerusalem
and Constantinople, though his letters suggest a certain pre-
eminence of the two first, which shared with Rome a Petrine connexion. On his accession, Gregory sent the customary profession
of faith to them all; to Antioch he sent a reliquary of the keys of
the Apostle, to Alexandria a cross containing filings from St.
Peter's chains. With Constantinople he inherited a quarrel from
his predecessor. For a century and a half the complimentary title
of Ecumenical Patriarch had been applied by others to the Bishops
of Constantinople, Rome and Alexandria; in 587 Constantinople
for the first time applied the title to itself, and Pope Pelagius at
once protested. Gregory took no immediate steps, though in 593
he quashed the sentences passed on two priests within the jurisdiction of the Eastern capital. But in 595 Patriarch John the Faster
wrote using the objectionable title in almost every line; to this
Gregory replied what he called a "sweet warning to check the
appetite for vain glory;" and to the Emperor he declared that the

name could only be used by a forerunner of Anti-Christ. For himself, the Pope preferred a humbler designation, which has been borne by his successors ever since, that of "servant of the servants of God." The date of the dispute is significant, for in 595 Gregory was planning his mission to the English, and nothing could be allowed to limit the papal claim of ecumenical jurisdiction. For the moment, the breach was healed by the death of John the Faster in September of that year; but Constantinople had not abandoned its pretensions, and within a century the Popes themselves were using the same title.

By comparison with Old Rome, the bishop of the new capital was a parvenu. But Constantinople atoned for its lack of antiquity by amassing a vast collection of relics, for which the appetite was already evident in 594, when the Empress asked Gregory to send her a part of St. Paul's body; to this request he tactfully replied that all approach to the sepulchre was prevented by awe-inspiring prodigies. Two years before, the Emperor Maurice had published a law forbidding the ordination of civil servants, and preventing them, along with soldiers and men of curial rank, from becoming monks, until they had cleared their accounts with the public treasury and completed their term of service. Gregory, as it was his duty to do, published both the prohibitions, but he protested strongly against the second, saying that it would close the Kingdom of Heaven to those with a monastic vocation; he asked the Emperor, who had been raised by God's grace from the rank of a simple captain, what answer he would make at the Last Judgment if no soldier was allowed to be converted; and he succeeded in obtaining a modification of the law. He had further complaints to make against Maurice, over the government's failure to protect Italy, and in 602 he was delighted when that Emperor was assassinated by Phocas; details of the brutal murder may not have been known to him, and Phocas was at least willing to recognize the Roman See as head of all the churches; none the less, Gregory's ready acceptance of the usurper is the one serious stain upon his moral judgment.

It was the Lombards of Italy who provided him with his most grievous troubles. Their king Agilulf, an Arian by religion, controlled much of the North, and they had established duchies round Benevento and Spoleto, while the imperial exarch at Ravenna remained almost powerless. National resistance naturally centred on the Church, the more so as Justinian had already given the Italian bishops a voice in the election of governors, and had allowed the Pope to share with the Senate the right of inspecting weights and measures in Rome. In 591, on his own authority,

Gregory appointed a military governor for Nepi, and next year he sent a tribune to command the troops at Naples; when Rome was threatened simultaneously, he negotiated a truce on payment of five hundred pounds of gold; and though the government refused to endorse this truce, Paul the Deacon tells us that the Duke of Spoleto was "touched by divine grace, recognizing such power in the Pope's words that with humble courtesy he satisfied the most religious apostolic bishop." Agilulf marched on Rome in 593; Gregory rose from a bed of sickness to preach to the panic-stricken people, illustrating texts from Ezekiel by the sombre desolation of the scene, in sermons which were so topical that sometimes his message came to him extempore in the pulpit. Pope and king met on the steps of St. Peter's, and Agilulf was persuaded to withdraw. But two years later, the Emperor condemned the policy of peace, and Gregory had to defend himself with some asperity; however, his view of the situation prevailed, in 599 a general pacification was concluded, and though the conflict was renewed in 601, he was now certain of ultimate success.

The Lombard menace was not only military, but also theological. While the invaders themselves were Arians, the Catholics of North Italy were divided into two separate churches over what was called the Three Chapters Schism, ever since Justinian had tried to reconcile the Monophysites by condemning a group of three writings that were suspected of containing Nestorian error. Gregory laboured to convert the heretics and reunite the ortho-dox, using as his chief instrument Theudelinda, Agilulf's Catholic Queen. It was especially for her that he wrote the four books of his Dialogues, on the miracles of the Fathers in Italy, attempting to show how heaven had confirmed the orthodox faith with signs following. A large portion of the work is occupied with the life of Benedict, but the author's credulity is remarkable; almost nothing is told of Rome itself, where direct evidence could have been produced, and of the three miracles whose truth can be tested all are demonstrably fictitious. The devil appears in full medieval regalia, there are instances of second sight, many visions and prophecies by the dying, much to encourage a belief in purgatory, and delightful tales like that of the nun who consumed a lettuce in her convent garden, without first making the sign of the cross, and consequently ate a little devil sitting on a leaf. But the legends, however fanciful, were intended to convey an assurance of God's continuing presence, even in troubled times, and they sprang in part from the author's biblicism; believing that the greater works, which Christ's disciples should do, would be similar to those

recorded of prophets and apostles, he tells several stories which
have a scriptural prototype.

Gregory was not the most learned man of his generation. That
title must be awarded to Leander's brother, Isidore of Seville, the
range of whose interests may be gathered from the subjects dealt
with in the twenty books of his so-called *Etymologies:* I Grammar,
II Rhetoric and Dialectic, III Arithmetic, Geometry, Music and
Astronomy—so far we have the *trivium*, and in Book III the
quadrivium, of the seven liberal arts—IV Medicine, V Law and
Chronology, VI Scripture, Canon Law and Ecclesiastical Offices,
VII God, Angels and Saints, VIII The Church and the Sects,
IX Languages, Races, Kingdoms, X An etymological Word-list,
XI Men and Monsters, XII Animals, XIII The Universe and its
Parts, XIV The Earth and its Parts, XV Buildings and Lands,
XVI Stones and Metals, XVII Agriculture and Botany, XVIII
War, Games and Pastimes, XIX Ships, Building Materials, Dress,
XX Food, Drink and Furniture. Gregory's interests were much
more narrowly confined; he praised Benedict for leaving Rome
"willingly ignorant and wisely uneducated," and he reproved
Bishop Desiderius of Vienne for lecturing on classical literature
because "the same mouth cannot sing the praises of Jupiter and
of Christ." But within his narrower range, Gregory's mind impressed itself more deeply on the future. He took a mediating view
of Christian art, treating holy pictures as visual aids for religious
instruction, and telling an iconoclastic Bishop of Marseilles that
they should be neither worshipped nor destroyed. He was deeply
versed in Scripture, the divine authority and inspiration of which
he accepted without question; while he delighted in the spiritual
meaning, which he compared to the wine at Cana, he agreed that
allegorical exegesis must conform basically to the uniform teaching of the Bible as a whole; the subject matter of all Scripture, and
the key to every book, he declared to be the revelation of God in
Christ; and he taught that obedience is more important than intellect, since "we hear the words of God if we act upon them."
Along with Scripture, Gregory accepted tradition, but chiefly in
the role of interpreter, rather than as an independent source. His
own theology was based on that of the great Augustine, modified
by the popular religion of the day, and his thought, seldom
original, forms a link between the patristic and scholastic periods.
In refusing to allow for the possibility of human ignorance and
liability to temptation in Christ's Person, he held what was tantamount to a docetic doctrine of the Incarnation. To the meaning of
Redemption he devoted careful study, viewing it under three
aspects as: first, deliverance from the devil, who was deceived by

the flesh of Christ into exceeding his just claims upon humanity, when he ventured to lay hold on One Who was both Man and God; second, deliverance from the wrath of God through the sacrifice of a sinless human Victim, Who "appeased the indignant Judge" by a life of obedience, by death and by continued intercession; third, deliverance from sin by incorporation of the elect in Christ, their great Exemplar, through spiritual illumination and mystical communion. Thus Christ has made redemption possible; but it has to be apprehended by human effort, so that no one in this life can be sure of his salvation; and though original and actual sin be remitted in baptism, the believer must thereafter satisfy by his own good works and penances, or else suffer purgatory as a temporal punishment for unrepented post-baptismal sin. Augustine had spoken of purgatory merely as a probable opinion: Gregory was the first to define it as a dogma which ought to be believed. The Old Testament saints, he thought, had been released by Christ's harrowing of hell where, despite their faith in the promised Redeemer, they had been held by their original sin. On the doctrine of angels, saints and demons, Gregory spoke more confidently than anyone in the West had done before, organizing the heavenly host in a hierarchy of nine ranks, similar but not identical in detail with that found in the sixth-century Greek writings falsely attributed to Dionysius the Areopagite. He emphasized the sinfulness of all humanity except for Christ, which would seem to imply a denial of Mary's immaculate conception, and he never mentions her assumption, though belief in the latter was at that moment for the first time being popularized by Gregory of Tours. On the doctrine of predestination he was logically inconsistent, holding a semi-Pelagian position which saw merit in the effort of human free-will, denied irresistible grace, and yet taught that man without God can initiate no good thing. The Eucharist he regarded as both sacrament and sacrifice, writing in his commentary on Job that Christians "satisfy their hungry soul with Christ's flesh by the daily sacrifice of His immolation." He himself celebrated daily, and wished other clergy to do the same. How great his liturgical reforms may have been, is a matter of controversy, but it seems clear that the Sacramentary which bears his name, together with his Antiphonary, even in their original forms marked an important stage in the codification of liturgy and chant. He introduced the Lord's Prayer at the end of the Canon of the Mass, apparently thinking that the apostles used this prayer alone at the consecration of the communion elements. It is uncertain whether he founded the Roman song-school, but he took a decided interest in it, and future ages were shown the couch on which he reclined to listen, and the whip with which he chastised the boys.

By the year 601 he was writing to say that his infirm body was dried up and ready for burial, and thereafter he was largely confined to bed, except that he rose to celebrate. He died on 12th March 604, a dutiful priest and a military leader, a preacher of righteousness and a mystical recluse, a politician and at the same time a compiler of superstitious legends. Few men have better summarized an epoch in their persons; Gregory founded the medieval papacy, and after Jerome, Augustine and Ambrose, he is reckoned as the fourth Doctor of the Latin Church.

CHAPTER II

BONIFACE AND THE CONVERSION OF NORTHERN EUROPE

IN HIS *Mission of St. Benedict,* CARDINAL NEWMAN WRITES:

> St. Benedict found the world, physical and social, in ruins. . . .
> The new world which he helped to create was a growth rather than
> a structure. Silent men were observed about the country or dis-
> covered in the forest, digging, clearing and building; and other silent
> men, not seen, were sitting in the cold cloister, tiring their eyes and
> keeping their attention on the stretch, while they painfully de-
> ciphered and copied and re-copied the manuscripts which they had
> saved. There was no one that "contended or cried out" or drew
> attention to what was going on; but by degrees the woody swamp
> became a hermitage, a religious house, a farm, an abbey, a village,
> a seminary, a school of learning and a city. . . .

During the Dark Ages the monks were the great salvagers both of
waste land and of unwanted learning, and occupied as they were
primarily with salvage and salvation, it was they who provided
most of the outstanding missionaries. The world was then best
served by those who had forsaken it.

By the seventh century, the West had evolved two distinct
types of monasticism, the Benedictine and the Irish, widely differ-
ing in temperament, but both of them interested in scholarship
and mission. In the one, the Celtic urge to go on pilgrimage, and
in the other, the strenuous bidding of the papacy, contributed a
stimulus for the evangelization of the heathen; and these heathen
of North Europe, unlike the converts of the early Church, were
to be given not only a gospel, but also a civilization. There was as
yet no Order of monks in the later sense of the word, for each
monastery remained independent and self-governing, but whereas
Benedict's houses had a common Rule provided by the founder,
the Irish discipline was based rather on oral tradition and personal
obedience to the abbot, with the result that the Irish monks were
more individualist than the Benedictine. They all acknowledged
the Pope as primate of Christendom; but the Benedictines were
employed from the start by the papacy as its personal agents,
while the Irish followed their own customs and wandered where

they pleased. External divergences, like the date of Easter and the shape of the tonsure, were comparatively trivial; the great contrast was in ethos, the Italian being humane and practical, the Irish heroic and austere. Thus Benedict used corporal punishment only as a last resort, but Columban awarded six strokes of the lash for failing to respond Amen when grace was said at table. We find Celtic saints mortifying their flesh by standing neck-deep in cold water to recite the Psalms, or remaining for hours in prayer with the arms stretched outward in the form of a cross; Benedict advised that his disciples, when rising for the night-office, should "encourage each other gently, since the sleepy ones are apt to make excuse." Ireland, looking back to the pristine fervour of monasticism in Egypt, where the hot climate allowed men to subsist with little food or sleep, regarded the ascetic life as a sort of martyrdom; Benedict, with the Roman genius for ordered living, gave his monks more than eight hours' sleep in winter, permitted a siesta on summer afternoons, allowed a pint of wine as their daily ration, and though he forbade them to have any personal possessions, he made them at least as comfortable as the peasants of the day. The monks of the West were on the whole more aristocratic than their brethren in the East; the sons of noblemen were attracted to the movement, and convents became the recognized depositaries for their unmarried daughters. Many of the Celtic saints were supposed to be of royal blood (though that claim might perhaps have been made by most Irishmen) and the Benedictine discipline likewise appealed to the upper classes. Although Benedict directed that on important matters the whole community should take counsel together, and although monasticism was in essence a democratic institution, none the less under both systems the rule of the abbot was almost unlimited by constitutional checks. But here there was an important difference. Benedict allowed and encouraged neighbouring bishops to intervene in cases of disorder; the Irish had no diocesans to control them, and Columban made his foundations in the Vosges without episcopal licence or supervision. The same thing was done by many of his compatriots, who wandered across the face of Europe preaching penitence, and however fervent their appeals may have been, they lacked the organization to produce permanent results. But they did possess a remarkable standard of scholarship. The ancient classics had come to Ireland as part of the Christian heritage, and they were studied more widely than elsewhere in the Irish monastic schools which, during the seventh century, admitted English pupils free of charge. Scholars were also produced by the Benedictine discipline, though rather as a by-product than as part of its primary aim; its Rule encouraged reading of Scripture and the Fathers, especially on Sundays and during Lent, at the beginning of which a special book was handed out to each of the brothers; and as the monks had to educate boys whose parents had dedicated them to God, they usually collected libraries and provided centres of such learning as there was. For a time the two systems of monasticism continued as friendly rivals, and there are cases in France where both rules were observed jointly in the same house. But its practical utility, coupled with the support of Rome, caused the Benedictine discipline to triumph, and all that at last remained of the Irish system was a memory of its ascetic zeal.

Both systems influenced England in the seventh century, and it was a combination of Celtic missionary enthusiasm with Roman order and obedience which inspired the labours of Boniface as apostle of Germany. Before his birth about 680, the Synod of Whitby had already accepted the Roman Easter; and Wilfrid, travelling to Rome to defend his title to the see of York, had been blown by the winds to Frisia where, in the course of a brief winter, he inaugurated a mission which was to attract several of his fellow-countrymen. But Wilfrid, despite his Roman proclivities, had originally been a product of the Celtic school at Lindisfarne; and although Theodore of Tarsus, the forceful Greek monk who then occupied the throne of Canterbury, was a papal nominee, none the less Celtic influence was still strong in schools like that of Malmesbury, where Aldhelm acquired his curious learning from the Irish monk Maildubh. However, one result of far-reaching consequence had followed from Augustine's mission to Canterbury. It was now accepted in England that, before exercising jurisdiction, an archbishop must receive his pallium from Rome; the request for it must be accompanied by a profession of orthodox faith, and receipt of the gift bound the recipient in obedience to the Pope. The very term "archbishop," as used to designate a metropolitan, was English; both the office and its Roman ties were to be introduced to the Continent by Boniface.

Born at Crediton in Devon, his baptismal name was Winfrid. He first felt called to be a monk when some visiting preachers stayed at the family home; but his father, a military thane, objected to the proposal, and it was only when the boy kept insisting on his desire to study sacred letters that he was at last allowed to enter a small monastery at Exeter. Here as an oblate, or child dedicated to God, he pursued elementary studies for seven years, moving on for higher education to a Benedictine house, which was almost certainly Nursling near Southampton. His training was thus completed under the learned stimulus which flowed from Theodore and Hadrian at Canterbury; but one side of his interests, a strange love of cryptograms, acrostics and grammatical puzzles, seems to be typically Irish. Early works which he composed include a Latin grammar, some Latin verses and a treatise on prosody; a crisp epistolary style which he developed, much less involved than that of Aldhelm, points forward to the vigorous and lucid Latinity of the Carolingian Renaissance. He was ordained at the usual age of thirty, taught pupils in the monastic school, and was employed on business for the Church; everything suggested a successful ecclesiastical career at home, to be crowned by an abbacy or bishopric, when he announced his intention of forsaking all and sailing overseas on mission.

Frisia was then the obvious strategic base for a Christian advance into Saxony, and it was particularly their kinsmen on the Continent that the Anglo-Saxons felt called to evangelize. During the early years of the seventh century, a beginning had been made in this direction by a hermit from Aquitaine called Amandus, who worked somewhat unsuccessfully in the region of Ghent, and better results were obtained under the leadership of Eligius, distinguished not only as Bishop of Noyon, but also as a silversmith; but the real penetration of virgin territory was commenced by Wilfrid, who found himself storm-bound in Frisia during the winter 678–9, and made a number of converts. The later difficulties of evangelism in that district were largely political, for the Frisian King Radbod was on the defensive against the advance of French armies, and had no love for the religion of his would-be conquerors. But in England the strategy of mission had been carefully thought out, with the encouraging source of strength which Roman support afforded, and in 690 the Englishman Willibrord landed near Utrecht with eleven companions. The number was the normal one for an Irish missionary group, showing the sense of apostleship with which they sailed. Willibrord himself had been educated at Ripon, where he must have felt the Romanizing tendencies of Wilfrid; but in 678 he left Ripon, probably because of Wilfrid's own difficulties there, and spent twelve years studying at an Irish monastery. He was therefore doubly equipped to lead the resumed mission. From Charlemagne's great-grandfather, Pepin of Heristal, he obtained political support; but he considered it more important to win papal sanction, and for this purpose he journeyed to Rome in 692. Three years later the mission had so far prospered that, on a second visit to Rome, he was consecrated archbishop, and given the new name of Clement which, like the later change of Winfrid's name to Boniface, must have signified reception into the Roman community; but although he was given

the pallium as a metropolitan, and had his own see fixed at
Utrecht, Willibrord was never able to organize a hierarchy with
subordinate bishops under his jurisdiction. In fact the passive
opposition of Radbod forced him to pass on into Denmark,
where the most that he could do was to enlist thirty Danish boys
for training as future missionaries; and on the way back, stopping
at the holy isle of Heligoland, he rashly baptized two persons in
its sacred springs, for which act of sacrilege he was nearly murdered by the pagans. Thereafter he was for a time obliged to confine his work to French-occupied Frisia, and even this was
recovered by Radbod after Pepin's death in 714.

It was at this point, when the churches had been destroyed and
the mission dispersed, that Boniface or, as we should still call him,
Winfrid arrived, having sailed from the port of London in 716.
But the situation was so unpromising that in less than a year he
returned home; this early baptism of fire had shown the need for
more careful planning, and above all for more powerful support.
Accordingly, rejecting the desire of the Nursling monks to make
him their abbot, he set out for Rome in 718, bearing a letter of
commendation from his friend Bishop Daniel of Winchester.
Impressed by his keenness after several interviews, Pope Gregory
II gave him the name of Boniface, together with a roving commission, though he was still only in priest's orders, to evangelize and
baptize the heathen. Thuringia was pointed out to him as a suitable mission-field, and he went there in the early summer of 719;
but seeing at once that nothing could be done without the secular
arm of government, he travelled on to the court of Charles Martel,
where he learnt that Willibrord had returned to Utrecht. Since
King Radbod was now dead, the obstacles to evangelism had been
removed, and so to Utrecht Boniface went, serving under his
older colleague for the next three years. The experience was as
valuable to the new missionary as his assistance was to the veteran,
and Willibrord sought to retain Boniface as co-adjutor for the
work in Frisia; but pleading the original directive of the Pope, the
younger man left him, and Willibrord laboured on through the
increasing weakness of old age, to die at the monastery of
Echternach in 739.

Meanwhile, Boniface explored the virgin soil of Hesse, where
his independent apostolate began. Here and also in the neighbouring district of Thuringia he made thousands of converts, and
a report of his success resulted in a summons to appear at Rome in
person. After supplying the Pope with a profession of his orthodox belief, he was consecrated on St. Andrew's Day 722, as
regionary bishop without fixed see for all Germany east of the

Rhine, taking an oath of fealty to the Roman See which is sufficiently important to be quoted in some detail. "I, Boniface,
bishop by the grace of God, vow to thee, St. Peter, Prince of the
Apostles, to thy vicar the holy Pope Gregory, and to his successors, in the name of the undivided Trinity, and by these thy most
sacred relics, that I will loyally and sincerely maintain the holy
catholic faith, and by God's help continue in the unity of the
same . . . and will at all times persevere in holding pure and faithful communion with thee, and in closely following the customs
of thy Church, which God has granted the power of binding and
loosing. . . . And if I ever learn that the conversation of any
clerics is contrary to the ancient institutions of the Fathers, I will
have no dealings or communion with them, but rather will prevent their actions to the best of my ability, and wherever I cannot
check them, I will faithfully and immediately send information to
my apostolic lord" at Rome. This was in fact the common form of
oath taken by the Pope's immediate suffragans, with the omission
of an unnecessary clause which professed their allegiance to the
Greek Emperor, and with the addition of a promise to avoid
communion with disorderly ecclesiastics, a promise considered
necessary from one who would probably be working in contact
with the errant Irish. One of these, Virgil or Fergal of Salzburg,
was to be reproved for his belief, then considered heretical, in the
existence of the Antipodes. But up till now it was only bishops in
the neighbourhood of Rome who had promised such fidelity to
the Pope as their metropolitan; to exact a similar profession from
a bishop of Germany meant that the Church which Boniface
would found must be drawn into equally close dependence on the
Roman See. There is no indication that Boniface objected; for the
papacy, his oath implied an immense advance of jurisdiction. It is
easy to suggest that if the Popes had been willing to allow a
greater amount of local freedom to the churches, the later
national tensions which helped to produce the Reformation might
have been avoided. But in the circumstances of the eighth century,
central direction and control from Rome were undoubtedly
needed to organize a stable mission, and were warmly welcomed
by the missionaries. Henceforward Boniface occupied the position not only of an evangelist, but also of a papal legate; he tried
faithfully to avoid communion with undesirable elements, and his
promise to do so later caused him qualms of conscience among the
highly secularized prelates of the French.

The Pope provided him with letters of commendation to
clergy, people, and monarchs, and Charles Martel, without men-
tioning the papal commission, granted him a safe-conduct for his

travels. A letter, written some twenty years later to Daniel of Winchester, indicates the importance of government protection: "without the patronage of the French Prince I cannot rule the church's members or defend the clergy, monks and nuns, nor can I even stop the pagan rites and idolatrous sacrilege of Germany. . . ." The power of the sword, as well as the sermons of a preacher, was to be needed for the taming of the heathen; but Boniface himself preferred to use spiritual methods of persuasion, and it seemed that the psychological moment had arrived for a dramatic gesture. At Geismar there was a giant oak-tree, sacred to Thor and hallowed by the worship of centuries; in the presence of a great concourse of both pagans and Christians, Boniface approached the tree, axe in hand; it was to be an appeal to heaven, a contest of the gods, while the human spectators watched and waited; and the evangelist, himself an expert woodman, was aided by a mighty gust of wind, which sent Thor's oak crashing to the ground in four fragments forming a cross. Such was the virtual end of paganism in Hesse.

But the prodigy, however spectacular, could not by itself instil deep Christian convictions, and it was the outstanding merit of Boniface to realize that he must plant strategic centres of learning and religious education, from which the faith might spread. For this purpose he founded monasteries; one of them, Fritzlar, grew out of a chapel which he built with the timber of Thor's oak. To staff his foundations, Boniface brought out monks and nuns from England; his correspondence shows how wide an interest his mission had aroused at home; and at one time or another his helpers included many famous English names. There was his own distant cousin, Walpurgis, a teaching nun who became Abbess of Heidenheim, and through the misfortune of dying on May 1st, has been involved in the folk-lore of the witches' sabbath on that date. Lioba, learned in Scripture, the Fathers, canon law and chronology, wrote shyly to Boniface from her convent in Dorset asking that she might regard him as a brother, and enclosing the gift of some remarkably unoriginal Latin verses; she was invited to come out and take charge of the double monastery, for both men and women in separate sections at Tauberbischofsheim near Würzburg, where in later life she was consulted by bishops on matters of faith and order, and became the intimate friend of Charlemagne's Queen Hildegard; we are told that though an expert in spiritual contemplation she was always gay, and like Boniface himself, to whom she had proved a tower of strength, she was at last buried in the great monastery of Fulda. Amongst the men who assisted him, were Lull of Malmesbury, who succeeded to leadership of the mission on the death of Boniface; Willibald, the brother of Walpurgis, who had gone on pilgrimage to Palestine and spent ten years at Monte Cassino; and Wigbert, also an Englishman, who was made Abbot of Fritzlar. In the latter house was placed a well-born Bavarian lad called Sturm, who had been given into the care of Boniface in 735; two years later a letter directs that the boy should take charge of the kitchen, after which he was ordained for mission work in Hesse. But he desired to be a monk, and on a trek through virgin forest, in peril from Saxon raids, he found an ideal site for what was to become the monastery of Fulda. Building began in 744; in 748 Sturm was sent for two years' training at Monte Cassino; and he then became abbot of the new foundation which, by the time of his death in 779, had grown to contain over four hundred monks. Fulda provided Boniface with a happy retreat and headquarters for the later stages of his campaign; before the middle of the next century it had become one of the outstanding centres of Christian learning in the whole of Europe. If a pagan country is to be watered with the gospel, spiritual reservoirs are needed as a constant source of supply, and it was precisely this function that was fulfilled by the German monasteries.

We possess over a hundred letters written by Boniface to a wide circle of friends, together with a number of replies, and the collection is an invaluable source both for painting his own character and for tracing the history of the period. Even when writing to the Pope, he regularly calls himself "servant of the servants of God," a designation which, though beloved by Gregory the Great, had been used before him in slightly different forms by Pope Damasus and by Augustine of Hippo. However, when writing to Archbishop Egbert of York, he uses the more formal title "German legate of the Apostolic See." Continually he asks his friends at home for books, commentaries, copies of the Bible; an English abbess is requested to provide a special text of St. Peter's Epistles in gold ink, to impress the pagans with a reverence for Scripture; and towards the end of his life, he begs Daniel of Winchester to send out a Book of the Prophets, which had belonged to his late teacher and was written in a clear, large script that his failing eyesight could decipher. Though himself a total abstainer, Boniface sends to Egbert two little casks of wine for a feast with the brethren in pledge of mutual love; to Daniel he despatches a small gift, a towel with which to dry his feet. Other gifts were exchanged between the letter-writers. King Ethelbert II of Kent sends a silver drinking cup and two woollen cloaks, asks for the saint's prayers, and hints that a pair of German falcons would be useful. As early as about 720, while Boniface was still on his Frisian mission, a young English nun called Bugga wrote as follows: "I have not been able to get the Martyrology for which you asked, but I will send it on as soon as I can find a copy. My dear friend, give me the joy of receiving the collection of Scripture texts which you promised in your delightful letter. I am sending you two pounds for an altar frontal, which is the best gift that I can manage; small as it is, it goes with real affection." The letters which Boniface himself wrote show his inward life of daily prayer and meditation on the Bible, of frequent communion and unshaken trust in God; they also show his love of the English countryside, remembered with longing in his exile.

His sermons display a deep interest in Scripture, Christian history and theology, expressed in a sometimes tortuous train of thought, but their primary concern is moral and ascetic. A specimen of his simple ethical appeal may be provided by the following extract:

Listen, brethren, and ponder carefully what it was that you renounced at baptism. You renounced the devil and all his works and pomps. What are the devil's works? Pride, idolatry, ill will, murder, slander, lying, perjury, hate, strife, fornication, adultery, stealing, drunkenness, magic, witchcraft, the use of amulets and spells. . . . You promised to believe in Almighty God, in Jesus Christ His Son and in the Holy Spirit, One God Almighty in perfect Trinity. These are God's commandments which we must observe and keep: love the Lord, in whom you have professed your faith, with all your heart and mind and strength, teach your children to love God, and your households in the same way. Reconcile those who are at feud. Let the judge give just judgment, without taking bribes, which blind the eyes even of the wise. Keep the Lord's Day, gathering at church, and praying there without vain repetitions. Give alms according to your ability, for charity blots out sin as water extinguishes the fire. Be hospitable, visit the sick, care for widows and orphans, pay tithes to the church, and do not to others what you would not have them do to you. Fear God and Him alone. . . . Apply yourselves to learn the Lord's Prayer and the Creed, and teach them to your children. . . . Fast, love righteousness, resist the devil, receive communion at the appointed seasons. . . . Believe that Christ will come again, that there will be a bodily resurrection, and a general judgment of all men. Then the evil will be divided from the good, and the one will go to eternal burning, the other to eternal bliss, to enjoy life everlasting in God with no more death, light without darkness, health without suffering, joy without fear, happiness without sorrow; peace there shall be for evermore, and the righteous shall shine like the sun, for eye hath not seen, nor ear heard, neither hath it entered into the heart of man to conceive what things God hath prepared for them that love Him.

In 726 Boniface was writing to Rome, as Augustine of Canterbury had done before him, to seek guidance on the moral questions which arose among a newly converted people. At this period he was fully occupied, not only with his own converts, but also with a refugee problem produced by Saxon raids, and the papacy provided him with a code of canons for the direction of his church. Equally significant was the gift of the pallium in 732, which constituted him a regionary archbishop, with power to consecrate suffragans, but still without a definite see of his own. On a third visit to Rome in 738, he offered to resign and go on a roving mission to the Saxons, but Gregory III, who was now Pope, insisted that he should continue the work of consolidation, and widened his authority so as to include Bavaria and Allemania. Next year, on the death of Willibrord, Frisia was also included in his circuit, if we may thus describe so vast a region, and although he then had no suffragan bishops, by 741 he had appointed eight. These were the years which organized a settled hierarchy for the growing church, but for Boniface it was a time of constant travelling, and it was quite needless for the Pope to write, as he then did, "you are not free, my brother, to stay in one place when your work there is done . . . wherever God opens you a door for the salvation of souls, go on with your preaching." Boniface did the work, not only of a visiting evangelist, but also of a founding father; a church council, which he held in 740, seems to have been the only one to meet anywhere in the French kingdom throughout the long reign of Charles Martel; and by 742 the organization was almost complete. Further, Charles had by then been succeeded by his sons Carloman and Pepin the Short, who took a much warmer interest in missionary progress. Gregory III died at the same time, in 741, and to his successor, a Calabrian Greek called Zacharias, Boniface complained of a rumour current in Germany that pagan superstitions were being practised at Rome. The new Pope replied indignantly that these had already been suppressed; the incident should not be over-emphasized, but it does indicate that the fidelity of Boniface to Rome was not uncritical.

For the next seven years, the main scene of his labours was France under the pious Carloman, who invited him to preside over a series of councils, composed of clergy and lay nobles, to remedy abuses in the Church. The result was to tighten the links between France and Rome, so that when Carloman had retired to a monastery, his brother Pepin wrote to the Pope about his own anomalous situation; in theory the last of the feeble Merovingians was still King of France, and Pepin was no more than Palace Mayor, but in practice, as he delicately hinted, it might be right

to recognize as king the actual ruler; to this transfer of authority
the Pope agreed, being happy to find a protector against the Lombards, and in 751 Pepin was crowned and anointed by Boniface
in his capacity of papal legate. Five years later the new monarch
rewarded Rome by transferring his Italian conquests to the
papacy, and thereby founded the temporal principality of the
Papal States. Meanwhile Boniface, whom Pepin had intended for
the see of Cologne, had been appointed Archbishop of Mainz
about 747, and in 753 his claim to administer Willibrord's old see
of Utrecht was confirmed. To this region, the sphere of his earliest
work, the eyes of the aged missionary turned; parting sadly from
his designated successor Lull, he packed his shroud and sailed
down the Rhine in early summer with a picked band of volunteers; the old fervour returned, mass baptisms followed, and
churches were rebuilt around the Zuider Zee. Next year he penetrated farther to Dokkum, but on a 5th of June, while he was
preparing to confirm his converts, both he and his party, to the
number of fifty, were massacred by a heathen tribe. The date is
uncertain; it was 754 in the tradition of Fulda, but 755 in that of
Mainz. His body was taken back for burial at his beloved Fulda,
and almost at once Archbishop Cuthbert of Canterbury informed
Lull that an English synod had decreed an annual commemoration
of the martyrdom, in token that Boniface, along with Gregory the
Great and Augustine of Canterbury, was recognized as a patron
saint of the English Church.

To the Continent he had brought, amongst more important
gifts, the English institution of religious confraternities to pray
for the souls of departed members, and the record of these obits
helped to form the genesis of monastic chronicles; he also took
the custom of dating by the year of Our Lord, an idea invented by
Dionysius Exiguus in the sixth century, but first popularized by
Bede and Willibrord in Britain, because there the multitude of
petty kings made it impossible to date events by regnal years. The
Empire of Charlemagne and the papal supremacy in Northern
Europe were in a sense built upon the achievement of Boniface;
but it is on his work as an organizer and educationalist, still more
as a preacher of the gospel, that his lasting fame depends. The
work of conversion proceeded slowly, and often superficially; but
although mass baptisms for reasons of political expediency might
prove a sandy foundation, there was always some genuine faith.
In the ninth century Anskar, a native of Picardy but said to have
been of Saxon stock, laboured in Denmark and Sweden, doing
much to check the horrors of the slave trade; but he was hampered
by the well-meant backing of Louis the Pious, and when the

sturdy Scandinavians accepted baptism in the tenth and following centuries, they did so from English missionaries who constituted no threat to their political independence. Before that, the Norsemen who settled in what came to be called Normandy had accepted the Christian faith under their first duke, Rollo, as part of a treaty concluded in 911 with the King of France. There was thus a variety of motives, political as well as religious, but the gospel was being preached throughout the heathen world then known.

CHAPTER III

ALCUIN AND THE CAROLINGIAN
RENAISSANCE

FREQUENTLY THE MORE TRIVIAL INSTITUTIONS OF AN EPOCH
show the greatest capacity for survival. Thus the Carolingian
monetary system of 240 pennies to the pound was adopted by
King Offa of Mercia towards the end of the eighth century, and it
has lasted longer in England than in its original home. The same
monarch, who was the first to style himself King of England, and
who began the tribute to Rome later known as Peter's Pence,
copied the ceremony of anointing by which King Pepin had compensated for his lack of royal blood; and although it was left to
Dunstan in the tenth century to elaborate a full English coronation service, none the less the sacramental inauguration of English
monarchs dates from Carolingian times. The remarkable learning
of that age is largely forgotten; but the beautiful Carolingian
script in which its books were written was revived shortly before
the Reformation, to provide the model for our modern style of
print. After the dark and wintry period that had gone before,
there was then a real springtime of scholarship; its literary products fill some thirty to forty volumes of Migne's *Patrology*, rang-
ing from grammar to history, from arithmetic to canon law; and
no remark so hopeful and self-confident can be found in the later
Middle Ages as the words which Alcuin wrote to Charlemagne,
"if your purposes succeed, a new and more splendid Athens will
arise in France."

In the vast multi-racial society ruled by Charlemagne religion
was the only factor that could provide a common bond; it is
therefore not surprising that he should have stressed the preaching
duties of the clergy, and sought to improve the standards of
clerical education. So large was his empire that he had to move its
headquarters from Paris to the Rhine, so prominent his religious
interests that the magnificent court chapel gave its name to Aix-
la-Chapelle. But there was another reason why the ruler wanted a
well-educated clergy. The Merovingians had used laymen, Mayors
of the Palace, as their great officers of state; Pepin and his descendants could not afford to encourage a similar lay family which

might come in time to supplant them; and so for their administration they used clerics, with the title of arch-chaplain and later of
chancellor, who could found no dynasty, and could be paid by the
gift of a rich abbacy or bishopric. Two consequences followed. In
the first place, the Carolingians kept too close a control of Church
appointments and Church property; there was an ugly story that
Pepin's father, Charles Martel, who won his name for hammering
the Moslems at Poitiers in 732, had been condemned body and
soul to hell because of his rapacity, and that Boniface, accompanied by the Abbot of St. Denis, on opening his tomb had found
it tenanted only by a snake. In the second place, then as now a
profitable career in administrative work was open to graduates,
and the demand created a supply. As early as 789 we find a capitulary, or royal ordinance, laying it down that "in every bishopric
and monastery there should be teaching of the psalms, music,
chant, computus (i.e. the calculations that were required, especially for fixing Easter) and grammar, and they must have carefully
corrected books." Revision of texts, both Scriptural and liturgical,
was an important part of the Carolingian achievement. The capitulary indicates the two main centres of education that then existed,
namely cathedral and monastic schools. It is true that in Italy
there still were lay teachers who purveyed learning privately in
return for fees; much later on, a proud pupil was to write, "my
education cost my uncle 2,000 shillings.... I am indeed thoroughly
learned." But the classical public schools had come to an end with
the Gothic invasions, and the one subject that really survived in
Italy was law. Elsewhere, education became almost exclusively
clerical, the curriculum being determined by professional considerations. If a bishop wished to maintain his staff of clergy, he
had to train them himself, or else appoint a senior priest to do so
for him; teaching was considered to be one of the most important
episcopal duties, and the bishop's throne was at the same time an
academic chair. Thus any sizable cathedral was likely to contain
a number of boys who were being brought up to serve as clerks.
They would receive the tonsure, an old Roman rite of adoption,
by which the bishop became responsible for their maintenance on
the one hand, and on the other was entitled to their services for
life. If on growing up they decided to marry, they would be
allowed to do so, and in that case could not proceed to holy
orders; but they would still perform subordinate duties about the
cathedral, and would still belong to the bishop's "family." It is
probable that the majority chose this course, but for those who
remained celibate a long career of ecclesiastical preferment was
open to talented men, and indeed the Church was the one profes-

sion in which it was possible to rise out of one's inherited social class.

The subjects studied in the cathedral schools were such as would be of use to future clerics, choristers and scribes: enough Latin and grammar to read the service-books, enough knowledge of Scripture to give simple expositions, enough practice in chant to lead the singing, and enough calligraphy to pen a document. On the other hand the monastic schools tended to be more definitely theological in emphasis, for they were concerned not with the vocational training of clerks, but with the spiritual preparation of men of prayer, who would not be engaged in pastoral duties, and might not even proceed to orders. None the less, in practice there was considerable overlapping; for example, clerks required a nodding acquaintance with astronomy in order to calculate the incidence of Easter, and monks had to be able to tell the time for the night-office by the stars. Moreover, the conditions were somewhat similar in both types of school, since both provided instruction in a resident community. The monasteries were primarily concerned to educate their own oblates, and a capitulary of 817 directed them to confine their activities to these; but in fact this was interpreted to mean that, if they taught external pupils, they must do so in a separate school outside the monastic enclosure. Two movements of reform in the eighth century brought the two types of community closer together. In 782, Benedict of Aniane founded a monastery on his estates in Languedoc, to be a model for strict observance of the Benedictine Rule; but as he allowed less time to manual labour, and elaborated the liturgical offices, his monks became more prominently concerned with the worship of a great abbey church. Episcopal schools had always built their life around the cathedral; and about 755 a relative of King Pepin, Bishop Chrodegang of Metz, compiled a rule under which the canons of his cathedral were to live together in community, as the clergy of Augustine had done at Hippo, observing a semi-monastic discipline, but at the same time fulfilling pastoral obligations. The bishops' chancelleries were bound to be concerned with the production and duplication of documents. Similar work was undertaken by the monks, when they began to turn from agriculture to the copying of manuscripts; such labour was found eminently suitable to their vocation, since it was toilsome, meditative and of practical utility, and Dom Cuthbert Butler has pointed out that the invention of printing left a gap, not easily filled, in the monastic routine. Strict discipline was normally maintained in all the schools; later on, we find in a Durham manuscript of the early twelfth century the warning

Afficitur plagis qui non vult discere gratis ("boys who will not learn are beaten"), and the initial A is formed from a lively picture of a master birching a boy. Girls were not entirely forgotten; double monasteries for both sexes in separate sections were common in England; and at the same time as the cathedrals were instituting discipline for their canons, parallel regulations were being drawn up for communities of "canonesses," which had previously tended to provide springtide homes for unmarried young ladies of the nobility. In eighth-century England, both main types of school were represented: the monastic pre-eminently by Wearmouth and Jarrow, whose chief ornament was the Venerable Bede, and the episcopal by the school of York which, under Archbishop Egbert, was the first attempt at an English University.

The founder of Wearmouth and Jarrow was Benedict Biscop—this recurrence of the name Benedict indicates its popularity. By birth a Northumbrian thane, and by inclination a close friend of Wilfrid, he visited seventeen continental monasteries in order to study their practice, and he brought home from his travels the rich library which made possible the scholarship of Bede. He also served for a time as Abbot of Canterbury, and made a total of five journeys to Rome. The monastery of St. Peter at Wearmouth was founded in 674, that of St. Paul at Jarrow eight years later; both were under the Benedictine discipline, and both enjoyed some papal privilege, now lost, which seems to have confirmed the monks' liberty of electing their own abbot. An enthusiastic admirer of the Roman liturgy, Benedict Biscop brought the arch-cantor of the Roman Church to teach the chant in England. Bede was entrusted to his care at the age of seven. There is a touching legend, that when the community was prostrated by illness the little boy and his abbot recited the offices alone; and it is not improbable, for a letter of Alcuin relates Bede's remark: "I know that angels are present when our monks chant the office and meet in chapter—what if they did not find me there?"

Northumbria was Bede's home for the remainder of his life; all the books that he needed had been gathered there, and there is no record that he travelled. He knew the sacred tongues, was well read in pagan authors and in the sciences, had studied Jerome, Ambrose, Augustine, Isidore and all the works of Gregory the Great; he refers in all to nearly two hundred books, though some of these were known to him only at second-hand from quotations in other writers. Humble about his own attainments, and at the same time highly sensitive to criticism, his great work was to assimilate and transmit the knowledge of the past; with a scholar's care he used special signs to mark the patristic borrowings in his commentaries; and he delighted in such studies, remarking on Proverbs 13 : 23 that "much food is to be garnered in the meadows of the Fathers." A devout student of the Bible, he was aware of its problems, but confident of solving them; he thought it unimportant that St. Mark should have attributed a text from Malachi to Isaiah, since all Scripture is ultimately written by the same Author. Allegory is essential to his method of interpretation. Thus, he finds the existence of Elkanah's two wives quite unedifying to priests and Christians, and so he insists that they must symbolize the Jewish synagogue and the Church. The building of Solomon's Temple provides him with a fertile field for the exercise of ingenuity; here he takes the fancied significance of numbers as a clue to the meaning of history and human life, seeing intimations of the Trinity in the 30,000 workmen and the 3,300 overseers; the cedars of Lebanon are men of renown cast down from the mountain of their pride, and the windows of the Temple are holy doctors who behold and pass on the light of celestial mysteries. When he turns to the gospel parables, he says that the lost coin represents the divine image in man, the nine other coins are the nine orders of unfallen angels, and the lamp is the Light of the World. The mustard tree typifies the Church, its branches are priests and preachers, and the birds who rest upon them are the laity. But he produces a more homely touch when he comes to interpret the text "faith as a grain of mustard seed:" mustard makes a good gargle if it is ground fine and mixed with honey, and in the same way faith must be pounded by temptation and sweetened with charity. Discussing the appearance of Christ in the Book of Revelation, he says that the long robe is "a priestly vesture, showing Christ's priesthood by which He offered Himself for us on the altar of the cross as a victim to His Father;" the last three words here are notable in view of the medieval theory, derived from Origen, that Christ paid a ransom not to God but to the devil. Bede's greatest work was his *Ecclesiastical History of the English Nation*, completed in 731, and despite its shortcomings still a source of primary importance. There was a popular demand for miracles, and he himself enjoyed telling a good story, but he was not uncritical in this respect, believing that miracles had largely ceased since the time of the apostles. In connexion with Wilfrid, for whom he had little sympathy, he relates only one supernatural occurrence. Cuthbert, on the other hand, has an eagle to feed him and seals to dry his feet; when he reproves the crows for stealing thatch from the guest-house at Farne, they atone by bringing him a piece of swine's fat with which to grease his shoes; and his knee is healed with a poultice prescribed by an

angel on horse-back. Bede, who believed that his own tongue had
been cured while singing Cuthbert's praises, certainly accepted the
value of prayer and spiritual healing; but he adopted a sensible
attitude to both, suggesting that exorcism will only be successful
if the patient confesses all his sins and if the best medical advice is
taken, and writing "it may be that our requests for others cannot
be granted, but the love which we give them will otherwise
obtain a response from God." Near the time of his own death,
which took place in 735, Bede said: "I have lived long, and the
merciful Judge has wisely ordered my life; the time of my departure is at hand, for my heart longs to behold Christ, my King, in
His beauty."

In the year of Bede's death, his friend and pupil Egbert received
the pallium as Archbishop of York; whether a cathedral school
already existed there is unknown, but it certainly received a decisive stimulus, if not its first foundation, from the new Archbishop,
who was concerned not only with clerical training, but also with a
general reform of the Church. Here Alcuin studied as a pupil
before teaching as a master, so that he stands in the succession at
one remove from Bede. He was born in or near York about 730,
of a noble family related to Willibrord; his immediate teacher,
Aelbert, succeeded to the see in 767, and Alcuin then took charge
of the cathedral school. By this time he had been ordained deacon
but, like many of the professional scholars of the period, he never
advanced to the priesthood. His training had been rigorously
orthodox, for he tells us "my master taught me to stand up with
everything I had to the defence of the catholic faith." Aelbert
made several journeys to the Continent in quest of books and
learning, and Alcuin went with him at least once to France and
Italy, on which occasion it is possible that he may have been
introduced to Charlemagne. That monarch was looking for
scholars to direct his educational programme, and although he
brought them from several countries, the English contribution
was to be the most important. In 778, the year of the minor action
at Roncesvalles later immortalized in the *Song of Roland*, Aelbert
resigned his bishopric, which made it easier for Alcuin to contem-
plate leaving York; three years afterwards, as he returned from
Rome with the pallium for Aelbert's successor, he was pressed by
Charlemagne to take up residence at the French court. This was a
peripatetic body, moving at the call of politics or war; in the next
fourteen years, the king was to keep Christmas at ten different
places; and thereafter Alcuin, too old for constant travel, had to
retire to the abbacy of Tours. But in the meanwhile he threw
himself into the life of the palace. We read of merry banquets, the

exchange of poems and letters, even a swimming-party at Aix-la-Chapelle with Alcuin and Charlemagne discussing a Scriptural problem in the middle of the pool. The king was no ascetic, but he attended mass daily and kept the canonical hours, pointing with a stick at the clerk whom he desired to read the lesson, and coughing loudly when he felt that the service ought to end. He could read, but preferred to be read to, and his favourite book, on which he sought to model his government, was Augustine's *City of God*. Some sort of college had existed at the court from the time of Charles Martel, but only as a finishing school for young nobles; Charlemagne turned it into a learned academy to stimulate a general revival of education, by training the country's intellectual leaders and by providing the requisite literature, textbooks of the various subjects, collections of sermons, standard editions of both Bible and liturgy. The result was a wide but ephemeral diffusion of culture, derivative rather than original; it was precisely a renaissance of the past, not a new creation, and the one fresh development was in church music for which, however, a notation had to be borrowed from the Byzantines. Here, the long-drawn-out musical sequences to the accompaniment of elaborate ceremonial may have provided the germ of medieval drama.

It must be remembered that Charlemagne was primarily a warrior, defending Christendom from the menace of pagan neighbours, and his great achievement was to incorporate Germany within the sphere of Roman civilization; to attain this result, he used the method of forcible conversion and he exacted tithe for the Church by statute, thereby shocking the gentle Alcuin, who declared that Christian missionaries should be preachers and not predatory animals. But the king, like many active soldiers, had a respect for scholars, and in the circle of the court he joked and argued with them as an equal. Before Alcuin arrived, Charlemagne was already attended by two Italians, Peter of Pisa and Paulinus of Aquileia; a third, Paul the Deacon, came from Monte Cassino in 782, but left five years later; and it was Alcuin who settled permanently and had the chief influence. This learned circle called its members by nicknames: the king himself was David, Alcuin was Horace, his beloved disciple Rabanus was surnamed Maurus after the favourite follower of Benedict, and Homer was the designation of Abbot Angilbert of St. Riquier, to whom Charlemagne's daughter bore two illegitimate sons. We may suspect that the names originated from Alcuin, for he certainly loved to address one of his pupils, who became a bishop, as his Venerable Fowl. Charming verses were written in the circle, especially by Alcuin, who composed a poem on the cuckoo and a lament for a lost nightingale. But there was also more serious study in the fields covered by the seven liberal arts. Here Alcuin did much to create a favourable climate of opinion in ecclesiastical circles; he admitted that the "lies" of Virgil should not be studied for their own sake, but he pointed out that the classics could provide a useful preparatory discipline, and he suggested that a study of astronomy had converted Abraham to the worship of the true God. The dialogues in which he recorded his views on grammar and kindred topics are wittily written, but quite elementary. When Charlemagne asked him about dialectic, he replied that there were five species of the subject, called Isagogae, Categories, Forms of Syllogism and Definition, Topics and Periermeniae. This strange list becomes clear when it is realized that the first and last items are the plurals of Greek titles which can be translated "Introduction" and "On Interpretation;" and in fact the five so-called species of dialectic are simply the titles of textbooks which Alcuin had read. Greek was not his strong point, and his very superficial acquaintance with it was derived from Jerome. None the less, the intellectual horizons of Western Europe were definitely widening; Charlemagne exchanged embassies with Harun al-Rashid, bearing gifts which included an elephant and a striking clock.

A general and semi-popular education was to be provided by the seven liberal arts; but these were intended to lead on to theology and exegesis. Here also, Alcuin desired to be a popularizer. His earliest surviving letter, addressed to a certain duke in the year 787, begins by congratulating the recipient on his love for Scripture. Later, Alcuin tells Charlemagne that he is delighted to hear how a layman has been asking questions about the Bible; this layman was apparently troubled over the Christian attitude to war, for he asked why on one occasion (Luke 22 : 36) Christ ordered His disciples to buy swords, and on another (John 18 : 11) told Peter to sheathe his weapon; in the true allegorical tradition, Alcuin solves the difficulty by saying that in the two contexts the sword symbolizes two different things. Yet another letter gives the famous mystical interpretation, derived from Augustine, of the 153 fish which the disciples caught (John 21 : 11). If the number 153 be represented by individual dots, these can be arranged in an equilateral triangle with 17 dots on each of its sides; and the number 17 is made up of 10 and 7, signifying respectively the commandments and the graces of the spirit. Moreover, 7 is itself made up of 3 and 4, representing faith in the Trinity which is sent to the four corners of the world. Alcuin adds that the net did not break because it contained none save the elect and those ordained to eternal peace.

This mention of election raises a theological problem which was to be vigorously debated in the next century. Alcuin believes that the future is already present in the sight of God, and he loves to speak of divine predestination in the course of history; at the same time he writes in his treatise on the Trinity: "free-will remains in men even now by nature, and where God is so pleased, He deigns to free it by grace, to deliver them from an evil will . . . (since the Fall) free-will itself has been deprived of good-will . . . without the help of grace, free-will can neither turn itself to God nor advance in Him . . . thus, if there is no grace of God, how shall the world be saved; and if there is no free-will, how shall it be judged?" In the same treatise he teaches something which sounds very like justification by faith.

> For those who desire to reach true blessedness, faith before all else is needful, as we are taught on apostolic authority which tells us, Without faith it is impossible to please God. It is agreed that none can reach true blessedness unless he pleases God, and none can please God except through faith. For faith is the foundation of all good things, the beginning of man's salvation; without it none can attain to the fellowship of God's children, since none can receive the grace of justification without it in this world, nor in the world to come can he enjoy eternal life.

This highly Scriptural approach is reinforced in the next section of the treatise by a reference to the entire Scripture of the Old and New Testaments as being "divinely inspired." And Alcuin, unlike some modern writers, was able to give especial authority to the teaching of Jesus, since he believed that throughout Christ's human life He was fully conscious of His deity; indeed, he goes so far as to suggest that when the Son of Man declared that He knew neither the day nor the hour of judgment, this was no more than a figure of speech called metonymy, implying that while He Himself knew, He preferred to keep men in ignorance. In his Trinitarian doctrine Alcuin teaches a double procession of the Spirit, from both Father and Son, and he devoted a special treatise to that subject, which was beginning to be debated with the Greeks.

The sort of problems, some trivial and some profound, which were being raised at the time, may be illustrated from his *Questions and Answers on Genesis*. Why is the Fall of Adam mentioned, that of the angels not? "Because God has not fore-ordained that He would heal the angels' hurt, but He has determined to cure that of men;" and the reason is that man, unlike the angels, was tempted from an external source. Why did God curse earth and not water? Because, among other reasons, "God fore-ordained that He would wash away in water the sin which man contracted from the fruit of earth." Why did God expiate human sin by Himself and not by an angel? "Because the merit of one angel would not suffice for the redemption of the whole human race; and the devil would not have incurred such guilt in the slaughter of an angel as he did in killing the Creator." Abel was accepted because he sacrificed "the best gifts of nature," but Cain offered "poorer gifts, as it is thought, such as human invention devised;" and Abel's three great marks of righteousness were virginity, priesthood and martyrdom, in all of which he is a type of Christ. When Eve was formed out of the side of Adam as he slept, it "assuredly signified by reason of a mystery that Christ fell asleep upon the cross for the Church's sake, and from His side the fount of our salvation flowed." The Church, he writes to King Ethelred of Northumbria, "is the bride of Christ, and he who seeks to violate her or to steal her goods, is punished by Christ our God, the husband of His holy Church;" kings should be nursing-fathers to widows, orphans and the poor, and while it is the bishops' duty to reform monasteries, "it is the part of lay people to obey their preaching." The Pope is the undoubted successor of St. Peter. To Hadrian I Alcuin writes: "I know that by enrolment of holy baptism I belong to the fold of that Shepherd who shrank not from laying down His life for His sheep; and these He entrusted to the pastoral care of blessed Peter, Prince of the Apostles, for his thrice-repeated declaration of great love; on him the Lord bestowed in heaven and earth an eternal power of binding and loosing; and of his holy see, most excellent Father, I recognize you as the Vicar, and confess you to be the heir of his wondrous power." On the question of baptism he writes to his Venerable Fowl, the Bishop of Arno, "the priest washes the body with water, the Holy Spirit justifies the soul by faith;" and the three outward signs are of no avail unless the three unseen powers work inwardly. On Holy Communion, he has a comment on John 6 : 52 which begins with a quotation from Augustine: "the faithful may recognize the Body of Christ, if they fail not to be the Body of Christ; they become His Body, if they are willing to live by His Spirit." To this quotation Alcuin adds, "he who would live must believe in Christ, and spiritually eat the spiritual Food, and thus be joined to Christ's Body." Much of Alcuin's material is taken from Augustine, though he also makes use of Jerome, Chrysostom and other Fathers. He has been described as a living but unoriginal encyclopedia, with a fund of bibliographical knowledge and a profound capacity for administration. In his correspondence he often begged for relics, especially for those of the "life-giving cross," and he introduced the Feast of All Saints to France. With Charlemagne he discussed a vast variety of topics, including Septuagesima, leap-years and eclipses. The range of his interests was enormous, but always connected somehow with the Church.

His main theological controversy was concerned with the Adoptionist heresy in Spain. This country was not within Charlemagne's dominions, though a Spaniard like Theodulf could be appointed Bishop of Orleans, and over the territory of the Spanish March Charlemagne did exercise a certain jurisdiction. When the Spaniards were converted from Arianism at the third Council of Toledo in 589, they accepted the Creed with the addition of the *Filioque* clause, an unauthorized addition which was later to cause friction between the Eastern and Western Churches; but for the moment it was merely a safeguard against the Arian denial of Christ's deity, since it asserted that the Spirit proceeds from the Son as well as from the Father, and Theodulf of Orleans composed a treatise in support of the doctrine, deducing it from a number of patristic texts. But the Spanish liturgy still contained phrases which suggested something less than a true union of the divine and human natures in the Incarnate Person of Jesus Christ; it spoke of "the man who was assumed," implying that the Son of God assumed, not human nature, but an individual man who must then have been adopted by the Godhead. Felix, the learned Bishop of Urgel in the Spanish March, upheld this heretical position, declaring that Christ as a man must be regarded as an adopted son of God; Pope Leo III later suggested that he had derived this idea from contact with Moslems, but it may have been no more than a revival of the old Arianism of Spain. At all events, the Pope condemned it as Nestorian, Felix was persuaded to recant at Ratisbon in 792, and two years later Charlemagne had his views condemned at the Council of Frankfurt. But when Felix returned to Urgel he relapsed into his heresy; he and Alcuin exchanged polemical treatises upon the subject; and one result of the controversy was that the custom of reciting the Creed at mass spread throughout Western Europe.

Other labours undertaken by Alcuin included an important revision of the text of the Vulgate Bible, and an attempt to standardize worship on the basis of the Gregorian Sacramentary. Some peculiar Gallican practices continued for a time, but Alcuin's hand is traceable in the Roman Missal of today. He provided elaborate prefaces, with a special intention for the service of each day of the week; but among his more ornate liturgical compositions, there occurs a simple private prayer for use on rising, which is very similar to the morning blessing contained in Luther's

Short Catechism; there is no evidence that Luther borrowed from Alcuin, but both prayers breathe the same spirit of a simple, popular piety. Charlemagne had asked for the standardization of the liturgy, and it was he also who obtained from Monte Cassino an authoritative text of the Benedictine Rule. With this Alcuin was not directly concerned, for it appears that he never made formal profession as a monk; but he was appointed Abbot of Tours in 796, and unlike other non-monastic commendators of abbeys, he resided in his house, established a flourishing school and ruled it carefully. Here he died in 804, an extraordinarily typical Englishman in his love of the *via media*. Neither a priest nor a layman, he remained content with the diaconate. Leading an abstemious life, and accepting the charge of a monastery, he did not trouble to become a monk. By nature of a retiring disposition, he yet craved friendship. He accepted wealth and endowments, though disapproving of Church tithe. With a mind that was neither original nor philosophic, he laid foundations for the later scholasticism. His peculiar gift was for stimulating others; all his pupils spoke of him with grateful admiration; and he came to be regarded as the ideal scholar, poet and divine.

Of the part he may have played in the wider political issues of the time it is impossible to speak with confidence, for the matter is a subject of keen dispute. But it is at least possible that he contributed to the iconoclastic controversy, and also to the revival of the Western Empire at the coronation of Charlemagne in the year 800. Both of these events were related to the growing rift between East and West. In the East, a reforming and somewhat puritanical Emperor had issued a decree, in 726, for the destruction of images in churches; his reasons need not detain us here, but he was at least partly influenced by a desire to refute Moslem accusations of idolatry. The decree, hotly resented by many Greek Christians, was eventually repealed by the Empress Irene at the second Council of Nicaea in 787. Papal legates attended and concurred, but the French Church was not represented, and when the acts of the Council were received at Charlemagne's court, they were found to contain a statement that images should be worshipped with the same reverence as is due to God; this was in fact a mistranslation of the Greek original, and although there is no confirmatory evidence, there is much to be said for Hauck's idea that the mistranslation had been deliberately introduced by the iconoclastic remnant, in order to prejudice the West. Whatever the truth may be, it was at once decided that an answer must be made to this blasphemous error, and the so-called *Caroline Books* were composed, upholding the doctrine of Gregory the Great that

images should be neither worshipped nor destroyed. Was Alcuin
the author of these books? He appears to have been away on a
visit to England at the time of their composition, but he could
have dealt with the matter by correspondence; they were the
work of a skilled theologian, put out under the name of Charlemagne, who would naturally have turned to his scholarly adviser;
and there is nothing improbable in the idea that Alcuin was the
real author of the books.

Whatever their authorship, they were intended as a polemic
against the Empress, for whom the West felt an increasing sense
of irritation. Since the deposition in 476 of Romulus Augustulus,
that doubly diminutive phantom, there had been no resident
Emperor in the West, and the sovereigns who ruled from Constantinople were theoretical heirs of the whole Roman Empire;
but they had signally failed either to govern or to protect Italy,
and when threatened by the Lombards, the Popes had depended
increasingly on Frankish help. After his solemn anointing by
Boniface, Pepin had been anointed a second time, along with his
Queen and two sons, by Pope Stephen II who conferred on him
the vague but high-sounding title of Patrician of the Romans.
About the same time a remarkable forgery was perpetrated. The
so-called Donation of Constantine purported to record a grant
from the first Christian Emperor to Pope Silvester and to his
successors, of spiritual supremacy over all the churches and of
temporal sovereignty throughout an undefined region of the
West. Renaissance scholars, working at the Vatican in the fifteenth
century, had no difficulty in proving the spurious nature of this
document, but it is none the less a fiction which points to an undoubted fact; for by moving his capital to Constantinople, the
Emperor created a power vacuum in the West, which the papacy
alone had the international status to fill. Gregory the Great had
acted almost as an independent sovereign; Pepin had created the
Papal States for Gregory's successors; and by about 780, Pope
Hadrian I had dropped the regnal years of the Byzantine Emperors from the date of his official documents, substituting the
formula "in the Reign of Our Lord Jesus Christ." Meanwhile the
East was in a state of schism because of its iconoclasm, and men
were bound to ask who was the actual ruler of Western Europe.
An answer was foreshadowed in 774, when Charlemagne visited
Rome just before Easter, and was greeted with palms and processions as "coming in the name of the Lord." The Empress
Irene did reverse the religious and political policy of her predecessors, suggesting a marriage between Charlemagne's daughter
and her son; but she was an impossible person, who shocked the

world in 797 by having the same son blinded and imprisoned in
the porphyry chamber where he had been born.

Events now moved to a swift climax, and strangely enough, the
immediate prelude to Charlemagne's imperial coronation was an
accusation laid against the Pope. Hadrian had belonged to the
Roman nobility; his successor, Leo III, was an ecclesiastical
bureaucrat of humble origins, and therefore opposed by the party
of the nobles. Charlemagne wrote to him somewhat patronizingly,
telling him to lead a godly and honest life, and remarking: "it is
our task, with the help of the divine mercy, to defend the Church
of Christ in every place by arms against the attacks of pagans and
the ravages of unbelievers, fortifying it within and without by
profession of the catholic faith; it is your task to raise your hands
to God like Moses and thus to aid our struggle." In plain terms,
the Pope was told to confine himself to spiritual functions; and in
the *Caroline Books* it is expressly stated that the Church has been
committed to the king for government. But in 799 a riot forced
Leo to flee from Rome to the king's court at Paderborn, with
charges levelled against him of immorality, adultery and perjury.
This at once raised the question of whether any human court was
competent to judge the Pope; and Alcuin insisted that he could
be judged by God alone. Charlemagne restored him to his dignities, but sent a commission to investigate the charges. In the
summer of 800 the Norsemen were busy raiding, and the king
could not come to Rome in person till November. Though treating Leo with respect, he held a synod on December 1st, at which
the Pope's accusers conveniently failed to appear; and on December 23rd Leo purged himself on oath at St. Peter's, declaring that
he did so voluntarily and without creating a precedent for judgment of the Pope. At the same moment, a legate arrived from the
Patriarch of Jerusalem, bringing to Charlemagne the keys of the
Holy Sepulchre and the banner of Jerusalem, in recognition of
his status as defender of the Church. On Christmas Day, the king
went to mass at St. Peter's; as he rose from his prayers, Leo
placed a crown upon his head, while the people cried: "Long life
and victory to the most religious Charles Augustus crowned by
God;" and the Pope, following the Byzantine fashion, prostrated
himself before the newly created Emperor. His biographer records
that Charlemagne later said he would not have gone to church
that day if he had known what was to happen, because the title
brought him ill-will from the Byzantine court, where an acute
diplomatic tension in fact lasted for the next fourteen years. But
too much importance should not be attached to a casual remark,
made after the event and after its consequences were apparent.

D

The coronation was obviously pre-arranged, and the people had been told what they were to shout; Charlemagne must have known of the plan in advance, although he may have wished to let it appear that the dignity was thrust upon him; and Leo, despite the fact that it enabled him to restore his tarnished reputation, was in no position to risk offending Charlemagne by staging a surprise. The ceremony did no more than recognize the actualities of the political situation, and there was no thought of supplanting the Greek Empire; it was merely a revival of the Empire in the West, with the Pope acting as the representative of Rome. But Charles had no legal title to his new dignity, apart from that which papal sanction gave him; and later ages forgot the Pope's prostration, remembering only that it was he who had bestowed the crown. On the one hand, the papacy had raised up a monarch on its doorstep, who was to prove more overbearing than the distant ruler of the East. On the other hand, the theory came to be accepted that only the Pope can make an Emperor.

Charlemagne may have come to regret the details of the ceremony, for in 813 he brought his son Louis the Pious to the chapel at Aix, harangued him on the duties of a ruler, and then bade him take his crown from off the altar, without any ecclesiastical participation. But in the months before Christmas of 800, he must have consulted with his advisers about the course he was to pursue in Rome; and again the question arises, whether it may not have been Alcuin who suggested that he should assume the imperial title. Earlier, Alcuin had occasionally referred to what he called the Empire of the French. In June 799, he was writing to Charlemagne about the three world powers, the Papacy then under a cloud, Constantinople which was tottering, and the French Kingdom; he continued: "all hope of the churches of Christ rests upon you alone, to you it belongs to avenge crimes, to direct the wayward, to comfort the afflicted and raise up the good." If Alcuin in fact suggested the imperial coronation, he was responsible for a political concept which, as the Holy Roman Empire, survived at least in name until 1806.

With Charlemagne's death in 814, the guiding hand was removed from the centre of affairs; his dominions fell apart, and the Partition of Verdun in 843 gave birth to the separate nations of Germany and France. But the interest in education which his reign had stimulated did not immediately vanish. That there was a popular demand for religious instruction, such as would have gratified Alcuin, is shown by vernacular translations into Old German of the Creed, the Lord's Prayer and the *Gloria in Excelsis*; two attempts were made to supply a popular version of the life of

Jesus, the one an anonymous poem called the *Heliand*, written about 830, and depicting the apostles as lusty knights of the Saviour, the other a prose life written about a generation later by the monk Otfrid. Alcuin's own pupil, Rabanus Maurus, was appointed Abbot of Fulda in 822, and he made that monastery the intellectual capital of Germany under Louis the Pious, becoming Archbishop of Mainz in 847, promoting the work of evangelism, and writing copiously on exegesis, grammar, philosophy, canon law and even domestic economy. He was also a prolific poet, and the hymn *Veni Creator Spiritus* may be from his pen. In turn, his pupil Walafrid Strabo took up the learned succession: before he was eighteen Walafrid had written the *Visio Wettini*, which is one of the precursors of Dante's *Inferno*; and some of his comments on the Bible seem to have later been incorporated in the vast compilation which, growing under many hands, eventually became the standard *Glossa Ordinaria* of the Middle Ages.

Claudius, the warlike Bishop of Turin, took up the sword against the Saracens and criticized what he called paganism in the churches. He disapproved of images and saints' days, saying "they have not forsaken idols but merely changed their names;" he objected even to adoration of the cross, preferring to worship the glorified Christ, with His work complete; and he derided the Petrine claims of the papacy, writing: "we should not call him apostolic who sits in the apostle's seat, but rather him who performs the office of an apostle." Archbishop Agobard of Lyons was, like Claudius, a native of Spain, holding similar views but expressing them more calmly. Images, he thought, are innocent in themselves, but their worship is idolatry; he was equally concerned to prohibit superstitious Christians from asking wizards for meteorological information; he criticized trial by ordeal, because it was a process of "tempting God"; and he denied the complete verbal inspiration of Scripture, though he accepted the divine origin of the ideas which it contains. Both Claudius and Agobard were influenced by the more spiritual side of Augustine, "whom to contradict," as Paschasius Radbertus wrote, "is not permissible."

Above all, there was the enigmatic figure of John Scotus Erigena, born in Ireland about 810 and trained there as a classical philologist. He was a typical don, of slender build, irascible temper and mordant wit. Charles the Bald appointed him head of the palace school in France; and when the king, sitting opposite him at dinner, asked what was the difference between Scot and sot, he is reputed to have answered "this table." He composed an epitaph on his enemy, Archbishop Hincmar of Rheims, during the lifetime of that prelate:

> Here Hincmar lies, a thief on avarice fed,
> His sole achievement this—that he is dead.

The French atmosphere seems at last to have become too hostile, and a not very reliable tradition records that he was invited to England by King Alfred, taught at Malmesbury, and there was stabbed to death by the pens of his rebellious pupils. Erigena was always a solitary figure, the loneliest figure in the whole of medieval Europe. At a time when there was mutual misunderstanding between East and West, he alone among the Latins studied Greek theology; as William of Malmesbury puts it, "he deviated from the Latin tradition while keeping his gaze fixed upon the Greeks, and for that reason was reputed to be a heretic." That his views were in fact heretical it is difficult to deny, for he followed out the Neoplatonic philosophy to a conclusion that is extremely hard to distinguish from pantheism. He did not mean to be a pantheist, for he held that God, as the supreme cause and source of being, is above and beyond the universe; but he also said that creation out of nothing is the same as creation out of God, since God, in His utter otherworldliness, is really the negation of everything that is, although He is not less but more than material existence. Like a magnet, God causes in all things a love which returns to Him at last; He is the beginning and likewise the end of all, so that Erigena can say that the Divine Artificer "makes and is made in everything." From God, the uncreated Nature which creates, proceed thoughts as the prototypes of things, at once created and creative; from the divine thoughts comes the created and uncreative matter of the universe; and to God, as the ultimate goal, neither created nor now creating, the universe returns, that God may be all in all. No substance can ever be destroyed, for though the thoughts of the wicked perish, those thoughts are vanity and therefore unreal. In order to have been logically consistent, Erigena should have followed Origen in accepting the doctrine of universal restoration; but although he holds that the righteous are in some sense deified, not by absorption into the divine Nature, but by contemplation and love, he yet believes that to the unrighteous the sight of God will somehow be a torment, just as sunlight is painful to weak eyes and pleasant to the strong. Paradise is not a place, but a state of being; its four rivers are the cardinal virtues, the serpent is sensuous delight; Adam represents the mind, Eve the senses, and the division of humanity into two sexes is a result of the Fall, which will vanish when the spiritual body, as first created, reappears. The bliss of heaven is the climax to a process which began in Christ's resurrection, and man will glow with divine love while still remaining man, just as iron glows in the furnace without changing nature, since "he who understands fully, becomes that which he understands." Creation cannot have taken place in space and time, since there can be no movement outward from the Immutable; the Incarnation was not a single historical event, but it points rather to the eternal connexion between the actual and the ideal; and Erigena writes, "as many as are the souls of the faithful, so many are the theophanies," adding that Christ is daily conceived through the Spirit, and born and nourished in the womb of faith.

All of this appears to be philosophical mysticism rather than theology. Erigena wrote: "authority proceeds from right reason, not reason from authority. . . . I think that rightful authority is nothing else than truth discovered by rational means, and committed to writing by the holy fathers for the benefit of posterity." But at the same time he could speak of "the unshaken authority of Holy Scripture," and say that "the authority of Holy Scripture is in all things to be followed." However, he tended to give the Bible a waxen nose, capable of being pulled in any direction, because he admitted a potentially infinite variety of allegorical meanings. As a specimen of his own exegesis, it may be remarked that to him the prodigal represents humanity, the elder son the angels, and the fatted calf Christ. Erigena was deeply influenced by the Platonic strain in Augustine. But his main work was done in translating the books falsely attributed to Dionysius the Areopagite, which were held in high honour because of their supposedly apostolic origin; and he also translated a commentary upon them by Maximus the Confessor, together with a treatise by Gregory of Nyssa. It was a useful, if dangerous, service to introduce the West to the subtleties of Greek speculation. The charge of heresy was not made against Erigena until after his death, and it was only in 1225 that he was finally condemned. Attempts to trace his influence on subsequent thinkers have been unsuccessful, except in the case of a few obscure heretics, but he represents a perennial type of human thought which reappears, without conscious derivation, in the later medieval mystics and in the idealist philosophy of Hegel.

He was involved in the two great theological debates of the ninth century, on Predestination and the Eucharist; we may take the latter first. Soon after 830, Paschasius Radbertus, monk and later Abbot of Corbie near Amiens, wrote a devotional treatise for monks, insisting on the Real Presence and the Eucharistic Sacrifice; such ideas were becoming part of the common assumptions of the period, but they now received their first full-scale treatment. Paschasius collected accounts of strange miracles, where pieces of human flesh had allegedly been found between the fingers of doubting priests, and he seemed to suggest that in the Sacrament the very Body that had been born of the Virgin was locally present with all its limbs, merely veiled and shrunken down in size, and suffering the Passion once again. To this Rabanus Maurus, Alcuin's disciple, replied in 845: "to receive the Body of Christ is to be united to Him by faith, thus making one Body with Him." Ratramnus, another monk of Corbie, expressed similar views with greater clarity: the sacrament is a memorial or figure, the consecrated Host is the Body of Christ spiritually but not corporally, and it is spiritually received by the faithful alone. Cranmer and Ridley later studied Ratramnus, claiming him as a supporter of their own sacramental doctrine; in the meanwhile, his treatise had been wrongly attributed to Erigena, and condemned as such at the Council of Vercelli in 1050. But Erigena would himself have accepted the doctrine it contained, for he elsewhere wrote that the sacramental elements are "not the identical Body . . . but only a memorial," "a typical similitude of spiritual participation in Jesus, which by faith we enjoy in the mind alone." There was a long but inconclusive debate; eventually, despite the learning and weight of the opposition, the views of Paschasius won the day, though not expressed in the grossly materialistic manner which he had employed.

The doctrine of Predestination was connected with that of the Sacraments, for it raised the question of their universal efficacy. Gottschalk, the leading figure in this controversy, was a poet of a high but melancholy order; his pessimism arose from the accident that his parents had forced him unwillingly into the monastery of Fulda as a child oblate. In his early twenties he obtained a dispensation from monastic vows, but this was cancelled through the opposition of his abbot, Rabanus Maurus, and after an attempt at missionary work, he then absorbed himself in the study of Augustine. By concentrating on a single aspect he made the doctrine of Predestination more terrible than it had been in the hands of the African saint. He denied all human freedom and held that the divine decrees, which predestined both the saved and the damned either to heaven or hell, had been determined even before the Fall of Adam. This supralapsarian double predestination appeared shocking to the majority of churchmen and Gottschalk spent most of his remaining life in a monastic prison, where he died around 870 without the sacraments, refusing to recant. Various writers, including Ratramnus and Walafrid Strabo, defended him, but he was attacked by the powerful Hincmar of Rheims who, having had the worst of the argument, called in the heavy artillery of Erigena to help him. Unfortunately, Erigena approached the problem without much knowledge of theology, and with too great reliance on ready-made logical formulae; he said that since God's Nature is simple, He cannot have a double will, both for salvation and for judgment, and that since evil is ultimately non-existent, no one can be predestined to it. These statements did not increase Erigena's reputation nor did the quarrel improve his liking for Hincmar. Violent passions were aroused on either side, but a compromise was finally reached at the Council of Thuzey in 860, which maintained the theology of Augustine without going to the lengths of Gottschalk.

The Carolingian Renaissance produced a reflected afterglow at the court of King Alfred, but the lights were already going out again in Europe. As early as 793 the Vikings had attacked Lindisfarne, which Alcuin thought a divine judgment on private and public sins. Jarrow was molested in the following year, and in 835 the Danes landed on the shore of Kent, while the Vikings, pushing on into France, threatened Paris ten years later. Meanwhile, the Moslems disembarked in Sicily in 827, and by 846 they had sailed north to the gates of Rome itself, forcing Pope Leo IV to construct the walls of the Leonine City for defence. There still were strong Popes, but by accepting a temporal sovereignty, the papacy had exposed itself to the turbulent factions of the Roman nobles, and in the tenth century it was to sink to its lowest pitch of weakness and degradation. Another ominous sign was the diversion of scholarship to the production of literary forgeries. In defence of the forgers, it must be said that written records were scanty, and they used their learning to produce an accurate replacement of what they believed to have been true. The result was that dogma began to create history, a trend which is well illustrated by the spurious Donation of Constantine. About the middle of the ninth century a scholarly workshop, probably at Le Mans, turned out a vast amount of fabrications including the False Decretals, on which later Popes were to base many of their claims. The immediate purpose of these forgeries was to strengthen the local bishops against their metropolitans by exalting the comparatively distant papacy, and at the same time to protect Church property from the greed of lay impropriators. In so far as the churches frequently lacked title deeds, the forgers were supplying a legitimate want; but it was tragic that scholarship should be thus prostituted to purposes that were political or worse.

There remained one permanent result. Books had come into their own, and although much of the ancient heritage had been lost in preceding centuries, what survived would be sedulously copied and re-copied and preserved. Alcuin got the books he needed reproduced from York, and in order to secure copy, elaborate arrangements were made for the loan of manuscripts, sometimes ending in disaster. We may conclude with a note from a medieval volume, which might be echoed by many a modern librarian: "This book is the property of Saint Maximin; Hatto had it written for the glory of God and of the Saint; and if anyone shall remove it from this place, without intending to return it, may he be damned in company with the devil."

CHAPTER IV

THE EAST FROM LEO THE ISAURIAN TO MICHAEL CERULARIUS

UNLIKE THE WEST, CONSTANTINOPLE NEVER ENDURED A Dark Age; there indeed were periods of anarchy and decadence, but Byzantine art, learning and administration continued virtually without a break. Professor Toynbee has recently attempted to argue that the Eastern Roman Empire died of decrepitude at the end of the sixth century, and that Leo the Isaurian then created a new Empire in response to the challenge of Islam; however, although the dynasty of Leo did for a time embark upon new and revolutionary policies, Bury and Gibbon before him were more correct in pointing to the continuity that endured through change. It was in essence the Empire of Constantine that lasted until the fall of Constantinople in 1453. As a result, the Byzantine clergy and people inherited an older attitude to Church affairs than that which was becoming prevalent throughout the West. In the early centuries, Christians had been obliged to organize themselves on a basis that was almost congregational, for they were scattered in small cells over the face of a vast Empire; when the last of the apostles died, there was little or nothing in the way of effective general oversight, so that responsibility was bound to devolve upon the local leaders; and although these leaders were called bishops, for at least three centuries they were pastors rather than prelates, in intimate personal contact with their flock, to whom they themselves regularly ministered the Word and Sacraments. With the growth of the Christian communities, some delegation of sacramental powers to the inferior clergy was inevitable, if the principle was maintained that, to avoid schism, there must not be more than one bishop in a city; and with increasing facility of communication, particular regions increasingly looked for guidance to their most ancient mother-church, especially if that metropolis, like Rome, Alexandria and Antioch, possessed an unbroken link with the apostolic age. Congregational autonomy was balanced by the harmony which was expected to prevail among the churches under the leading of the same Spirit. None the less, it is doubtful whether at any time since Pentecost all professing Christians have formed one visibly united body; the divisions which St. Paul deplored at Corinth continued to be manifest, sometimes for causes that were genuinely theological, often for motives of mere personal rivalry, and almost always for a variety of reasons that were neither entirely creditable nor the reverse. The ideal of one Church is noble and inspiring. But nearly 2,000 years of Christian history should at least raise a doubt whether Providence intends such unity to be expressed on the plane of outward institutions; whether the Church is not meant to grow like a human body, by reduplication of separate individual cells, rather than by mere extension of an undifferentiated mass; whether the bond of mutual charity is not preferable to the fetter of uniformity.

Rome was the one Church in the West of undoubtedly apostolic foundation, and in her own sphere her metropolitan standing could never be seriously contested. St. Peter and St. Paul had both been teachers of the Roman Church, in whose defence they were believed to have shed their blood. Moreover, Rome was the seat of government, the spot on which all roads converged; Christians the world over, even if they did not accept Roman ecclesiastical jurisdiction, yet looked up to Rome and to her Bishop with affection and respect. When Constantine removed his capital to the Bosporus, he left the papacy free to develop its claims both spiritual and temporal; and although there were few outstanding Popes before the fifth century, Rome had usually managed to take the right side in doctrinal controversies, thus acquiring a reputation for orthodoxy, if not as yet a dogma of infallibility. The conversion of the barbarians was very largely organized from Rome; the Empire of Charlemagne received its sanction at the hands of the Pope; and by now, virtually all Western Christians regarded the papacy as supreme head of the Church on earth, in a way that was personal, all-embracing and unique, even if the precise limits of its authority had not been adequately defined, and even if some theologians were prepared to grant the secular power a large measure of external influence in Church affairs.

But the situation looked very different when viewed with Eastern eyes. Constantine had taken the Roman Empire to the East, so that the Bishop of his new capital became the leading court prelate at a time when Rome had fallen into ruin; if the Pope were allowed some sort of honorary precedence in the Church as a whole, for reasons that were now purely historical, that was the most that he could legitimately claim; and if Rome had been the See of Peter, there was now a convenient legend that

St. Andrew had helped to found Constantinople. Moreover, Constantine had called the Council of Nicaea, and as further problems of theology arose, they were settled at subsequent Ecumenical Councils; the East passionately believed that the supreme ecclesiastical authority, the appointed organ of the Holy Spirit, was not the papacy but a council representing the entire Church; and it thought that in matters of jurisdiction, its four Patriarchs, at Constantinople, Alexandria, Antioch and Jerusalem, possessed an authority co-ordinate with that of Rome. The communion of the Church was maintained by the communion of the Patriarchs, including the Pope, with one another; each incumbent on election was expected to send a profession of faith to his four brethren; and they were at perfect liberty to withhold their communion from him, if they found his faith unacceptable. Again, it was a Christian Empire which Constantine had founded; he had taken the chief seat at the Council of Nicaea; and although it was the duty of bishops to preach the law of God to Emperors, it was the Emperor's privilege to promulgate and execute that law. In the turmoil of Western society, the Popes had succeeded to the imperial function of acting as the fount of law and justice; but in the East the Byzantine Emperor, surrounded by the liturgical adoration of his court, became an ecclesiastical person, if not a semi-divine being, and it was for him alone to order the affairs of both State and Church. In consequence, the Church's ethos was much more laicized in the East than in the West; Eastern clergy have never refused the cup to lay people at communion. Clerical dominance was accentuated in the West by the fact that few apart from the clergy could even sign their names, whereas in the East education was much more nearly universal, there was a highly efficient civil service from whose ranks the superior clergy were frequently recruited, and the laity always took a passionate interest in theological disputes. A key to much of Byzantine history is to be found in the persistent strife between the circus factions of the "Blues" and the "Greens." For under an autocratic rule, the games in the circus provided the sole occasion on which popular feeling could express itself, and the supporters of the rival sides were organized as public corporations. The "Greens" tended to be radical in politics and liberal in theology, while the "Blues" were orthodox, conservative and loyal; and the religious undercurrents, nowadays present at a Scottish football match between Celtic and Rangers, were equally manifest at the Byzantine sports.

Constantinople was not only a well-educated city, it was also extremely wealthy. When Pope Agatho sent envoys to the capital in 680, he apologized for the comparative poverty of his legates, explaining that the Roman clergy were poor men who had to work with their hands. In 968, Bishop Liutprand of Cremona came from the West as ambassador for the Emperor Otto I, and was amazed at the wealth of the Greek ecclesiastics; but he also noticed a servant problem which often occurs in a highly developed economy, and he remarks that the Greek bishops, rich as they might be, were obliged to do their own shopping. Constantinople reckoned her wealth chiefly in the multitude of relics she had gathered. The Virgin Mary was prominently honoured, and when the city was besieged by Avars in 626, the Patriarch Sergius had her image painted upon all its landward gates. Images were of course hateful to Jews and Moslems, and there was always some Christian opposition; the pilgrim Arculf, passing through Constantinople in 670, saw an image of the Virgin destroyed by a solitary but zealous iconoclast. And from about the same date, the Empire was relying for its defence upon the more practical invention of Greek fire, a secret preparation of naphtha projected from flame-throwers and said to be capable of burning even on the surface of the sea. Its armed forces were professional and efficient, with religious services held morning and night, and lay orators who acted as field preachers for the troops. Medical science was cultivated; the monastery of the Pantocrator had a hospital with fifty beds, a medical staff of sixty, five wards for different types of illness, a consulting room, and a special unit to deal with epileptics. Higher education was greatly valued; professors received good salaries, parents often made real sacrifices to educate their children, and we read of one student who earned his University fees by working as a stoker in the public baths. The secular University was separate from the patriarchal school of theology, and the monasteries taught only monks. So firmly implanted was the principle of State control over religion that in 1931, when the monks of Mount Athos wished to start keeping hens, they solemnly applied to the Greek Foreign Office for the requisite permission. Yet in this highly civilized society, whose kings were theologians and whose theologians were honoured almost as kings, criminals and political enemies were savagely mutilated as a legal punishment, with the approval of the Church, which regarded mutilation as preferable to the death penalty because it allowed the criminal time to repent. Even Emperors, when their fortunes waned, were not exempt from punishment. Of the hundred and seven Emperors who ruled at Constantinople between 395 and 1453, only thirty-four died in their beds; eight fell in battle or through some accident; and the remaining sixty-five perished or disappeared in the course of revolutions. But the Church survived each change of dynasty, for in the cosmopolitan society of the East the orthodox religion was the great common bond, and the Orthodox Church was both the people's possession and their pride.

As the centuries passed, misunderstanding grew. The language barrier increasingly became an iron curtain, for a knowledge of Greek died out almost entirely in the West, and the East had little need for Latin apart from its legal studies. Eastern services were conducted in the language of the people, while the Latin rite was intelligible only to the priests. Behind the particular points of controversy, as to the use of unleavened bread for communion, and the right of priests to be married or to shave their beards, behind even the doctrinal difference over the *Filioque* clause of the Creed, there lay the immemorial contempt of the Latin for the Greekling, answered by the disdain of the legitimist Empire of Constantinople for the upstart Empire of the West. The Greeks regarded the Latins as barbarians, and themselves as the true heirs of ancient Rome; on their part, the Latins were horrified when the Greeks refused to acknowledge the divine institution of the papacy; and two rival doctrines of the Church, papal and conciliar, confronted one another in irreconcilable opposition. On the one hand, there was a State-Church, with full lay participation, governed by the Emperor, headed by a college of equal Patriarchs, and guided in doctrine by the inspired pronouncements of Ecumenical Councils. On the other hand was ranged a hieratic theocracy, in which the laity played no part, controlled by Popes who could make and unmake kings, who alone could define doctrine and issue ecclesiastical laws, and who claimed an active supremacy over the entire Church of Christ. When either side felt strong enough to assert its point of view, friction and even schism were bound to follow.

The evils of State interference were apparent in the seventh century, as they had been at intervals since the fourth; strong rulers sought to pacify their subjects by issuing statements on controverted points of theology, with the perennial but unfulfilled hope of reconciling those dissident Christian communities which had separated from the main Orthodox Church. In 622 the Emperor Heraclius was on the brink of a seven years' struggle with Persia which was later reckoned by William of Tyre as the first of the Crusades; and no sooner had Persia been defeated, and the relic of the True Cross been restored, than a prolonged conflict broke out with the new and rising power of Islam. In such circumstances the Emperor opened negotiations with the large

sect of Monophysites, who insisted so strongly on the deity of
Christ that they believed His human nature had been absorbed in
the divine. The Orthodox, together with the Catholics of the
West, believed that real humanity together with deity subsisted in
the one Incarnate Person; but it was thought that all might unite
in the belief, designated by the name Monothelite, that Christ
possessed only one centre of psychological activity or, in other
words, a single divine will. This mediating doctrine was proposed
by Patriarch Sergius of Constantinople, who wrote in 634 to
Pope Honorius I, exaggerating the success of the efforts made for
reunion, and minimizing the theological concessions which it
involved. The Pope, who had just healed a schism in North
Italy, was anxious for unity and he did not regard these concessions as important; he advised Sergius to leave the counting of
centres of activity as a riddle for schoolmasters to set before their
boys, but he did clearly accept the doctrine of a single will in
Christ. It later became apparent that this would deny the reality
of His temptations and of His agony in Gethsemane; but in 638,
the year of the Pope's death, the Emperor published an official
document, asserting one will and ordering further argument to
cease. Argument however continued, both in East and West.
Sophronius, the Patriarch of Jerusalem, had been vigorously
opposed to Monothelitism. It was condemned at the Lateran
Council of 649 by Pope Martin I, who was arrested for this
temerity by imperial officers and, although confined to bed with
gout, was taken to Constantinople, exposed in his bed to the
insults of the populace, and died in exile and great poverty, the
last of the Popes to be venerated as a martyr. But by 680 the
heretical doctrine had lost its political advantages, for the Moslems had then captured the great centres of Monophysite population and there was no further hope of religious unity. The sixth
Ecumenical Council met at Constantinople in November 680,
continuing its sessions until September of the following year.
Steps had been taken to ascertain the views of the whole Church,
and even as far away as England, Archbishop Theodore of Canterbury discussed the problem at the Synod of Hatfield. With the
agreement of the Emperor, the Council solemnly condemned
Monothelitism and all its supporters, including Honorius I, who
was described as an ex-Pope in the official acts, perhaps because
of an idea then widely current that, if a Pope should fall into
heresy, he would *ipso facto* be deposed. And the reigning Pope,
Leo II, when confirming these acts explicitly stated that Honorius
had defiled the hitherto spotless faith of the Roman See. Papal
apologists naturally claim that the error of Honorius was personal

and not official, no more than a careless slip in correspondence; but when one infallible pontiff publicly condemns the doctrine publicly professed by an equally infallible predecessor, it becomes difficult for the simple-minded to understand the conditions under which an *ex cathedra* pronouncement can reliably be made. Had the incident involved an Eastern Patriarch, it would have raised no problems, since they never laid claim to infallibility; but to the papacy it was extremely damaging, and it added to the existing grounds of discord between East and West.

Meanwhile the pressure of Islam continued, in a crescent-shaped attack menacing the under-belly of Europe. Flushed with their initial successes, and fired by the inspiration of a new and simple faith, the Moslem armies penetrated along the North African littoral until the further horn of their attack had pierced Spain and France, only to be flung back by Charles Martel at the battle of Poitiers in 732. On the Eastern side, they were besieging Constantinople as early as 673, and though beaten off by Greek fire, their fleet returned each spring for the following four years. The capital held firm, but within its walls Emperor succeeded Emperor and confusion reigned until in 717 the strong hand of Leo the Isaurian took control; born in Syria and brought up in Thrace, he had gained the favour of Justinian II by a timely gift of mutton for his troops, and this success in the commissariat led to a military command in Anatolia, and so, after a revolution, to the throne. Immediately on his accession Leo had to defend the capital from yet another siege, and he then turned to a radical reorganization of the Empire.

Heavy fresh taxation was resented by the populace. The Emperor himself began with a prejudice against the monks, who enjoyed some fiscal exemptions and diverted potential recruits from his armies; but he did revise the imperial law, with a more marked emphasis on Christian morality, especially in matters of marriage and divorce. His earliest seals bore a traditional picture of the Virgin, but this was quickly dropped; for Leo and his soldiers, coming from the Eastern provinces, had been taught by the Moslems to show a healthy distaste for idolatry, and he felt that the superstitious inhabitants of Constantinople were trusting in images rather than in their own right hands to save them. According to the Syrian sources, Leo published an edict against the use of images in 726; the Greek sources mention nothing so formal as an edict, and suggest that there was only a strongly worded propaganda from the government. Whatever the niceties of the legal situation, the attitude of the Emperor was obvious by 727, when he had an image of Christ removed from the palace gate, and some women were executed for interfering with the workmen by pushing down their ladder. It should be remembered that in earlier times Christ had always been represented symbolically, as the Good Shepherd or the Lamb of God, and it was only in 692 that canonical permission was first given by a Church Council for representations of the actual human figure of the Saviour. But devotion to holy pictures was firmly entrenched in the Greek-speaking population, especially among the women and the monks; and the latter, already disliked for other reasons by the military Emperor, made considerable profits from painting icons and attracting pilgrims to their shrines. They did not go so far as to make graven images, sculptured in the round, but they saw no theological objection to flat portraits of holy persons, and in theory they were careful to distinguish the veneration paid to such objects from the worship which is properly due to God alone. John of Damascus, the greatest theologian of the period, at once published a defence of images, maintaining that the Second Commandment had been abrogated since the Incarnation, which made it possible for men to see God in human form; he added that contempt for material things implied a Manichaean dualism, and was tantamount to a denial of the Word made Flesh. For such fear of heresy there was some reasonable cause. In the part of Asia Minor from which Iconoclasm drew its strength, the heretical sect of the Paulicians was numerous; these people were certainly dualists in their belief that the world was made by an evil spirit called Satanael, they taught that the Incarnation of Christ was docetic or phantasmal, and they opposed not only images, but even the Christian sacraments. With such extreme views Leo had no sympathy; he and his family were devoted to the symbol of the cross, that triumphant symbol under which Constantine had marched to victory; and his one desire was to restore a pure and simple creed, which might serve as an effective ideology against the militant advances of Islam. Nor was the iconcoclastic movement in its origins merely political and secular; it also had supporters among the clergy, and before Leo began his propaganda three bishops of Asia Minor had been destroying images in churches. In general, the upper classes and the intellectuals favoured iconoclasm, while it was opposed by the peasants and the monks, and the dispute formed one chapter in the incessant strife between liberals and conservatives, or "Greens" and "Blues." Germanus, the Patriarch of Constantinople, was persuaded to resign in 730; Leo appointed as successor one of his own secretaries called Anastasius; and the policy of iconoclasm was then reinforced by an ecclesiastical decree. At Rome Pope

Gregory II, already embittered by the increase in government taxation, wrote a letter of protest, from which it appears that Leo had ventured to call himself both priest and emperor, and had appealed to the Old Testament example of Hezekiah destroying the brazen serpent. So far from paying attention to the papal protest, Leo removed the provinces of Sicily and Illyricum from the ecclesiastical jurisdiction of Rome and transferred them to that of Constantinople; they already belonged to the civil administration of the East, and the transfer was only a piece of bureaucratic reform; but the Popes had always asserted themselves in both these regions, and Gregory was grievously annoyed.

However, there was little persecution in the reign of Leo, and it was his son Constantine V who made a determined effort to destroy both images and those who worshipped them. He wrote a book, declaring that the communion elements are the only material symbols of Christ which Christians should employ; he condemned not merely images, but also invocation of the saints, the cult of relics, even the titles Saint and Mother of God; and in 753 he convened a Synod of 338 bishops to enforce his views. The assembly agreed to condemn images, but further than that they would not go; from among the Patriarchs, it was only the court prelate of Constantinople who attended; and the Pope, despairing of protection from the Emperor, turned at this very moment to King Pepin and the French. None the less, Constantine now launched a veritable reign of terror, directed especially against the monks, many of whom were forced to marry or paraded through the streets hand in hand with nuns. The unintended effect of this persecution was to instil in its victims a desire for spiritual independence, and even an affection for Rome as the champion of freedom from State control. Constantine's son, Leo IV, was obliged to mitigate the persecution, and on his death in 780 his widow Irene, acting as regent for their young son, began to restore the use of images. Her efforts were at first frustrated by the army, which revered the memory of its warlike Emperors; but with the help of a complaisant Patriarch and the distant approval of the papacy, she succeeded in having iconoclasm condemned at the seventh Ecumenical Council, which met in 787 at Nicaea. Either by mistake or by deliberate falsification, the Latin version of the Council's acts asserted that images should be honoured with divine worship, and in answer to this blasphemy the *Caroline Books* were written, partly to uphold the old doctrine of Gregory the Great, and partly to detach the papacy from its renewed alliance with the Greek Empire; so puritan was the tone of these books that Roman Catholics in the sixteenth

E

century regarded them as a Calvinist forgery, but in fact it was
the abuse of images, and not images as such, that they condemned.
Thus ended the first period of iconoclasm; it was followed by a
second, from 814 to 843, in which similar events were closely
repeated. Again a military Emperor of Eastern birth, Leo the
Armenian, sought to purify the faith of his subjects by destroying
images; again a Patriarch was forced to abdicate, and there was
persecution of Greek monks who turned for support to Rome;
again a widowed Empress, Theodora, reversed the policy of
iconoclasm; and in 843, on the conclusion of the struggle, a great
Feast of Orthodoxy was instituted in honour of the icons and
their martyred supporters. Iconoclasm had proved too negative
to kindle an enduring faith; instead, by acting as a persecutor, it
had increased the devotion of its enemies.

Moreover, the growing cleavage between East and West had
been still further emphasized. In the best Latin tradition, John of
Damascus had declared that kings should not legislate for the
Church; but though the doctrine of the Greek monks on images
had triumphed, their Romeward leanings were abhorred; and
henceforward the liberal intellectuals were to champion the cause
of Greek nationalism and loyalty to the State. On balance, the
Emperors had gained rather than lost prestige. Improving on the
splendours of the Abbasid court at Baghdad, the Emperor
Theophilus built himself a new throne-room about the year 830,
where the awed envoys of foreign powers were received amid the
roars of golden lions and the music of mechanical birds upon a
gilded plane-tree. With the papacy the Emperors were now again
in theological agreement; but the Popes regarded the restoration
of images as poor compensation for the loss of Illyricum and
Sicily; and when the heathen kingdoms of the Balkans displayed
a readiness to accept the gospel, there was to be a keen struggle
for their ecclesiastical allegiance between Constantinople and
Rome.

In the year 858, these two leading sees came to be occupied by
two forceful characters. The Pope, Nicholas I, belonged to the
old Roman nobility and had had a distinguished career of service
in the Curia; with high-handed authority, he was to attack even
so powerful a prelate as Hincmar of Rheims, and to depose two
German Archbishops for their complicity in a royal divorce; and
his political interventions, coupled with his integrity of character,
were to make him an example to future Popes. The Patriarch,
Photius, was a learned professor and successful civil servant, who
was appointed in an attempt to conciliate the two rival factions at
Constantinople. His scholarship produced a digest of several

hundred books, called the *Myriobiblion*, which is a mine of information on works now lost. He had been Professor of Philosophy at the University of Constantinople, and in that capacity it is said that, with donnish delight, he once concocted a neat little heresy just to see how the then Patriarch, who affected to despise logic, would be able to deal with it. This Patriarch, a somewhat narrow-minded monk called Ignatius, was instigated by the extremists to excommunicate a brother of the Empress Theodora; for this rash act of interference, it was decided in 858 that he must go. Photius was the obvious man to succeed; a moderate, but not too outspoken, and related to Theodora, he was duly consecrated Patriarch by bishops from both the rival parties. He had almost everything in his favour, learning, orthodoxy, wide popularity and imperial support, but his position suffered from three serious defects. In the first place, he had only been a layman when appointed Patriarch, and although exceptions were frequently permitted, the Church did not approve of raising laymen direct to the episcopate. Secondly, the bishop who presided at his consecration was the moderate leader, Gregory Asbestas of Syracuse; and Gregory, despite an appeal to Rome, had been suspended from his clerical functions by the previous Patriarch. Third, and worst of all, the predecessor of Photius had not resigned and was still alive. When Photius sent his profession of faith to Rome asking for recognition, Pope Nicholas at once saw his opportunity of fishing in the troubled waters; he first refused to acknowledge the new Patriarch, and then "for the good of the Church," proposed a bargain, by which recognition would be granted if the disputed provinces of Sicily and Illyricum were returned to the Roman jurisdiction. Meanwhile, the old supporters of Ignatius, angry at the change in patriarchal policy, were scheming to restore their fallen leader; with the result that, at a synod held at Constantinople in 861, Photius was obliged to allow arbitration by the Roman legates. This was the first time that the East had ever permitted such interference by the papacy in its domestic discipline, and the legates, overjoyed at the concession, at once took the side of Photius. But the Pope had not recovered the provinces he coveted; he repudiated his legates' action, and in 863 he had Photius formally deposed by a synod which met in Rome.

The situation was now complicated by the dreams, which both sides entertained, of missionary expansion in the Balkans. Photius had a university pupil called Constantine, better known by the name of Cyril which he afterwards assumed; this man was sent in 861 to the Crimea, in response to a request from the heathen

Khazars, who were then discussing the respective merits of Christianity, Judaism and Islam; he spent a year among them, but most decided to become Jews, and his one material success was the discovery of a body in the sea, alleged to be that of Clement of Rome, and identified by an anchor mentioned in a legend. This precious relic he was afterwards to take to Rome; but meanwhile in 862 a Moravian embassy arrived at Constantinople asking for Christian missionaries. Prince Ratislav wished to make his country Christian, but at the same time to avoid the Romeward leanings of the neighbouring German Church. Cyril had some knowledge of the language, for the writing of which he invented the Glagolitic script, and after translating portions of Scripture and the liturgy, he set out for Moravia, accompanied by his brother Methodius. The willingness of the Byzantines to permit worship in the local vernacular was of great advantage to missionaries; Rome, though sometimes making exceptions, normally insisted that the service must be conducted in Latin, Greek or Hebrew, the three languages in which Pilate had written the inscription on the cross. However, the Pope felt it advisable to use discretion, and in 867 he invited Cyril and Methodius to Rome, where they were both consecrated bishops; Cyril then died, and his brother returned to Moravia, which through the influence of German prelates eventually fell to the Latin sphere. At the same time, in 865, King Boris of Bulgaria had accepted baptism at the hands of Greek clergy, with the Greek Emperor standing godfather; but Constantinople refused to let him have an independent Bulgarian Patriarch, and for this he turned to Rome. Pope Nicholas wrote a diplomatic letter, pointing out that Constantinople was not really apostolic and should only be ranked fourth among the leading sees; and Boris was delighted to hear from the Pope that he and his subjects, both men and women, could continue wearing trousers and could bathe on Wednesdays and Fridays without pain of sin. The accusation of schismatic practices, especially in allowing the ordination of married men, was now first made against the Greeks. But Rome was no more willing than Constantinople to create a Bulgarian Patriarch, and the Bulgars, attracted by the Slavonic liturgy, at last sided with the East.

Rivalry between the two Churches in this mission field embittered an already tense situation. In correspondence, both Photius and Nicholas had agreed that the words of Matt. 16 : 18 refer to Peter's faith and not his person as the rock on which the Church is built; but Nicholas had accused the Greeks of schismatic practices, and to this Photius replied with a charge of doctrinal error. The Creed, as formulated at Ecumenical Councils, did not contain the *Filioque* clause; this had slipped in almost unnoticed at a series of Spanish synods, but its use was now widespread in the West, and although the Popes admitted that the addition was unauthorized, they were not prepared to check it. The Greeks did agree that the Spirit proceeds from the Father through the Son, and this form of statement seemed theologically adequate to the Latins; but the burden of the Greek complaint was that the West, on its own sole authority, had disrupted the communion of the churches by adding to the work of inspired and universally accepted Councils. This was regarded as an instance of papal usurpation; and to it, Photius added a number of minor charges, arising out of points on which Eastern practice differed from the West. In 863 he wrote to the Frankish ruler Louis II asking for the removal of the tyrannous Pope; and in 867, with the backing of his own Emperor, he declared Nicholas deposed. But in the same year, that Emperor was murdered by Basil the Macedonian, a poor equerry who had won court favour through his skill in breaking horses and his readiness to marry a discarded imperial mistress. Basil founded a new and glorious dynasty, which was to recover much of the Byzantine conquests; and at once he changed his ministers, dismissing Photius and restoring Ignatius to the patriarchal throne. An Ecumenical Council, attended by papal legates, confirmed the deposition of Photius and renewed the concord of the churches; but immediately afterwards, disputes over jurisdiction in Bulgaria threatened a resumption of the schism; and when Ignatius died in 877, all parties were strangely willing to accept Photius as his lawful successor. The Bulgars themselves solved the Bulgarian problem by deciding for the East. But Photius, after yet another change of government, finally fell from power in 886; primarily a scholar and a politician, he is honoured in the Greek Church as a saint, and he inspired his successors to fight for national independence against Rome. Relations were again at one point so strained that some authorities have wrongly thought there was a second Photian schism. In point of fact the churches remained in an uneasy truce until 1054; but concord had been seriously shaken, and in his attack upon the *Filioque*, Photius had given his compatriots a powerful weapon of offence.

After Nicholas, the moral stature of the papacy declined. One of his successors, who had offended a party of the Romans, was exhumed from his grave, posthumously unfrocked and thrown into the Tiber. Another Pope was said to be the lover of a notorious lady called Marozia; their illegitimate son succeeded to the papacy in his early twenties, and a grandson of Marozia, who became Pope at the age of eighteen, had to be deposed for flagrant immorality. At this point, the highest office in the Western Church had become a plaything of the Roman aristocracy; and in the latter half of the tenth century, the revived German Empire intervened to restore a semblance of decency and order. The Emperors appointed good men to the papacy, thus helping to reform the Church; but these same good men, once in power, began again to assert their spiritual authority against the Empire. Moreover, the insistence on clerical celibacy now acquired a new importance in the West; bishoprics and benefices must not be allowed to descend from shameless fathers to their offspring; and although the married clergy of Milan appealed to the Bible and to their great Archbishop Ambrose, although Guibert the Archdeacon declared that marriage was lawful for laity and clergy alike "because all the sons of the Church are priests, be they laymen or clerks," none the less the reforming Popes insisted that everyone in major orders must be celibate, thus underlining yet another divergence between East and West. For the Greek Church, while preferring celibate monks as its bishops, always allowed married men to receive the priesthood, and although it forbade marriage after ordination, it encouraged candidates to marry before they were ordained.

Meanwhile, under the Macedonian dynasty the Greek Empire recovered ground from Islam and expanded in the Balkans. The remnant of the Paulician heretics was settled on the Bulgarian frontier, where their dualist doctrine inspired the Bogomils of Bosnia, later spreading to the Albigensians of southern France. An event of vast importance for the future of Europe was the conversion of Russia to the Orthodox Eastern Faith. In 957 the Grand Duchess Olga was baptized, a solitary convert, on a State visit to Constantinople. About thirty years later her grandson Vladimir, rejecting the teetotal religion of Mohammed because "drinking is the delight of the Russians," rejecting Judaism because the Dispersion seemed a token of divine displeasure, and rejecting Roman missionaries because they ordered him to fast, sent an embassy to Constantinople which reported that the wondrous worship in St. Sophia was like a foretaste of celestial glory; and moved by this glowing report, he contracted a marriage alliance with the Greek imperial family which involved acceptance of the Greek religion. On his baptism Vladimir took the name of Basil, by which the reigning Emperor was called; government pressure produced a fairly rapid conversion of the Russian people, but their Church remained an alien institution, closely tied to the State; and until 1237, with two exceptions, the Metropolitan of Russia was always a Greek. Such was the enormous expansion of

Byzantine influence. In the capital, a Patriarch was strong enough to excommunicate the Emperor Leo VI for contracting his fourth marriage with the black-eyed Carbinopsina. The marriage, secretly performed by a court chaplain in 906, was approved by Marozia's lover, Pope Sergius III; but the Patriarch, Nicholas Mysticus, refused communion to Leo, and though deposed for a time, was reinstated by the repentant Emperor on his death-bed in 911. A century later, in 1009, the Patriarchs stopped the custom of praying for the Popes in church, and events were again moving towards schism; a result which became inevitable after 1028, when the Macedonian dynasty was represented only by two pious old ladies, the Empresses Zoe and Theodora, too weak to control an ambitious Patriarch.

In 1043 Michael Cerularius became Patriarch of Constantinople. Three years before, he had been moved by the suicide of his brother to take monastic vows. Cultured and honest, he had previously been chief minister of the imperial government, but after his elevation to the patriarchate, he regarded himself as at least equal to the civil ruler; and he was later to assume the purple imperial buskins and to be arrested in 1058 for an alleged attempt upon the throne. Such a man was bound to be intransigent in his dealings with the papacy, and from 1048 the Roman See was occupied by an equally forceful character, Leo IX, a product of the reform movement associated with the monastery of Cluny, who devoted his life to the correction of simony and other abuses in the Latin Church. Sufficient trouble had already been caused by the transfer of Illyricum from Roman to Byzantine jurisdiction; Sicily, the other province that went with it, though at the moment occupied by Moslems, was now to be the cause of further strife. From about 1040 a party of Norman adventurers, led by the sons of Tancred de Hauteville, had settled in South Italy, and their conquests alarmed not only the Pope but also both the Western and Eastern Emperors. By 1052 the three powers were drawing together in a military alliance which Cerularius, to maintain the independence of his Church, was determined on preventing. He therefore instigated a Bulgarian bishop, Leo of Ochrida, to write to the Bishop of Trani in South Italy; and the letter, attacking the Latin usages, was intended for transmission to the Pope. Its main attack was directed against the use of unleavened bread in the communion, which the East regarded as a Judaistic practice, reinforced by criticism of the Latin custom of fasting on Saturdays, eating things strangled, and of failing to sing Alleluia after the start of Lent. At the same time, with the tidy mind of a former bureaucrat, Cerularius insisted that all the congregations

in Constantinople must follow the same usages, and when the
Latin churches there refused to conform, he had them closed
amid riots in which the consecrated Host was said to have been
trampled underfoot. His letter to the West was couched in violent
language, obviously desiring to provoke a rupture; and it arrived
in Italy at a moment when the Normans had defeated the papal
army and made prisoner of the Pope. Leo received it through his
principal secretary, Cardinal Humbert of Moyenmoutier, who
knew a little Greek and in translating it did nothing to mitigate
its violence. The Pope himself was spending the time of his
captivity in learning Greek, but had not progressed far enough to
check Humbert's translation; deeply shocked by the contents, he
ordered Humbert to draft a reply, maintaining the papal supremacy
and defending the Latin usages. But this reply was in turn considered too violent to be sent. Meanwhile the Greek Emperor,
anxious to defeat the Normans, had persuaded Cerularius to
adopt a more conciliatory tone, though his correspondence continued to give offence by using the hated title of Ecumenical
Patriarch, and he made the unpardonable mistake of addressing
the Pope as "Brother" instead of "Father."

In such circumstances a papal legation, headed by Cardinal
Humbert, arrived at Constantinople in 1054, bearing a cordial
letter to the Greek Emperor and a rebuke for the impertinent
Patriarch, whose stubborn intransigence, coupled with the hot-
headed impulse of the Cardinal, was now to produce the final and
dramatic rupture. The major points in dispute were the *Filioque*
clause, clerical celibacy and the use of unleavened bread; minor
ones included liturgical divergences and the fact that the Latin
clergy shaved their beards. In Constantinople the Roman legates
could count on support from some of the monks, and they knew
that the Emperor was anxious to conclude a treaty; not realizing
the immense popularity of Cerularius, who was regarded as a
national champion, they felt able to treat him with studied disdain. But Pope Leo died in April, and his successor was not in
fact installed until twelve months later; in the interval, the lega-
tine powers of Humbert and his colleagues lapsed, so that they
ceased to have any legal standing. Nevertheless, on Saturday, 16th
July 1054, the three legates strode into the Church of St. Sophia
just as service was about to begin, laid upon the altar a bull ex-
communicating Cerularius and all his associates, and left shaking
the dust from off their feet. Few documents contain such a tissue
of inaccuracies as the bull which Humbert had concocted; he
even had the effrontery to accuse the Greeks of omitting the doctrine of the Double Procession from the accepted Creed, a state-

ment which was the exact opposite of truth. The Emperor made a fruitless attempt to mediate, but the people demonstrated in favour of their Patriarch, and on 24th July a Greek synod formally excommunicated the Roman legates, who by this time were safely on their way to Rome.

Both sides claimed a resounding victory. But Cerularius had been careful to leave it open for a future Pope to repudiate the legates. So far, the excommunication on either side had been levelled at persons and not Churches, and it took about a century for ordinary people to realize that East and West were in a state of permanent schism. The events of 1054 were not decisive in themselves; but they marked the climax to a long process of estrangement and misunderstanding. Thirty attempts at reunion were made; thrice the Churches were again officially united, in 1204, 1274 and 1439, but on each occasion it was a mere paper formality, achieved under political pressure, and without permanent effect. Mutual suspicion continued to increase, particularly in 1204 when a drunken mob of crusaders, accusing the Emperor of bad faith, sacked Constantinople and massacred some of its Christian population; and just before the fall of Constantinople in 1453, a prominent Greek official declared that he would rather live under the rule of the Turkish turban than that of the papal tiara.

CHAPTER V

THE HILDEBRANDINE REFORM

THE NAME OF HILDEBRAND, WHO REIGNED AS POPE GREGORY VII from 1073 until his death in 1085, is outstandingly associated with a movement for the reform of abuses such as simony and clerical concubinage; it was an attempt to realize the Kingdom of God on earth, by purifying the Church under the leadership of a high-minded Pope; and when it came into conflict with the German Empire, it led to a full-fledged assertion of the papal claim to universal sovereignty. But Hildebrand neither initiated this movement, nor was he able to bring it to a successful end. He died in exile, deserted by almost the whole Church, with an anti-pope established in Rome; and it was left to his successors, under the inspiration of his ideals, to complete the edifice of papal power. Other men, long before his time, had begun the reforming movement; a century before, when the papacy had become a byword for the immorality of its ineffective occupants, earnest souls were demanding a return to righteousness. The original centres of this demand were located, not in Rome or Italy, but rather in those Romance districts which were later to produce many of the new impulses of the Middle Ages, including the crusades and the scholastic theology. Burgundy, Lorraine and to a lesser extent Germany were the earliest homes of the reforming movement, which only captured the papacy a generation before Hildebrand. It was promoted, first, by the revival of monasticism radiating from the great mother-house of Cluny; second, by the renewed study of canon law, exemplified in the work of Bishop Burchard of Worms; and third, by the desire of the best German Emperors to rescue the Church from degradation.

Cluny, situated near Mâcon in Burgundy, lay on one of the cross-roads of Europe, hard by the river highway of the Rhône and not far from a pilgrim route to Rome. Its monastery was founded in the year 910 by William the Pious, Duke of Aquitaine, and placed under the strict rule of Berno of Baume as its first abbot. By an unusual privilege, the foundation charter permitted the monks to elect their abbot without interference from Duke

William or his successors, and thus from the outset Cluny was associated with the ideal of spiritual independence from lay control. Its life was based on a stringent observance of the Benedictine discipline, with special emphasis on devotion, both private and public, in the due performance of the liturgy. Before Berno's death in 927, some half a dozen neighbouring monasteries had accepted a similar discipline; under his successors, particularly Odo and Odilo, a large number of houses were affiliated to Cluny, so that by the eleventh century the Cluniac Order formed a compact international organization for the encouragement of its ideals. The worship in its huge abbey church was lengthy, impressive and elaborate. The life of its monks was well regulated, even in the smallest details: personal linen was clearly marked with the owner's name, and the laundry was regularly collected on Tuesdays and returned on Saturdays. Meat was eaten only by the sick in the infirmary, but, apart from their daily ration of wine and a pound of bread, the monks had a three-course dinner, of dried beans and vegetables, with fish on Sundays and Thursdays, and on other days cheese or eggs, of which four or five were served for every monk. There was a large guest-house with stables, where free horse-shoes were provided for travellers who needed them; for poorer pilgrims who came on foot, bread and wine were always available at the almonry. To dispense his charities, the almoner received a tenth of all the abbey's money tithes, and a tenth of all money offered in the church; surplus food from the monks' table was given to the poor, and there were extra allowances on certain feast-days and the anniversary of a monk's death; once a week, the almoner went round the town to visit the sick poor in their homes and to supply what they required. So reckless was the generosity of Odo that his prior sometimes complained. And the monks, whose prayers were frequently requested, took an interest not only in the living but also in the dead; Odilo sanctioned an annual day of prayer for the departed, which in course of time was observed throughout the Church on November 2nd as All Souls' Day. Other houses, not directly affiliated to Cluny, were influenced by its spirit; such were Monte Cassino, the ancient headquarters of the Benedictine observance, and Santa Maria on the Aventine at Rome, where Hildebrand was to receive his boyhood education. Meanwhile, although the first distinctively Cluniac house was not founded in England until 1077, a similar monastic reform was being carried out in the later tenth century by Dunstan, first as Abbot of Glastonbury, and then as Archbishop of Canterbury. The leaders of the Cluniac movement were men of noble families, who increasingly won the confidence of kings and popes. Hugh, who became Abbot of Cluny in 1049, was the intimate adviser of nine popes, beginning with Leo IX; he was also a close friend to the Emperor Henry III, who shared his reforming ardour, and he was the godfather of Henry IV, whom he attempted to reconcile to Hildebrand. Such abbots, when taking part in the councils of the Church, pressed for the remedy of abuses, and above all for the enforcement of clerical celibacy. They also helped to promote a sort of early Geneva convention, known as the Treuga or Truce of God, to protect the victims of war. As early as 990, the council of Le Puy threatened excommunication against those who should attack clergy, churches, or the poor; under the guidance of Abbot Odilo, similar measures were taken by synods in various parts of France; and in 1027, the council of Elne prohibited all fighting between Saturday afternoon and Monday morning, in order that the Lord's Day might be properly observed. About the same time, chivalry began to take its religious character, with the young knight dedicating his arms to the protection of widows, orphans and the Church.

Because of their contacts with both spiritual and secular authorities, the Cluniac leaders were anxious to promote understanding and co-operation between Church and State. A similar attitude characterized the earlier canon lawyers. During the first quarter of the eleventh century, an influential digest of Church Law was compiled by Burchard of Worms. He manifests no trace of hostility to the State, but rather regards it as a natural ally of the Church in the divine ordering of human society. On the other hand, he does treat the Church as an independent institution, with the papacy as its supreme court of appeal; and on the question, which was to become crucial, of the right of patronage enjoyed by kings and nobles, he insists that no bishop should be intruded against the will of the people. The ancient and canonical method of appointment had been election by clergy and people of the diocese, while in the institution of parish priests the bishop had a decisive voice. But feudalism had brought the system of *Eigenkirche* or proprietary churches; the local lord, having built and endowed such a church, appointed its incumbent without reference to ecclesiastical authority. The bishops had themselves become great feudal magnates, with large temporal possessions attached to their sees; hence, in order to preserve the unity of his realm, the king insisted on nominating the prelates, and on exacting from them an oath of homage. By these encroachments, the jurisdiction and the very unity of the Church were threatened. Feudalism represented an organic structure of society, a sort of pyramid linking all men through their lesser loyalties in allegiance to a common head; in such a unified organization, there was no room for two ultimate sources of power; and the subsequent struggle between papacy and empire was based on the assumption that in the last resort, one or other must be supreme. But the Teutonic tradition, especially as exemplified in Salic Law, brought another element which was to be of enormous service to the papacy. This was the idea of a *pactum* or elementary social contract between king and people, whereby the king at his accession promised to rule in accordance with the law; if he broke the law, his subjects might have a legitimate right of rebellion; and here an opening was provided for the papacy, as guardian of public morals, to judge between king and people in an alleged breach of contract.

Meanwhile canon law was passing from a conciliar to a papal phase. Its sources lay in Scripture, tradition, the canons of councils and the decretals of the Popes. For a long time in the West, it was enshrined in collections which had no more than local currency; of these the African and the Spanish were the most important. But at Rome in the sixth century, a Scythian monk called Dionysius Exiguus gathered together the decrees of the early councils, adding to them a series of thirty-nine papal decretals from the time of Pope Siricius in the late fourth century; this collection came into widespread use when Pope Hadrian I sent it, in an expanded form, to Charlemagne as the official law-book of the Roman Church, and it was not finally superseded until the twelfth century by the work of Gratian. About the year 850 an expert school of French forgers produced the False Decretals, written under the assumed name of Isidore of Seville; this collection contains many genuine documents, but supplements them with seventy spurious decretals attributed to the pre-Nicene Popes, and adds further fabricated material, including the Donation of Constantine, at a later date. Dionysius had placed papal letters alongside conciliar decrees; in the False Decretals, the papal element predominates, and the Pope appears as the sovereign lawgiver for Christendom. The purpose of this forgery was to protect the Church and clergy from feudal encroachments; it seems to have been known and approved by Nicholas I, but it was not until the time of Hildebrand that it was seriously employed as a weapon against lay control. Its spurious nature was not recognized until the fifteenth century.

In the meanwhile, those who longed for reformation hoped to achieve this through the civil power. Such intervention was unwittingly invoked by the papacy itself; John XII, one of the

earliest Popes to adopt a new name at his election, called on the
German ruler, Otto I, to protect him from the rising power of
Berengarius II in Italy. In 962 he crowned Otto as Holy Roman
Emperor; but only a year later, having plotted against his new
ally, he was deposed and succeeded by an imperial nominee. Otto
had consolidated his rule in Germany by controlling the episcopate; both he and his successors now applied the same policy in
Rome, and it was they who appointed the first German and the
first Frenchman to occupy the papal throne. But during a temporary weakness of the empire, the Roman nobles once again
acquired control of papal elections. The last of the puppet Popes
whom they created, Benedict IX, is said perhaps wrongly to have
been only twelve years old when he assumed the tiara in 1033.
Twelve years later, faced by an anti-pope whom the rival faction
had installed, weary of office and perhaps contemplating matri-
mony, Benedict sold the papacy to a Roman priest, John, in
return for a pension which was to be paid him out of Peter's
Pence. John, who took the name of Gregory VI, supported the
reform movement, and by acquiring the papacy had hoped to
further its ideals; but Benedict repented of his bargain and resumed
office. With three rival pontiffs, each holding one of the principal
churches in Rome, the Emperor Henry III felt obliged to intervene. He descended on Italy, held a synod at Sutri in 1046,
deposed the three rivals or compelled them to resign, and installed
a worthy German of his own choice as Pope. This cleansing of
the papacy was welcomed by most of the reformers; Peter
Damian, the pious prior of a hermitage at Fonte Avellana, compared the Emperor to David and the Roman nobles to Goliath.
But despite the fact that Henry was an ardent reformer and a
friend to the Cluniac Abbot Hugh, there were others who looked
askance on this invasion of Church prerogatives by the secular
power.

When he went into exile in Germany, Gregory VI took with
him his chaplain, a young relative named Hildebrand. Born about
1020 to poor parents at Soana on the borders of Tuscany, Hildebrand had spent his entire youth at Rome, where he not only saw
the tribulations of the papacy, but also was educated under
Cluniac influence at the monastery of Santa Maria on the Aventine, of which one of his uncles was the abbot. Diminutive in
stature and unprepossessing in appearance, he made good use of
his German visit, although he tells us that he had left Rome with
great reluctance; Germany was at this period the great centre for
the revived study of canon law, and it was from this that Hildebrand derived his theocratic conceptions of authority. On

Gregory's death in 1047 he seems to have taken refuge in a monastery: at Cluny itself according to a contemporary writer, Bonizo of Sutri, but Bonizo is often ill informed and his statement must be treated with reserve. However, there can be no doubt that Hildebrand was a monk, since otherwise there would have been no point in his enemies' later description of him as a false one; precisely where and when he made his profession we do not know, and it may be that he had been a child oblate from his youth.

At Rome, two popes had died in rapid succession; both were believed to have been poisoned in the interests of the dethroned Benedict IX. There was in such circumstances a certain dearth of candidates for the papacy; but Henry III conferred it upon a cousin of his own, Bishop Bruno of Toul, who took the name of Leo IX. Though appointed in 1048, Leo insisted on going to Rome to win the approval of the Roman clergy and people, in addition to the Emperor's nomination, and it was only when their approval had been secured in the following year that he formally began his pontificate. He brought with him a number of reforming friends from Germany, including Humbert of Moyenmoutier, whom he made a Cardinal Bishop, and Hildebrand, who was given the humbler task of restoring discipline in the monastery of St. Paul. In the Church at large there was a crying need for reformation; one of Leo's first acts was to excommunicate a Bishop of Langres for simony, murder, adultery and sodomy; and to deal with such cases direct papal intervention was often required, since under the ancient and more cumbrous canonical procedure, seventy-two witnesses must be produced to substantiate a charge against a bishop. The strange complexities, the divided loyalties, of medieval life are illustrated in the tale told by Ordericus Vitalis of a French bishop, who was also by right of birth a baron; in his first capacity this schizophrenic person was strictly celibate, but in the second he was married with the hope of heirs. At his Easter Synod of 1049, Leo attempted to enforce celibacy on all clerics from the rank of sub-deacon upwards, though for some time to come this was to remain no more than a pious ideal; in the same year, at the Synod of Rheims, he grasped the nettle of simony at its root, by enacting that prelates should be freely elected by their flocks. Both measures were repeated ten years later by Pope Nicholas II, who decreed, at the Roman Synod of 1059, that no cleric should be instituted by a lay patron, and that the people should boycott services conducted by an unchaste priest. But these were mere opening salvoes in the campaign; the system of lay patronage, with its attendant vice of presents offered by the prospective candidate, was too profitable to both parties to be eradicated at once; and those of the clergy, who possessed wives or concubines, protested that for many men celibacy was an impossible and even unchristian standard.

None the less, Leo travelled extensively, holding synods in Italy, Germany and France for the furtherance of reform; and he strengthened his administration by making the college of cardinals a more distinct body, to which he appointed like-minded men from outside the Roman Church. The Pope's immediate entourage comprised, first, the seven suffragan bishops of the suburbicarian sees, who presided in turn for one day each week at the services in the Lateran; second, the priests of the *tituli* or parish churches inside Rome, at this period about twenty-five in number; and third, the seven regionary deacons, each assisted by two sub-deacons. These cardinal bishops, priests and deacons were employed not only for the government of the Church in Rome, but also as the Pope's personal legates to other parts. Their counsels were divided over the subject of relations between Church and State. Peter Damian, who belonged to the older school of thought, welcomed the support of pious rulers like Henry III. But Humbert, the impulsive architect of the schism in 1054, insisted on ecclesiastical supremacy, writing as follows in his treatise against simoniacs: "in the Church, priesthood is like the soul and kingship like the body . . . just as the soul rules and commands the body, so the priestly dignity is superior to the royal, as heaven is to earth." With an attitude like that of John Knox's *Blast of the Trumpet*, Humbert disapproved particularly of investiture to Church offices by a woman. On the question of simony, he followed the extreme views of Guy of Arezzo in declaring this vice to be a heresy, which made all the ministerial acts of a simoniac invalid. In defiance of tradition, he insisted that no heretic can perform a true sacrament; and the novelty of such views may be illustrated by the fact that, whereas the early Church had condemned Cyprian's practice of rebaptizing converted heretics, Humbert warmly approved the line which Cyprian had taken. To all of these extreme assertions the more moderate Peter Damian was opposed; his dream of harmonious co-operation between Church and State, though rejected for the moment, was later to be revived by Dante, who wrote much of his *Divine Comedy* in a cell at Damian's hermitage of Fonte Avellana. Meanwhile, Hildebrand played a subordinate part in the work of the papal curia; he was by no means prominent until after Humbert's death in 1061; but while only a sub-deacon, he was sent as legate to France, Milan and the German court, and in 1055 he deposed six French bishops for simony.

The Emperor died in 1056, to be succeeded by his son Henry IV, then a six-year-old boy of headstrong will, whom his mother had difficulty in controlling; young Henry first came into collision with the papacy at the age of seventeen, when he tried to divorce a wife whom he had married only a year before. But for the moment, the regency of the Empress Agnes gave Rome an opportunity for more independent action. Victor II, the last Pope to be appointed by the Emperor, died after a brief pontificate in 1057; his successor Stephen IX was elected at Rome without reference to the German court. And Stephen, whose family name was Frederick of Lorraine, had been a staunch ally of the anti-imperialists in the curia; he had accompanied Humbert to Constantinople on the fateful embassy in 1054; and thereafter he served as Abbot of Monte Cassino, while his brother Duke Godfrey of Lorraine married Countess Beatrice of Tuscany who, along with her daughter Matilda, was for years to be a fervent supporter of the papacy. Stephen's death a few months after his election allowed the Roman nobles to make one last bid for power; they set up a respectable nonentity as Pope Benedict X; but the cardinals, now a strong, international and coherent group, rejected him, fled from Rome, and after mature deliberation elected the Bishop of Florence, who was enthroned as Nicholas II in January 1059.

His first care was to regulate the procedure for future papal elections, by a decree promulgated at the Roman Synod held three months after his accession. The cardinal bishops were to take the lead, in consultation with the remaining cardinals, clergy and people of Rome; if no suitable candidate could be found within the Roman Church, the Pope might be chosen from elsewhere, and if their freedom of action was hampered inside Rome itself, the cardinals might hold their conclave at any safer spot; and the new Pope, even if prevented from entering Rome, should exercise his full powers at once. These provisions, of which Humbert was probably the chief author, sanctioned the peculiar circumstances under which Nicholas had himself been elected; their purpose was to rescue the conclave from pressure by the Roman nobles, and in their main outlines they have governed papal elections ever since. Nothing was said about the place of the Emperor, except for a studiously vague clause, safeguarding "the honour and reverence due to our beloved son Henry" and such of his successors as might be granted the same privilege. There is another version of the decree, which gives the Emperor a place along with the cardinals in managing the election; but this seems to have been altered in the imperial favour by Archbishop Guibert of Ravenna. To protect himself both from the German Empire

F

and from the Roman nobles, Nicholas relied on the support of Countess Beatrice, the Normans in South Italy, and the Patarine or democratic party amongst the Lombards, who were in chronic revolt against the rich married clergy of Milan. But on the death of Nicholas in 1061, all the hostile elements united, with the approval of Henry IV, to secure the appointment of an anti-pope, Bishop Cadalus of Parma, described as "rich in silver, poor in virtue," who took the name of Honorius II. Meanwhile the cardinals regularly elected a member of the reforming party, Bishop Anselm of Lucca, who was installed at Rome by the Normans under the name of Alexander II. In the ensuing contest, Alexander was enabled to win by a change of government in Germany; and Hildebrand, who had been Archdeacon of Rome since 1059, was now more and more the power behind the papacy. It was on his advice that the Norman Conquest of England was sanctioned by the gift of a papal banner; legates were sent in 1067 to the distracted city of Milan, following up the work begun there by Peter Damian nine years before; a force of militia was raised, by Hildebrand, to curb the factions inside Rome; and when Henry, who had come of age in 1065, began to show a mind of his own, his chief counsellors were excommunicated in 1073. A few days afterwards, Alexander II died; Hildebrand, now almost the sole survivor of the reforming circle which had gathered round Leo IX, was the obvious choice as his successor.

He was seized by the crowd during Alexander's funeral, hustled unwillingly to the Church of St. Peter ad Vincula, and there acclaimed as Pope; the cardinals then hurried through the formalities of an election, and Hildebrand was accepted with the unanimous support of Rome. But he himself shrank from the responsibility; "not of my own will did I enter the priesthood," he wrote, "with force they placed me on the apostolic throne, for which I was far from fit;" and he besought his correspondents for their prayers. The picture of him as an ambitious schemer, now at last successful, is neither correct nor just. Fully aware of the vast problems facing the Church, caught as it so largely was in the meshes of the feudal system, he confided to Lanfranc soon after his election that he was mainly concerned to deal with "kings who opposed divine justice and bishops who set a bad example." But he was determined at whatever cost to continue the progress of reform. At first he hoped to do so on the lines traced out by Damian, by working together with King Henry; it was only when that monarch failed to co-operate that he fell back on the theocratic policy of Humbert. He took the name of Gregory VII, probably not in imitation of the first Pope who had borne that name, but rather in memory of his own early patron, Gregory VI, who himself had hoped to revive the papacy. He wrote much about the love of God; none the less, he paid no attention to those charitable measures of poor relief which had so strongly marked the pontificate of Gregory the Great. Rather, Hildebrand regarded it as his chief duty to enforce the gospel ethic upon others; "we have received a mission," as he wrote in 1074 to Herman of Metz, "to evangelize mankind—woe to us if we preach not the gospel." His great ideal was the rule of right-eousness, *iustitia*, a word which appears in his letters about two hundred and sixty times. Thus a term which was to be crucial in the thought of Luther was also a key-word for Hildebrand; by it, the Pope meant not only a right relationship between the indivi-dual and his God, but also right relations for all humanity, an order of society based on the divine law. Contemporaries com-pared him to the prophet Elijah, and the Old Testament was prominent in his mind; his favourite text was the prophetic rebuke to King Saul (1 Sam. 15 : 22–3), "to obey is better than sacrifice . . . for rebellion is as the sin of witchcraft." Any opposition to himself he regarded as an attack upon God; against the foes of the papacy he confidently predicted divine judgment to come and in this world temporal disaster. To enforce his own will, which he thus equated with the divine will, Hildebrand relied not on material weapons but on God, "without Whom," as he wrote to a Moslem king of Mauretania, "we can neither do nor think any good thing." For himself, he sought to live always as in God's sight, and to others he recommended a similar discipline; he advised Matilda of Tuscany to receive communion daily, and so to live that she would be always ready to communicate. To the same lady, and also to Queen Adelaide of Hungary, he urged the practice of devotion to the Virgin, whom he described as "the highest Queen of heaven, exalted above all the choirs of angels, the honour and glory of womankind, the salvation and ennoble-ment of the elect." Hildebrand placed great emphasis on the intercession of the saints, and particularly of St. Peter, whom he solemnly invoked at moments of crisis, and of whom he regarded himself as the humble mouth-piece. The Pope no less that others must be subject to the "statutes of the holy fathers," a phrase which along with "righteousness" was often on Hildebrand's lips; he did not regard himself as an innovator, but rather as the restorer of divine ordinances for the government of men. And the moral order, which he represented, was universal in its scope. King Svein of Denmark, a just and obedient monarch, was re-minded that "the law of the Roman Pontiffs has reached farther than that of Emperors, their sound has gone out into all the earth, and where Augustus was the ruler, Christ now rules." As early as 1073, the Lombards were being told that the Roman Church is "your mother and, as you know, the mistress of all Christendom."

In the first year of his pontificate, Hildebrand exchanged friendly embassies with the Eastern Emperor Michael VII, and a year later he was planning a military expedition to assist the Greeks; earnestly desiring reunion between the Roman Church and what he described as "her daughter the Church of Constantinople," he confided to Hugh of Cluny in 1075 that he was "distressed with immense sorrow and infinite sadness, because at the instigation of the devil, the Church of the East is abandoning the Catholic Faith." To please the Emperor Michael, he excommunicated Robert Guiscard, a troublesome Norman in the South, though that breach in the Norman alliance was offset by the fact that Landulf of Benevento and Richard of Capua had shortly before become vassals of the Holy See. To Henry IV, Hildebrand hinted in December 1074 that he intended to lead an army to the East in person. But these dreams of reunion and reconquest bore no fruit, for throughout his life, the Pope was involved in pressing problems nearer home. Above all, there was the problem of Henry IV himself, an impetuous and autocratic monarch, with none of his father's interest in reform, supported by a German episcopate whose ranks he had recruited through simony, and surrounded by counsellors whom Alexander II had just excommunicated. Yet Hildebrand made a serious effort at reconciliation; he employed as intermediaries the Empress-Mother Agnes, now a nun, Beatrice and Matilda of Tuscany, Matilda's husband the younger Godfrey of Lorraine, Duke Rudolf of Swabia, and anyone whose influence might lead to peace. To these overtures Henry surprisingly responded, but it was political necessity and not love of Rome that moved him. In 1073 the Saxons had revolted, vexed by the re-imposition of feudal services which had been allowed to lapse during the young king's minority; the revolt was supported by the Saxon bishops, and dynastic jealousies combined to produce so strong a threat that Henry was obliged to make his peace with Rome. He wrote an abject letter to the Pope, confessing his sins and asking for papal absolution, promising obedience and help in Church reform; Hildebrand, accepting these professions at their face value, and rejoicing in their submissive tone, responded with alacrity, helped to pacify the Saxons, and sent a couple of legates early in 1074 to absolve the king. To Rudolf of Swabia he wrote, comparing priesthood and empire to the two eyes which jointly give light to the body of humanity; it was a perfect expression of Damian's theory of the two powers; but a bare couple of years later, disillusioned in his hope of co-operation, Hildebrand was comparing papacy to the sun and empire to the moon, which shines only by reflection from the greater luminary.

Meanwhile, the Pope pushed forward with his attack on the twin vices of simony and clerical concubinage. Both were related, since a cleric who purchased preferment would often wish to have sons who might inherit it; and the attack on both was an attempt to rescue the Church from the nexus of the feudal system. With a reference to Rev. 2 : 14–15, any lapse from celibacy by a clerk was described as the heresy of Nicolaitanism. Earlier decrees against both this and simony were renewed at Hildebrand's first synod held in Rome, during Lent of 1074, and his legates were instructed to enforce these at meetings of the episcopate in Germany and France. He expected obedience, for he regarded bishops as his delegates, and called their office that of a "vicarious dispensation;" but he aroused immediate and violent opposition. Liemar of Bremen complained that "this dangerous man," the Pope, "is ordering us about as if we were his bailiffs." Siegfried of Mainz, the other leading archbishop in Germany, procrastinated for six months and then timidly called a synod of his suffragans; St. Paul was quoted in favour of marriage, the meeting broke up in disorder, and Siegfried, after urging discretion on the Pope, tried to wash his hands of the affair on a plea of ill health. Elsewhere, when the decrees were published, riots followed; at Rouen, Archbishop John of Avranches narrowly escaped stoning by his clergy. More than twenty bishops, assembled at Trier on the Pope's orders to investigate charges against one of their number, acquitted the culprit and added a unanimous rider protesting against papal interference. Only in Saxony could Hildebrand still count on episcopal support. But he summoned the ringleaders of the opposition to the Roman synod of 1075, and when Liemar failed to appear, suspended him and some of his companions from office. The obnoxious decrees were repeated, the laity were urged to assist by imposing a boycott on guilty clerks. And, still more important, Hildebrand's first decree against lay investiture was passed.

Lay patronage, rightly or wrongly, was an established institution; royal nomination to the greater benefices was also the regular practice, and it could be justified by the size of the landed estates with which they were endowed. But rulers were now claiming not merely to nominate, but also to confer spiritual authority.

In the tenth century, kings were calling themselves "vicars of Christ;" by the early eleventh, the kings of England and France had so far advanced the spiritual aspect of their office that they claimed to heal diseases by the royal touch. Ruling by divine right, and anointed like priests at their coronation, such monarchs occupied a quasi-ecclesiastical status; they invested their bishops, on appointment, with ring and pastoral staff; and in Germany, such investiture was accompanied by a phrase, *accipe ecclesiam* ("receive your church"), which implied the bestowal of spiritual jurisdiction. To the exercise of such powers by laymen there were obvious theological objections, but it was the practical consequences of the abuse that chiefly troubled Hildebrand. In order to reform the Church, he must receive obedience from the bishops; and if they were to be made obedient, the Church must control their appointment. Thus the decree against lay investiture resulted from the plan of reformation; it was not passed until Hildebrand had been Pope for a couple of years, and it was not in itself the main objective of his policy. Realizing that it involved a change in long-established customs, he invited Henry to discuss its terms. In France, he waited for a further two years, until 1077, before he published it. And in England, where William the Conqueror was appointing bishops of reforming sympathies, he tacitly allowed the Crown to continue nomination.

None the less, the Pope was rapidly coming to a more authoritarian ideal of his position. It is at this point, in March 1075, that there appears in his *Registrum* a series of aphorisms called the *Dictatus Papae*; their author, sometimes supposed to have been Cardinal Deusdedit, was probably Hildebrand himself. Drawing almost entirely on earlier sources, including the False Decretals, he traces the outlines of an absolute papal autocracy. The Roman Church has been founded by God alone; it has never erred, nor ever will err, according to the testimony of Scripture; no one who does not agree with it may be called a Catholic. Only the Roman Pontiff is rightly entitled Ecumenical; he has power to depose both bishops and emperors; he can make new laws in cases of necessity, and absolve the subjects of wicked rulers from their allegiance; princes should kiss his feet, and he may use the imperial insignia; no council should be called Ecumenical without his sanction, nor any book of canons be accepted without his authority; the more important cases from every church should be referred to him, and while his sentences are final, he himself can be judged by no man; if canonically ordained, he is without doubt by the merits of St. Peter rendered holy.

For a few months Henry remained silent; he had not yet been

crowned as German Emperor, and he seems to have been engaged in secret negotiations for this purpose with the Pope. But suddenly, in September 1075, he sent ambassadors into Italy, to make an alliance with the restive Lombard bishops and the excommunicated Robert Guiscard; he appointed bishops to two vacant Italian sees; and at Milan, where there had been a disputed election and continued strife, he installed his own nominee, Tedald, as Archbishop. So flagrant a breach of the recent decree against lay investiture could not pass unnoticed; Hildebrand sent him an angry reminder of the fate of Saul, coupled with a verbal threat of excommunication. To this ultimatum Henry replied by summoning the German episcopate to a council at Worms in January 1076; here two archbishops and about twenty-four of their colleagues renounced allegiance to the Pope, while the king composed an indignant letter bidding the false monk descend from Peter's throne. The North Italian bishops quickly signified their assent, and at the Pope's Lenten synod of 1076, an ambassador arrived to inform him that he had been deposed by the King and Church of Germany. Calmly protecting this ambassador from the shocked fury of his Roman audience, Hildebrand proceeded to depose the rebellious bishops; and then, solemnly calling on "blessed Peter, Prince of the Apostles" to "hear the servant whom you have nourished from his childhood and delivered from the hands of his enemies until this day," the Pope excommunicated Henry and released his subjects from their oath of allegiance. Righteousness must triumph; an unjust ruler must not be suffered to remain in power; and although at this point he did not lay much stress upon it, Hildebrand had in fact deposed the king.

Europe was overawed by the papal thunderbolt, all the more effective because it answered an unwarranted attack upon the Pope. The Bishop of Utrecht, who had ventured to publish the sentence against Hildebrand, had his cathedral struck by lightning and himself died a few weeks later. The German bishops began to waver, the Saxons revolted yet again. The princes of the Empire, whose desire for autonomy was later to assist Luther in rejecting Rome, now from the same motive helped Hildebrand to reject their king. At a Diet held in October, the princes met two papal legates, and agreed that if Henry had not satisfied the Pope by the following February, they would regard him as deposed; meanwhile, they summoned a council to meet in February at Augsburg, where Hildebrand was invited to preside and settle the future of the kingdom. For the Pope, this invitation offered the brilliant prospect of acting as the arbiter of nations; for the king, it meant utter ruin, and Henry, almost deserted except for his

North Italian allies, resolved on the desperate step of throwing himself upon the papal mercy. Crossing the Alps with a few friends early in 1077, he made his way to Matilda's castle of Canossa, where Hildebrand was awaiting an escort to conduct him into Germany. To a written message, the Pope had replied that Henry must face his accusers at Augsburg. But now, the king appeared in person beneath his windows, bare-foot, clad in the garb of a penitent, standing patiently for three days in the January snow. The delay is a measure, not of Henry's humiliation, but of Hildebrand's anxiety. Confronted with a sincere penitent, no priest could justly refuse absolution; but to absolve the king would frustrate the expected triumph of the Pope in Germany. There was an agonizing conflict between Hildebrand's duty as a priest and his ambitions as a statesman; to his credit, he finally allowed his ministry of reconciliation to prevail. His companions, including Matilda and Hugh of Cluny, urged him to be merciful; some of them described his stubborn delay as a sign "not of apostolic discipline, but rather of tyrannous ferocity." So, in one of the great dramatic moments of history, he absolved his penitent; an action which had the automatic effect of allowing Henry to resume the throne. In a patently apologetic letter to the German nobles, he later explained that he had done nothing to alter the status of the kingdom; but in fact, Henry had fulfilled the conditions demanded of him, and in the Pope's own account of the proceedings he is consistently described as king. Yet Hildebrand had little cause to trust his assumed penitence; similar professions had been made in 1073, only to be thereafter broken; and the Pope was still bent on attending the projected council to settle the affairs of Germany. He therefore extracted from Henry, not only a general promise of obedience, but also a specific guarantee of safe conduct for his journey north. That journey, in the distracted state of Germany, he was never able to undertake; and despite an outward humiliation, which to medieval eyes was a sign of grace rather than dishonour, the real gainer at Canossa was the astute King Henry.

The papal party in Germany felt that it had been betrayed. But it was still determined to reject Henry; a diet, held at Forchheim in March 1078, confirmed his deposition and elected Rudolf of Swabia as the new king. With these measures the papal legates who were present concurred; but for the moment Hildebrand withheld his sanction, ostensibly until he could determine which king had the juster title, actually with the purpose of regaining his place as arbiter. In the meanwhile, he occupied himself with fresh and vigorous legislation, repeating in stronger terms his previous decrees against abuses. He pronounced the sacraments of married clergy invalid, ordinations performed by simoniacs null and void. At this a severe critic of the papacy, the monk Sigebert of Gembloux, was moved to complain that "the Roman Pontiffs proclaim themselves successors of the Apostles, and in fact they might really be so, if only they had not sought their own glory, and to that end prophesied under their own inspiration, without fear of shaking the spiritual edifice which rests on apostolic doctrine."

The question of sound doctrine was now brought to the fore-front by the views of Berengarius of Tours. Educated under the scholarly Bishop Fulbert of Chartres, he himself taught at the school of Tours and served as Archdeacon of Angers; he acquired a reputation for learning and administrative skill, but appears to have been of an aggressive character, over-confident in his dialectical ability. The eleventh century witnessed some develop-ments in eucharistic practice: withdrawal of the cup from the laity, and further elevation of the consecrated Host. Berengarius reacted against the type of doctrine which these practices implied; he found a copy of the treatise by Ratramnus of Corbie, and wrongly attributing this to Erigena, professed himself a disciple of the latter. Late in 1049 he wrote somewhat curtly to Lanfranc, challenging a debate on the subject; the letter, forwarded to Rome, was there read by its recipient to a council which he was attend-ing; and Berengarius was summoned on a charge of heresy. Unable to come since he had meanwhile been imprisoned for refusing to pay taxes, Berengarius was condemned in absence, felt himself to be a martyr, and embarked on a personal vendetta against Lanfranc. His case was again considered at the Council of Tours in 1054, which Hildebrand attended as papal legate; here Berengarius agreed that after consecration the bread and wine are "the true Body and Blood of Christ," a statement with which Hildebrand was perfectly satisfied; but the opposition insisted that the substances of bread and wine are annihilated, and owing to the death of Pope Leo IX the debate had to be postponed. So far, Berengarius had sought to maintain a real but spiritual presence. But his courage failed him when he had to face a Roman council in 1059, and he there agreed that Christ's Body and Blood are actually (*sensualiter*) touched by the hands of the priest and the teeth of the faithful. About ten years later, Lanfranc wrote a treatise *On the Body and Blood of the Lord*, asserting a substantial presence, to which Berengarius replied with his work *On the Holy Supper*. Realizing that the majority was against him, he asserted that the Church is not infallible, that councils have no final authority, and that Scripture, as interpreted by the individual conscience, is the sole guide to truth; further, Christ cannot be materially present on the altar, since He will not return from heaven until the Last Judgment. At the same time, he seems to have held something not unlike Luther's doctrine of consubstantiation, since he wrote that "the consecrated bread, preserving its own substance, is the Body of Christ, not by losing what it was but by assuming what it was not." Summoned to defend himself at Rome in 1078, he had a long conference with Hildebrand, and went so far as to admit that the bread is the true Body of Christ, which was born of the Virgin, suffered on the Cross, and now sits at the right hand of the Father, while the wine is the very Blood which flowed from His side. All of this could still be interpreted spiritually, but Hildebrand declared it to be orthodox, adding that both he and Peter Damian regarded Lanfranc's views as too extreme: rightly so, since in 496 Pope Gelasius I had stated that "the nature or substance of bread and wine does not cease to exist." However, despite the Pope's effort to protect him, the council which met at Rome in 1079 demanded a stronger statement; under severe pressure, Berengarius was forced to declare that "through the mystery of holy prayer and the words of our Redeemer" the elements "are substantially converted into the true, proper and life-giving flesh and blood of Jesus Christ . . . not simply by way of sign and sacramental efficacy, but in their proper nature and true substance." After this, Berengarius disappears from history, a broken and disappointed man; he seems to have privately retained his former views, insisting that the denials had been wrung from him by force; but the debate which he provoked had been the means of eliciting an official doctrine virtually identical with transubstantiation.

Meanwhile, the Pope continued to hope for a council in Germany, but of the rival kings, Rudolf could not and Henry would not arrange for it to meet. At last in 1080 a peremptory demand arrived from Henry that his opponent should be excommunicated; this act of self-assertion convinced Hildebrand that docility, and therefore justice, lay on the other side. He therefore proceeded to a solemn and synodical decision, this time invoking both St. Peter and St. Paul: for continued falsehood and disobedience, Henry was excommunicated and deposed, while on the Pope's apostolic authority the kingdom was transferred to Rudolf. Next year, in a letter to his faithful supporter Bishop Herman of Metz, Hildebrand penned an elaborate defence of his decision. Quoting the text "Thou art Peter," he asked whether kings were exempt from the universal power of binding and loosing entrusted to the chief apostle: "Who, I ask, thinks himself to be exempted, unless perhaps he is a wretch who will not bear the yoke of the Lord, subjects himself to the devil's burden, and refuses to be numbered with the sheep of Christ?" Several of the authorities which he alleged were spurious, taken from the False Decretals, but he found one genuine and apposite quotation from Gregory the Great, to the effect that kings forfeit their dignity if they venture to violate a decree of the apostolic see; and with a telling allusion to the Roman Pontifical, he declared that even a lowly exorcist is ordained a spiritual emperor, with powers greater than those entrusted to any layman. The whole letter was a forthright assertion of papal supremacy, and Hildebrand expected that his second thunderbolt would prove as crippling as the first. But support for the papacy had dwindled in the interval since 1076; Henry was now in a much stronger position, and all those who valued stable government in Germany regarded the papal sentence as an attack upon the nation. The Bishop of Spires described Hildebrand as "an execrable disturber of laws both human and divine;" a council at Mainz deposed him, he was accused among other things of heresy in having attempted to protect Berengarius, and a second council, held at Brixen in June 1080, proceeded to elect Archbishop Guibert of Ravenna as a new Pope. Guibert was an apt choice, for although he led the Lombard bishops in their revolt from Rome, he was of blameless character and sympathetic to the programme of reform. It was therefore in vain that Roman propagandists compared him to the beast of the Apocalypse. And when Rudolf died in the following October, Hildebrand's position had become desperately serious.

Already, while the council of Brixen was in session, he had taken steps for his defence. The Norman Robert Guiscard had by now been excommunicated twice, and had occupied a slice of papal territory; but Hildebrand restored him to communion, confirmed the "unjust tenure" of his conquests, and in return received homage and promises of help. In the spring of 1081, Henry appeared at the gates of Rome demanding admission, but he had brought few troops, and it was not until a third attempt, in 1083, that he acquired a foothold in the city. Defections followed; thirteen cardinals, including the Roman Chancellor and Archdeacon, went over to the opposing side; on Palm Sunday 1084 Guibert was enthroned as Pope Clement III, and on Easter Day he placed the imperial crown on Henry's brow. Meanwhile, Hildebrand remained shut up in the Castle of Sant' Angelo. Guiscard, busy with an attack on the Greek Empire, had as yet sent none of his promised help; but with his own security threat-

ened by the German occupation of Rome, the Norman at last
moved north, and Henry was obliged to leave, taking his anti-
pope with him as far as Tivoli. Rome was then brutally pillaged
by the relieving Norman army; its populace turned in fury against
Hildebrand, who was removed in custody by Guiscard to Salerno.
Here on 25th May 1085 he died, defiant but deserted, with a
paraphrase of the Psalmist's words upon his lips: "I have loved
righteousness and hated iniquity, therefore I die in exile." The
sentence may be apocryphal, but it aptly summarizes his ideal.

Except for isolated instances, he had not attempted to assert a
direct temporal sovereignty. In Spain, the lands which were being
reconquered from the Moslems were claimed by him as papal
fiefs; he wrote more than once to the Spanish princes, reminding
them that "by its ancient constitutions" their kingdom belonged
to St. Peter and the Roman Church; and reversing the policy of
his predecessors, he enforced the use of the Roman liturgy in
Spain. For his claims here, the only basis lay in the Donation of
Constantine; but Spain was an exceptional region, and it was
natural that the reconquest should take place under the aegis of
the papacy. Hungary was a quite different case, for at the beginning of the century its first king, Stephen, had definitely placed
his realm under papal protection. Those Normans of South Italy
who desired a clearer title to their territories were willingly
accepted as vassals of the Holy See. But in England, although the
Pope's legates made some demand for papal suzerainty, perhaps
in virtue of the blessing bestowed upon the Norman Conquest,
the demand was stoutly resisted and it was quietly dropped by
Hildebrand himself; here he was able to obtain reform without
direct intervention, and in fact under William the Conqueror the
English Church remained both a reforming and a state-controlled
institution. France was weak and divided; Philip I, its greedy and
sensual monarch, had his fits of pious generosity to abbeys; and
when he indulged in simony, a mere threat of excommunication
in 1075 sufficed to bring his administration into line.

Only in Germany did Hildebrand take direct political action;
it was forced upon him by the opposition of King Henry; and
although it ostensibly took the form of asserting papal overlord-
ship, its basic purpose was to maintain the supremacy of moral
obligations. The Pope believed himself to be fighting for the rule
of righteousness rather than the rule of Rome, but the two were
so identified in his theocratic mind that even at Canossa he had
great difficulty in holding them apart. None the less, his policies
were aimed at promoting the Church's welfare, and did not arise
from mere love of power. In the interests of Church reform, he

went far towards establishing a centralized ecclesiastical structure that was closely parallel to the feudal organization of the State. By the use of legates, both temporary and permanent, he kept the papacy in constant touch with local affairs; by breaking up the old primacies, such as that which had once been exercised by the Archbishop of Sens over Gaul and Germany, he destroyed the local centres of allegiance; by obliging metropolitans to come to Rome for their pallium in person, he bound them even more closely to himself; and by strict supervision of individual bishops, he sought to function as a feudal head for the entire Church. All of these tendencies were reinforced under Hildebrand's successors; but even during his pontificate, bishops were beginning to take an oath of fealty to Rome. And although he could quote precedents for most of his assertions, although Nicholas I had already said that Rome is "head of all the Churches" and "the Pope holds the place of Jesus Christ within the Church Universal," yet Hildebrand inaugurated a new régime by translating such abstract principles into action, and he was in fact the first Pope who ventured to depose an Emperor. In his own eyes no more than a restorer of the old ways, he was accused by the German bishops, with some reason, of arrogating to himself new and unlawful authority in the *Dictatus Papae*. The papal theocracy, which he was largely instrumental in founding, degenerated over the years into a secularized dominion; yet at the outset the idea of a united Europe, under Christian leadership, with politics subordinated to morality, was by no means an unworthy vision.

The investiture controversy was settled for a time by the Concordat of Worms in 1122. This peace treaty between Church and State followed in its main outlines the settlement which had been already reached in England. A clear distinction was drawn between the secular and the spiritual functions of the episcopate; the king gave up the obnoxious practice of investing with the spiritual symbols of ring and staff, but he continued to exact homage for the temporalities, to which he instituted the incumbent by touch of the sceptre; and although he conceded the right of free and canonical election, this was effective only in Italy and Burgundy, whereas in Germany he retained powers of supervision which amounted to virtual control. Thus the bishops, in their spiritual capacity, were recognized as servants of the Church; but at the same time, their obligations as feudal magnates were guaranteed to the Crown. Before this compromise was reached, a storm of polemical literature had produced some fifty writings on the imperial side and sixty-five in defence of the papacy. Hildebrand's claims were buttressed by the canon lawyers

Anselm the younger of Lucca and Cardinal Deusdedit, the latter of whom is inclined to make tendentious interpolations in his sources; but another canonist, Ivo of Chartres, while he allowed the Pope very wide dispensing powers, also recognized the State's autonomy in its own sphere, and thus adumbrated the settlement which was to be reached at Worms. Defending the Pope's action in releasing Henry's subjects from their allegiance, Gebhard of Salzburg maintained that an oath cannot bind men to evil, and therefore that human sovereignty is limited by the rights of conscience. Manegold of Lautenbach, working on the theory of a tacit social contract, wrote as follows: "when the man who is chosen to defend the good and restrain evil himself embarks on wickedness . . . is it not obvious that he rightly forfeits his position, and that the people are freed from subjection to his rule . . . since he has broken the pact in terms of which he was made ruler?" On the imperial side, appeal was made to history rather than theory. Peter Crassus, a lay lawyer, cited the civil code of Justinian, and in answer to the pretensions of Rudolf of Swabia, he emphasized the hereditary principle as conferring an authority ordained of God. Henry himself insisted on the divine right of kingship, quoting the two swords of Luke 22 : 38 to justify the separation of Church and State. One of his supporters, Guy of Osnabruck, writing in 1084-5, went so far as to assert that papal elections are invalid without imperial assent.

But in all this vociferous appeal to public opinion, the most significant contribution was made by an unknown writer, usually called the Anonymous of York, though he may have been a clerk at Rouen before settling in England, who published his views in the earliest years of the twelfth century, and was surprisingly in advance of his times. Drawing his authorities largely from the Old Testament, he emphasized, as others had done, the sacred character of royalty; both kings and bishops are anointed "christs," but whereas the priest represents the humanity of Jesus, which is "an inferior office and nature," the king on the other hand is "the image of a superior one, namely His divinity." Thus the Christian ruler is consecrated to a spiritual function, which entitles him not only to bestow Church offices but also to judge the clergy. More important, the York Anonymous was the sole writer of the period to grasp the really weak point in the papal case. Hildebrand had asserted that righteousness is an essential qualification for kingly rule; in his great letter of defence to Herman of Metz, he stated "it is far better that any good Christian, rather than some wicked prince, should be deemed a king." But should not the same test be applied also to the papacy? In the *Dictatus Papae*, Hildebrand pronounced that the Pope, if regularly appointed, is sanctified through St. Peter's merits. To this the Anonymous replies by asking "if the Pope should issue his own laws, or seek his own glory, or do his own will and not Christ's, who then would venture to accept him as Christ's true apostle?" The papacy must be judged by the standards which it applies to others, and if an evil king forfeits his crown, an evil Pope must equally forfeit his tiara. It was precisely this point which was later taken up by Wycliffe, whose doctrine of "dominion by grace" is no more than a restatement of Hildebrand's view that only the righteous ought to rule; but whereas Hildebrand had used the doctrine to justify his deposition of an emperor, Wycliffe turned the same weapon against the papacy, by demanding its abolition after it had grown corrupt. In this salient feature of his theology, the so-called Morning Star of the Reformation had been anticipated, almost three centuries before, by an otherwise unremembered fellow-countryman.

CHAPTER VI

THE FIRST CRUSADE

WHEN MOHAMMED DIED IN THE YEAR 632, HE LEFT HIS followers the stimulus of a new religion which, combined with the pressure of over-population in their homeland, impelled them to a wave of rapid and extensive conquests. Without any preconcerted plan of campaign, they plundered their neighbours, found the resistance weak, and advanced yet farther, until they had occupied not only Persia and parts of the Punjab, but also Syria, Palestine, Egypt, North Africa and Spain. For Christians the saddest moment came in 638, when Jerusalem was surrendered to the Caliph Omar; Sophronius the Patriarch, murmuring through his tears "Behold the abomination of desolation, spoken of by Daniel the prophet," died a few weeks later from a broken heart. But the Moslems were tolerant to both Christianity and Judaism; regarding the elder faiths as immature versions of their own, they allowed to all whom they called People of the Book a quiet continuance of worship. Indeed the Christian sects preferred Moslem to Byzantine rule, since taxes were lighter and apart from a few civil disabilities, they suffered less interference from the new régime. Conversions to Islam were numerous; it appeared to John of Damascus and many others as a form, albeit unorthodox, of Christianity; and it was in fact the earliest type of successful Unitarianism. Moreover the Arabs no less than the Byzantines served themselves heir to Graeco-Roman culture. They studied classical philosophy, medicine and law, together with geography and astronomy; in the field of mathematics they transmitted from India the incalculable boon of the so-called Arabic numerals; their writers produced exquisite lyric poetry and a profound school of mysticism; their art contrived to be at the same time rich and puritanical. Little of all this was genuinely original, and much of it came from alien elements absorbed into the Moslem population. But in the Dark Ages and for some time thereafter, the Arab was infinitely more civilized than the Western European. His government, however, was a splendid despotism, for in the Abbasid court at Baghdad an executioner stood prominently beside the throne; and the Caliph, dressed on ceremonial

occasions in the sacred mantle of the Prophet, called himself the
Vicegerent of God. There was a strong police force, with a
system of spies and informers; the prefect of police, in his general
oversight of morality, prohibited the public sale of wine, found
suitable husbands for widows, protected slaves and animals from
excessive loads, and even inspected dolls to ensure that no
idolatry was creeping into the children's toyshops.

Meanwhile the Greek clergy continued to minister to their
diminished congregations. During the troubled period of iconoclasm at Constantinople, they turned hopefully to Charlemagne as
a protector; and the Caliph Harun al-Rashid, glad to find an ally
against Byzantine influence, encouraged the foundation of Latin
hospices and convents in the Holy Land. A small but steady
stream of pilgrims from the West kept contact with Jerusalem.
Medieval minds did not make a very clear distinction between the
actual city and its celestial counterpart. Relics were prized and
sought for, as a material pledge of spiritual realities; thus, when
King Athelstan's sister married Duke Hugh of France in 926, the
French ambassadors brought gifts to England, including Constantine's sword with one of the nails from the cross set in its hilt,
Charlemagne's lance, said to have been that with which Christ's
side was pierced, a piece of the True Cross and a fragment from
the Crown of Thorns. In 969 the Greek Emperor Nicephorus
Phocas swept down into Syria; six years later his cousin and successor, repelling the armies of the Fatimid dynasty in Egypt,
penetrated as far as Nazareth and Caesarea; but despite these vic-
tories, Antioch had to be accepted as the southern limit of Byzantine power. Nicephorus had used the language of a Crusade,
declaring that his war was a struggle for the defence of Christendom and the recapture of its sacred sites. But the Patriarch refused
to accept his suggestion that the war dead should be honoured as
martyrs, for the Greek Church, though admitting the sad necessity of warfare, never regarded participation in it as a religious
act. Very different was the attitude of the West, where the Latin
Church was only too anxious to employ the energies of bellicose
barbarians. A century before Nicephorus, Pope Leo IV had
promised heavenly rewards to any soldier who died fighting for
the Church, and a century later the institution of chivalry was
giving the knight a sort of consecration. Pilgrimages, encouraged
by the Cluniac movement as an acceptable divine service, became
more frequent in the tenth and eleventh centuries, with only a
short break under the mad Caliph Hakim around the year 1010;
and with the twin impulses of religion and land-hunger to prompt
them, as the Moslems had been prompted already, it would merely

be a matter of time until the Latins embarked on the armed pilgrimage of a Crusade. Some of them were already waging a holy
war, with papal blessing, against the infidel in Spain.

In 1071 the Eastern Empire suffered its most tragic defeat. A
group of Turkish adventurers, called Seljuks after the name of a
mythical ancestor, and playing a rôle in Islam analogous to that
of the Normans in Christendom, had established themselves as
the actual power behind the now decadent caliphate of Baghdad.
They annexed Armenia by 1067 and were raiding far into imperial
territory, where the defences had been permitted to decay and the
troops were composed chiefly of Varangians and other mercenaries. Mustering the best force that he could manage, the Emperor
Romanus Diogenes marched out to reconquer Armenia in the
spring of 1071; but on the field of Manzikert he was routed and
taken prisoner, while some of his soldiers deserted and the Norman contingent refused to fight. This Norman treachery was long
remembered at Constantinople, where it was to render their
crusaders suspect and unwelcome: deservedly so, since the Normans themselves regarded the annexation of the Greek Empire
as a natural step in the Crusade, and on the eve of Manzikert their
Italian leader, Robert Guiscard, had completed his conquest of
the Greek possessions in South Italy.

But the Emperor's need of troops was too pressing for him to
choose the source of their supply, and Michael VII was soon
seeking military assistance from Hildebrand; to the Pope the reunion of the churches was a more attractive prospect than the
recapture of Palestine, but he responded warmly to these Greek
overtures, and it was only his long conflict with the Germans that
prevented him from marching to the East in person. It was left
for his disciple, Urban II, to launch the Crusade, and to give it
that more visionary bent which directed it to the reconquest of
Jerusalem rather than the relief of the hard-pressed Greeks. In the
interval the Seljuks occupied Asia Minor, together with Syria and
Palestine, while the Normans, crossing the Adriatic to Dyrrhachium under Guiscard and his son Bohemund, invaded Mace-
donia and Greece. To repel them the Emperor Alexius, who succeeded at a fresh moment of crisis in 1081, was obliged to employ
the ships of Venice, and in return to recompense the Venetians
with trading privileges resented by his subjects. So empty was his
treasury that he had to debase the imperial coinage, which for
seven centuries had been the one stable currency in the world.
He was excommunicated by the papacy as a result of the revolution which brought him to the throne; and Greek antipathy to the
West became so violent that the death of Hildebrand was regarded

as a well-earned punishment for his alliance with the godless Normans.

Yet by 1095 the Seljuk power was declining through a divided inheritance and a civil war. At Rome, the statesmanlike Urban II had become Pope, after a distinguished career as Archdeacon of Rheims, Prior of Cluny and Cardinal Bishop of Ostia. An admirer of Hildebrand, and a loyal supporter of him to the last, he had a more flexible outlook, which permitted him to recover much of the ground lost by the papacy in the West, while in dealing with the East his first act was to remove the excommunication pronounced against Alexius. Guiscard was now dead, and the Normans had engulfed enough territory to satiate them for the moment. It was therefore in an atmosphere of mutual goodwill that Greek ambassadors met the Pope in 1095, at the Council of Piacenza, with a new request for military aid. Both he and his companions at the Council were impressed by the tale of Christian sufferings in Eastern lands; and as he crossed the Alps on further business which took him into France, Urban seems to have been meditating definite plans for a Crusade.

In August 1095 the Pope was at Le Puy, where he issued letters summoning a council of French bishops to meet at Clermont in November. The Bishop of Le Puy, Adhemar of Monteil, had gone on pilgrimage to Palestine about eight years before; with his experience, tactfulness and influential family connexions, he was at once taken into Urban's confidence, and probably designated as spiritual leader of the coming Crusade. It was to be a venture patronized and directed by the Church, but it would also require adequate military leadership, and Adhemar seems to have suggested a friend of his own, Count Raymond of Toulouse, who had already fought the Moslems in Spain. According to a contemporary chronicler, Raymond was to play the part of Aaron to Adhemar's Moses on the march towards the Promised Land. On 18th November, thirteen archbishops, two hundred and five bishops, and a number of lesser clerics assembled for the opening of the Council of Clermont; like Urban himself, the majority were Frenchmen, and it is significant that France, the home both of chivalry and of Cluniac devotion, supplied most of the manpower for the crusading army. After a week spent in dealing with the perennial problems of simony, lay investiture and clerical concubinage, and after the excommunication of the French King Philip for adultery, Urban announced that he would hold a public session for the purpose of making an important speech. The crowds, both clerical and lay that gathered, were too large for the cathedral to accommodate, and the Pope addressed them in an open field outside the city. Five accounts of what he said are extant, three of them written by men who seem to have been present in the audience; there are too many discrepancies between them for any of these sources to be regarded as a wholly authentic record, but by piecing together fragments from them all, it is at least possible to reproduce the impression which his speech left upon the hearers' minds.

He dwelt upon the sufferings of the Eastern Christians, and their appeal for help: "you must hasten to assist your brethren of the East, who need your aid and have often begged it . . . this is Christ's command." Jerusalem itself is trampled underfoot by pagan armies, while Christians waste their strength in fratricidal wars: "but this is no knightly service, when it rends asunder the sheepfold of the Redeemer." Therefore "it is right to enforce anew the Truce of God," so that "those who have been wont to wage private wars against the faithful may now conduct a successful war against the infidel." "If in ancient days the Maccabees won high religious honour by fighting for the ceremonial law and the Jewish Temple, you also, Christian soldiers, may justly defend your country's freedom by force of arms. . . . Remember the great deeds of your own ancestors, the glories of King Charlemagne and those others who destroyed the kingdoms of the pagans, and stir up your minds to martial valour." There will be material inducements, for "the possessions of the enemy will fall into your hands and you will spoil their treasure." Still more, there will be spiritual rewards of a character which anticipates the later papal indulgences: "if those who set out lose their lives . . . their sins shall be forgiven, and this privilege I grant to all who go in virtue of the powers vested in me by Almighty God." The venture will be a work of great religious merit, restoring "to its former stature the majesty of Holy Church;" it will be a true discipleship of Christ, and "any who desire to follow the Lord with pure heart and zealous mind, any who wish faithfully to bear His Cross, should at once take the highway to the Holy Sepulchre." "Under your leader Jesus Christ, as a Christian army, a conquering host, stronger than the Israelites of old, you shall fight for your Jerusalem and do battle with the Turks your Jebusites. Count it a noble thing to die for Christ in the city where Christ died for you. And if you happen to die upon the way . . . God pays the penny for the first hour as well as for the sixth. It is a vile thing to do violence against Christians, but a great virtue to draw the sword against a Saracen, and a great sign of love to lay down our lives for the brethren. . . . Short is the life and light the labour which brings you a crown that fadeth not away. . . . And you, my brethren and fellow-bishops . . . publish this among the churches committed to your care, and everywhere with free voice preach the pilgrimage to Jerusalem." "Thus let enmity depart from among you, let your quarrels end, let fighting cease, let all discord and controversy slumber. Take the road to the Sepulchre of Christ."

Urban was a skilled preacher of considerable power; the effect of his words was immediate and electrifying. Amid scenes of well-nigh revivalist enthusiasm, while the great crowd cried "God wills it," Adhemar knelt to receive his commission as papal legate, and hundreds came forward with him to take the Cross. As the Pope had presented it, the Crusade seemed "a new way of salvation" and taking the crusader's badge appeared almost as a second baptism. Looking back on the spiritual emotion of those days, Fulcher of Chartres described in the preface to his history how, "forsaking the honour of the world, parting from their parents, wives and property, men clung to God and followed Him in obedience to the counsels of the gospel;" and after alluding to their noble deeds done "in honour of the Saviour," he spoke with admiration of "the many thousands of martyrs who on this expedition died a happy death." Indeed, the response to Urban's appeal, far greater than he had anticipated, proved to be embarrassingly large. Pestilence, feuds and famine in preceding years had worked on imaginations that were all too easily excited; strange portents were reported in the skies, where angelic hosts were thought to be observed in combat; a huge shower of meteorites seemed to herald some momentous stirring of the peoples; and there was even a rumour that Charlemagne had risen from the dead to lead the expedition. Medieval man lived, like the early Christians, in imminent expectation of the Second Advent, and at the same time with an almost morbid consciousness of sin; the Church taught him that his faults could be expiated by journeying to a holy shrine, and when he heard tell of Jerusalem in the midst of his present miseries, he pictured a land flowing with milk and honey, or even heaven itself. To spiritual longings was added a harsh economic necessity, for with high food prices, with a growing population, and with much of the countryside uncultivated, there was a host of landless men, not only among the peasants, but also among the younger sons of the nobility, who hoped to carve out new acres for themselves by emigration. There were merchants in the Italian cities, eager to expand their Eastern trade. And behind all the mixed motives of the crusading movement, there lay the expansionist foreign policy of the reforming Popes, by which the military energies of Europe were harnessed to extend the spiritual domain of Rome.

Itinerant evangelists carried on the preaching of the Crusade. Urban had envisaged an orderly enrolment under the local bishops, but enthusiasm was kindled far more effectively by free-lance "revivalists" like Robert of Arbrissel and Peter the Hermit; the latter of these was a native of Amiens, who had been roughly handled by the Turks on an attempted pilgrimage some years before, and despite the fact that his face bore an unfortunate resemblance to the donkey that he rode, he had an incredible power of moving men. Some of the excitement which he aroused vented itself in pogroms against the Jews of Germany. None the less a throng of enthusiastic but undisciplined pilgrims, led by Peter and a knight called Walter the Penniless, arrived under the walls of Constantinople in the summer of 1096. Alexius had asked for military reinforcements, and instead the West had sent him a disorderly rabble, demanding to be fed; sadly disillusioned, he provided them with rations and shipped them across the Bosporus, with the sage advice to remain inactive until their comrades had arrived. But the pilgrims pressed on into Asia Minor, where by October all save a handful had been massacred, and thus the so-called People's Crusade ended in complete dis-aster. It was only the first wave of a much larger movement, but it had committed petty thefts and even savage cruelties against fellow-Christians on the way. To the Greeks it appeared like an invasion, and Anna Comnena, the daughter of Alexius, wrote in her memoirs that her father "feared the incursions of these people, for ... they were known to have an insatiable greed ... the entire West was on the move, bursting *en masse* into Asia with its goods and chattels."

Meanwhile the knights and nobles were making their more serious military preparations, and during the winter of 1096–7 three main contingents moved to Constantinople. The Lorrainers were led by Duke Godfrey of Bouillon, with his brother Baldwin; the Provençals marched under Raymond of Toulouse, accompanied by Bishop Adhemar; and the Normans of South Italy, as always more bent on pillage than devotion, followed Bohemund and his nephew Tancred. A smaller group, one of the first to arrive, was commanded by Hugh of Vermandois, the younger brother of the French King. Robert of Normandy and Stephen of Blois led the latest arrivals, who appeared at the Greek capital in May 1097. Chaplains, wives, children and a swarm of less reput-able non-combatants accompanied the troops, who comprised in all a formidable army. Fulcher of Chartres, one of the chaplains with the expedition, estimated its total at 600,000 men; this, like most medieval estimates, is an obvious exaggeration, and the figures given for the individual units, coupled with the time taken by the whole in crossing a bridge, suggest that the entire force numbered between fifty and a hundred thousand. Even so, it was comparable in strength to the total muster of the Byzantine army, and it was obvious to Alexius that he must come to an understanding with its leaders. He sent distinguished officers to meet them as they arrived in turn at his frontiers, and arranged to supply them with provisions as they crossed Greek territory. But there was constant friction, even a certain amount of looting, and in Holy Week of 1097 the Lorrainers, while encamped outside Constantinople, staged a minor attack upon the city. By lavish hospitality and judicious gifts, Alexius obtained the allegiance of the crusading nobles; he knew that once they had reconquered Asia Minor, they intended to found principalities for themselves, and he was not averse to having Christian buffer-states on his Eastern border, provided that at least in principle his suzerainty was recognized. Hugh of Vermandois, whose rank was much greater than his possessions, readily agreed to the proposal; overwhelmed by the magnificence of the Greek court, he took an oath of homage to the Emperor, who then used his influence to overcome the reluctance of the rest. Bohemund was surprisingly complaisant; but he was already experienced in dealing with Byzantines, and he hoped by the readiness of his submission to obtain from Alexius an appointment as commander-in-chief. In this he was disappointed, for the Emperor, though outwardly courteous, had fresh memories of the Norman attack upon Dyrrhachium; Princess Anna believed that the Normans were eager to obtain the Empire for themselves, and stated that she had never seen a man so dishonest as their leader. Godfrey of Bouillon at first objected to the oath, since he had already sworn allegiance to Henry IV of Germany; but his scruples were overcome by curtailing food supplies to his troublesome troops, and on Easter Sunday he professed himself the vassal of Alexius. Raymond of Toulouse alone refused to promise more than that he would respect the life and honour of the Emperor; aspiring to lead the whole Crusade, and regarding himself as the Pope's lay representative, he declined to entangle himself with further commitments. But through the tactful mediation of Bishop Adhemar, he parted from the Greek court on friendly terms, although he had previously spoken of the Emperor's "most false and detestable deceit." All of the Western leaders were dazzled by Byzantine wealth and brilliance, in contrast to which their own rough manners seemed uncouth; Stephen of Blois wrote to his wife Adela, the daughter of William the Conqueror, that although her father had been generous, his gifts were almost nothing compared with the munificence of Alexius. The successive contingents had been ferried across the Bosporus as soon as their leaders had done homage; and by early summer, to the Greeks' intense relief, the last of them were safely landed on the Asiatic shore.

Their first success came with the capture of Nicaea on 19th June, after the army had fortified itself by receiving communion. Both Raymond and Adhemar distinguished themselves during the siege, but the final surrender was due to the arrival of a Greek fleet; and although Alexius rewarded the crusaders generously, they were annoyed at not being allowed to plunder the city. However, they took heart from the victory, and Stephen wrote home to say that, unless Antioch resisted, they hoped to be in Jerusalem in five weeks' time. At Dorylaeum, in the mountain passes of the interior, they met the main Seljuk field army on 1st July; the battle was long and stubborn, but Adhemar turned the tide by outflanking the Turks with his own contingent; and the crusaders, depleted but triumphant, found the route through Asia Minor open. They had arrived at a moment when Moslem power was divided and consequently weak. Not only was there the outstanding discord between the rival caliphates of Baghdad and Cairo, but the Seljuks themselves had lost their former cohesion, and a number of emirs were acting independently. Local garrisons on the Aegean seaboard were easily reduced by the Greeks, who undertook to protect the crusaders' lines of communication; and with the help of guides provided by Alexius, they embarked on the hot and thirsty march round the great salt desert of Anatolia. Tancred and Baldwin made private expeditions into Cilicia, where they came to blows with one another, and Baldwin then broke away to establish himself as Count of Edessa, where the Armenian ruler had invoked his help. In the main body, although no individual was recognized as supreme commander, the nobles' council of war was held to a consistent purpose by the gentle remonstrances of Adhemar; and despite the difficulties of atrocious roads and cumbrous armour, augmented first by summer heat and then by the autumn rains, they had reached Antioch before the end of October. During the march their morale had remained high, and the close comradeship between men of so many different languages seemed to Fulcher like a Pentecost inspired of God; here again, the direct source of inspiration was doubtless provided by the Bishop of Le Puy, who himself led the van in crossing the Orontes.

But before Palestine could be invaded, Antioch must fall. It covered an area more than two miles long and one mile broad, with a plentiful water-supply, enclosing not only bazaars and houses, but also market gardens and grazing ground for sheep; its immense walls, built by Justinian and recently repaired, were strengthened with four hundred towers and crowned at their highest point by a mighty citadel; on the south side the terrain was too precipitous for an assault, and behind these massive fortifications, amply supplied with food and water, the Moslem garrison could confidently endure a protracted siege. The crusaders, on the other hand, had no siege-engines, nor was their army large enough to invest the place completely; and as they shrank from storming it at once, they were obliged to spend a dreary winter at its gates. Provisions ran short, famine prices began to prevail in the camp. Adhemar did what he could to see that the poorer soldiers were fed; he corresponded with the Greek Patriarch of Jerusalem, who had fled to Cyprus, and obtained some gift parcels from that source; after Christmas he proclaimed a solemn fast, but in the shortage of rations its observance made little difference, and soon one man in seven was dying of starvation. Yet there were also signs of hope. The arrival of thirteen Genoese ships in the harbour of St. Simeon had opened communications with the West by sea. Two Moslem relief forces were defeated, and the captured booty prompted that tireless correspondent, Stephen of Blois, to write: "You may know for a fact, my beloved, that I now have twice as much gold, silver and other riches." In March an English fleet, commanded by the exiled Edgar Atheling, sailed into the port, bringing a welcome supply of siege weapons and engineers from Constantinople. Finally the Fatimids of Egypt, who loathed the Turks as usurpers, sent an embassy offering to partition the Near East between themselves and the crusaders. But, to offset all the encouragement that spring had brought, news arrived that the formidable Kerbogha of Mosul was preparing a large army to relieve the beleaguered city. Fortunately he spent precious weeks in a fruitless attack on Baldwin at Edessa; and meanwhile Bohemund, all the time secretly determined to annex Antioch for himself, found a traitor within its walls who admitted him and his forces on 3rd June, 1098. By evening, apart from a few troops in the citadel, there was no Turk left alive in Antioch, and the Christian population under its Patriarch welcomed the crusaders. But only two days later, Kerbogha reached the Orontes.

It was now the turn of the crusaders to be besieged in the captured city. Food was again scarce, and there were some desertions. Panic-stricken fugitives took the false report to

Alexius, then campaigning in central Asia Minor, that Antioch had already fallen to the Moslems; and the Emperor judged it prudent to retreat, an act of apparent disloyalty which the crusaders considered sufficient to absolve them from their allegiance to the Greeks. But at this point, when all seemed well-nigh lost, hopes were rekindled by an opportune if questionable miracle. A poor peasant of Provence called Peter Bartholomew, whose previous life had by no means been distinguished for piety, came to Raymond and Adhemar with a tale of repeated visions, in which St. Andrew had bidden him look in the cathedral of Antioch for the Holy Lance that was used to pierce Christ's side. The Bishop was extremely sceptical, for he knew Peter's character, and he also knew that another relic, claimed as the same instrument of the Passion, was already in existence at Constantinople. But Raymond, with the simpler mind of a soldier, was deeply impressed. A priest named Stephen was visited in the night by figures of Christ, the Virgin and St. Peter, promising succour within five days' time; Stephen was a more reputable witness, and he was ready to swear on the Gospels that he had told the truth. Finally workmen were sent to dig into the floor of the cathedral, and after a long day's search Peter emerged from the excavations, triumphantly bearing a small piece of iron. Heartened by the discovery, the crusaders routed Kerbogha's forces on 28th June.

But they now fell into violent disagreement over their future plans. Bohemund, who had been able to take the lead during a temporary illness of Raymond, was determined to rule as Prince of Antioch. Raymond, reminding the nobles of the homage which all except himself had paid, insisted that the city should be returned to Alexius, its rightful owner. The common soldiers were eager to press forward to Jerusalem. And at the start of August, Adhemar fell a victim to typhoid fever. His death was an immense loss to the Crusade, of which he had been acknowledged as the spiritual director. Though his figure is a shadowy one in the surviving records, he seems to have presided more often than not over the war council of the princes; he bore his full share of the battles, intervening with decisive effect at Dorylaeum, and twice the man who carried his standard had been killed; most important of all, he had consistently worked for good relations with the Greek Empire and the Greek ecclesiastics of the East. With his gentle but guiding hand removed, the divided nobles dissipated their energies on minor and unco-ordinated actions; they wrote to the Pope, asking him to come out and lead them in person; and meanwhile Peter Bartholomew continued to prophesy in the interests of Bohemund's propaganda. At last, in January 1099, Raymond set out for Jerusalem, walking barefoot as a pilgrim, and accompanied by all of his own troops, together with Robert of Normandy and Tancred; nearly a month later, Godfrey of Bouillon was shamed into following; but Bohemund and Baldwin remained in their principalities of Antioch and Edessa.

The Fatimids of Egypt, having failed to make an alliance with the crusaders, had occupied Palestine as soon as they received news of Kerbogha's defeat; they were in control of the country as far north as Beirut, and past that point they were only prepared to admit unarmed pilgrims. Raymond made a leisurely progress, accepting the submission of some of the independent emirs, but wasting three months on a fruitless siege of Arqa near Tripoli. When he entered Fatimid territory he did not attempt to reduce the garrisons of the coastal towns, but pushed on to Jerusalem, arriving before its walls on 7th June; Ramleh and Bethlehem had opened their gates to him on the way, and he had by now been joined by most of the crusading army. Jerusalem was almost as well fortified as Antioch; its strong garrison had poisoned all the outside springs except for the pool of Siloam; supplies were difficult to obtain, since the coast was blockaded by an Egyptian fleet; and although a few Genoese ships managed to land at Jaffa, it was known that a relief army was on the point of setting out from Egypt. Religious processions were organized round the Holy City and sermons delivered by the best preachers among the chaplains. Meanwhile three large wooden towers on wheels were prepared in secrecy; and by moving these against the walls, the crusaders were enabled to storm the city on 15th July, 1099. A savage massacre of the Moslem and Jewish population followed, by which even Christian opinion in the East was shocked. But the Crusade had attained its objective, and although Pope Urban died before receiving news of the success, the ghost of Bishop Adhemar was believed to have been seen at the final assault.

A victory over the Egyptian troops at Ascalon soon secured the safety of the new conquests. But the problem of how they were to be governed proved embarrassing and delicate. Had Adhemar lived, he would probably have wished to place Jerusalem under nominal suzerainty of the Church, while allowing Raymond to exercise an actual control. But during the march from Antioch, Raymond had lost much of his popularity; he was thought to be a poor strategist, overbearing in his manners, and too friendly to the Greeks. Realizing that he would not be supported by the remainder, he declined a half-hearted offer of the crown, and eventually found himself a domain in Tripoli. The crusaders then turned with relief to Godfrey, who had been among the first to enter Jerusalem, and was regarded as the model of a pious knight; when inquiries were made about his private life, the only complaint that could be discovered was that he spent too much time on his devotions. Characteristically Godfrey refused to be crowned king in the city where his Lord had suffered, and he took up its government with the title Defender of the Holy Sepulchre. Most of the Greek clergy had fled to Cyprus, where their Patriarch had but recently died; to replace him Arnulf, chaplain to Robert of Normandy, was installed as the first Latin occupant of the see, and he began a period of oppression by torturing some of the native clergy to discover the hiding-place of the relic of the Cross. But Urban, before his death, had sent out a fresh legate in the person of Archbishop Daimbert of Pisa; this haughty Italian prelate, backed by a valuable Pisan fleet, soon managed to eject Arnulf and occupy the patriarchal throne. His dreams of establishing personal rule over Jerusalem were frustrated by the death of Godfrey, followed by the quick action of the troops in summoning his brother Baldwin from Edessa; and on Christmas Day 1100, in the Church of the Nativity at Bethlehem, Baldwin was crowned as King.

The result of the Crusade had been to found a cordon of small Christian states at Jerusalem, Tripoli, Antioch and Edessa, which could survive only so long as the Moslem emirs of the interior remained divided; but when Moslem power revived under Zenghi and his successor Saladin, Edessa fell in 1144 and Jerusalem forty-three years later, while a series of no less than eight Crusades, lasting until the close of the thirteenth century, failed to restore a permanent Christian occupation. At the outset, it had been a chivalrous adventure, undertaken in the spirit of religious idealism, but its motives very soon became more secular and more commercial. Venice quickly joined Genoa and Pisa in sending her ships to profit by the Eastern trade, which brought new foods and new luxuries back to Europe; cane sugar, lemons, muslin and damask, together with glass mirrors, were among the novelties imported, and the use of the rosary, if not originated at this time, was certainly stimulated by contact with the East. Arabic words made their way into the European languages, and the geographical horizon of men's minds was greatly widened. With the rising importance of the commercial cities, and the adoption of a monetary economy for distant trade, the structure of feudalism experienced considerable change. New military orders were founded, consisting of knights under monastic vows. The

Knights of St. John, wearing the Maltese Cross on their black
robes, had a hospital at Jerusalem which could accommodate
2,000 patients. The Templars, lavishly endowed by their patrons,
came in course of time to operate as a large banking firm, with
houses along the pilgrim routes where travellers' cheques could
be cashed. Great fortresses, like Monreal and Krak des Che-
valiers, were built to control the desert approaches into Palestine,
while in the pillared colonnades of their colonial residences, the
nobles enjoyed a colourful and cultured existence. They exchanged
courtesies with their Moslem neighbours, and developed a taste
for Eastern foods, women and religion which enervated, if it did
not entirely corrupt, the faith for which they were supposed to
fight. And in the homeland of Europe, although the influx of new
ideas provided an intellectual stimulus, the main effect of the
crusading movement was at once to exalt and to deprave the
papacy, by encouraging it to embark on schemes of conquest that
were political rather than religious. It is a striking fact that the
phrase "Church Militant" first came into use during the second
half of the twelfth century; before that time, the terrestrial portion
of the Christian fellowship was regularly described as "the Church
on Pilgrimage."

CHAPTER VII

ANSELM AND THE RISE OF SCHOLASTICISM

THROUGHOUT THE ELEVENTH CENTURY, CHRISTIAN SCHOLAR-
ship was beginning to acquire new methods and new
material. Gerbert of Aurillac, who died as Pope Silvester II in 1003, had been an early pioneer and, to his contemporaries,
a frightening portent. He not only revived the logic of Boethius
but also, having studied in the Spanish schools, he acquired from
the Moslems a fair knowledge of mathematics; hence in his teaching he was able to use the abacus, the monochord and a model of
the planetary system; and men believed that he had sold his soul
to the devil, so as to perform his strange scientific art by means
of magic. His pupil, Fulbert of Chartres, was better understood
and consequently better loved. Though a mathematician and a
poet, Fulbert was primarily a divine, with a marked gift for
arousing the enthusiasm of his scholars; in the evenings, when
work was done, he used to walk with them in a small garden
beside the chapel, talking of eternity; and despite the fact that he
wrote little himself, he founded a flourishing school of humanism
at Chartres. But one of Fulbert's pupils was Berengarius, whose
confidence in human reason led him to challenge Church authority; and everywhere in conservative circles the new learning was
suspect for its unorthodox trends. Peter Damian, an earnest
preacher and a solid churchman, rejects Plato, Pythagoras and
Euclid, advising his readers to content themselves with a knowledge of the Bible; for, as he puts it in his book *On Holy Simplicity*,
if logic were requisite for salvation, then God would have sent
philosophers and not fishermen as His apostles. The devil,
Damian thinks, was undoubtedly the first professor. Even Lanfranc, head of the monastic school at Bec, though ready to employ
rational arguments in defending the faith, is none the less fond of
quoting the text from 1 Cor. 1 : 17—"Not with wisdom of words,
lest the cross of Christ should be made of none effect." It was left
for Lanfranc's pupil Anselm to match a profound faith with an
equal profundity of intellect, and so to produce a deeply devotional philosophy.

The monastery of Bec had been founded in 1041, under condi-

tions of extreme poverty; its founder and first abbot, a knight
called Herlouin, built the church with his own hands. There was
little sign of intellectual promise at the start, for Herlouin himself
was an illiterate, who only learnt to read at the age of forty; but
he welcomed Lanfranc, an Italian lawyer wandering in search of
knowledge, and under Lanfranc's direction, Bec speedily became
the chief centre of scholarship in Normandy. The result was a
happy combination of Norman strength with Italian virtuosity,
whose products included the future Pope Alexander II. Anselm
was drawn to Bec in 1059, when he was twenty-six years old;
born at Aosta in what was then Savoy, he had from his youth
desired to be a monk—Eadmer, his biographer, records a boyish
dream in which he found himself climbing a mountain to see God
—but meeting with parental opposition he escaped from home
across the Alps. After a few months of study, he confided his
desires to Lanfranc, who sent him for guidance to the Archbishop
of Rouen; and that prelate advised him to enter the monastic life,
as the most natural vocation for a scholar at this period. In 1063,
when Lanfranc was appointed to the abbacy of Caen, Anselm
succeeded his old teacher as prior of Bec, with charge of the
school, and on the death of Herlouin fifteen years later he became
abbot of the monastery. Especially popular with the keen young
men who flocked to hear his teaching, he maintained a discipline
that was firm but wise; when a neighbouring abbot complained
that he could not improve his boys, however often he beat them,
Anselm asked the surprisingly modern question: "Have you tried
not beating them?" He loved nursing the sick in the infirmary,
and had an almost Franciscan sympathy for animals. Much later
on, as Archbishop of Canterbury, he was riding from Windsor
when a hare took refuge from its hunters underneath his horse;
dismounting with tears in his eyes, he rescued the palpitating
creature and delivered a short homily to the huntsmen, in which
he compared its plight to that of a harried soul departing from
the body. Anselm was not an outstanding preacher; his gifts
were for the study rather than the pulpit. But he was always ready
to address his fellow-monks on the spiritual life, or to talk with
laymen about their religious difficulties. With a singular capacity
for understanding the problems of honest doubt, he could penetrate the minds of his pupils and answer their unspoken questions. In his extensive correspondence, running to well over four
hundred letters, he is always sympathetic, anxious to believe the
best, but at the same time gently firm. His severest censures were
reserved for the rapacity of fellow-monks, at a time when monastic administrators had been seized by the passion for adding field

to field; to the Abbot of St. Albans he wrote, "there are many officers of our Order who, rather than dissipate their endowments, erase God's law from their hearts." But if his views were decided, his attitude remained consistently humble; when Lanfranc started addressing his letters to Dom Anselm, he asked, "why do you not write to me, instead of to this imaginary prelate?" Above all, his prayers are aflame with a passionate faith. "Grant that I may taste by love what I apprehend by knowledge, that I may feel in my heart what I touch through the Spirit:" such is his request in a Meditation *On the Redemption of Mankind*, and he continues, "Oh Christian soul, raised up from a dreadful death, bought and delivered from a wretched servitude by the Blood of God, awaken, remember thy resurrection, reflect on thy redemption and deliverance . . . rejoice in the contemplation of its preciousness."

Anselm's thought is thus firmly rooted in the faith. But at the same time, he seeks to understand the reason for the faith that is in him. As a teacher, he feels it incumbent upon him to show how Christianity provides an integrated picture of the universe, which is rational, harmonious and intellectually satisfying; not in order to put philosophy in place of revelation, but because the gifts of both mind and spirit come in a coherent pattern from one and the same God. "Faith in search of self-understanding" is his motto; "I do not seek to understand in order that I may believe," he writes, "but I believe in order to understand;" for "although the right method of procedure demands that we should believe the mysteries of faith before we venture to discuss them rationally, none the less it seems to me to indicate negligence if, after we have been confirmed in the faith, we do not study to comprehend what we believe." With this aim in view, he wrote several works of religious philosophy during his teaching days at Bec. The *Monologion*, whose original title was "An example of Meditation on the Rationality of Faith," sets out to prove the existence of God by arguments derived from human reason and not from scriptural revelation. Briefly, the signs of moral purpose and intelligent design, which are observable in nature, presuppose some perfect and self-existent Being as its Creator; all the varying degrees of goodness in the creatures must come to them from one supreme Good, their very existence must be due to participation in the supreme Being; and just as a community of qualities implies a common source, so a scale of degrees in perfection leads us to postulate an absolute standard of reference. Men may speak truly and act justly, but God is Justice and Truth; "when the same Spirit utters Himself, He at the same time utters all created things," which are thus an expressive revelation of their Maker.

The monks of Bec had asked Anselm to write this treatise for them, but he was not himself entirely satisfied with the result. He searched laboriously for one compelling proof of God's existence; until, as Eadmer records, the so-called Ontological Proof came to him during the watches of a tormented night, and he embodied it in his next work, the *Proslogion*. Here, he defines God as a Being so perfect that nothing greater is conceivable, from which it follows that He cannot be conceived as non-existent. For if He did not exist, some existing object would, by virtue of its mere existence, be greater than He; and so He would cease to be what He is defined as being. Thus, when the fool says in his heart that there is no God (Ps. 14 : 1), he can be convicted out of his own mouth, since in the very act of naming God, he has postulated the idea of a Being which must necessarily exist. The argument is obviously defective, for a definition of terms need not be a statement of fact. Gaunilo, a monk of Marmoutiers, at once pointed out that the same sort of argument could be used to demonstrate the existence of any mental concept, such as that of a lost island more perfect than any island known; to this Anselm answered that his proof only applies to the unique case of God, who is not the most perfect specimen in a particular category, but the perfection of Being itself. Both medieval and modern philosophers have been divided in their verdict. Aquinas, followed by Kant, denied the possibility of an *a priori* proof of God; Bonaventura, and later Descartes, accepted it as cogent, provided that it was properly expressed. Philosophically the objection remains that existence is not a predicate of the same kind as greatness. But the value of Anselm's argument is religious rather than philosophical. He starts from the conviction that God is omnipresent, present even in our doubt of Him, so that we can never argue about Him as if He were not there; in consequence, the proof quickly turns into a prayer—"therefore, O Lord my God, Thou dost exist so truly that Thy non-existence cannot be conceived." It is no more than a deduction from the data given by faith; once we know God, however imperfectly, we know that He exists.

Meanwhile, Anselm was drawn more and more from the quiet studies which he loved into the turmoil of administrative work. When he had become Abbot of Bec in 1078, he was obliged to pay several visits to the English estates belonging to his monastery; he thus acquired friends and a certain following in England, where the Church was being rapidly reorganized after the Norman Conquest. In theory, William the Conqueror did not claim any supreme headship, but in practice his ecclesiastical adminis-

H

tration differed little from that of the later Tudors. He indignantly
refused the request for an oath of fealty to the Pope, although he
did arrange for the more regular collection of Peter's Pence. He
appointed the bishops and greater abbots, investing them with
ring and staff. He refused to let any English prelate journey to
Rome without his permission, nor would he allow any papal
letter to be received without his knowledge. Although the episcopal courts were for the first time separated from the civil ones,
thus receiving a certain measure of independent spiritual jurisdiction, none the less the king's consent was required before the
excommunication of any baron or royal minister, and the prelates
were themselves answerable on serious charges to the king. This
refusal to tolerate foreign interference was the traditional attitude
of eleventh-century rulers, yet in 1079 Hildebrand complained
that "no-one else has been so lacking in devotion and humility as
to prevent bishops from visiting the threshold of the apostles."
Earlier, he had pleaded that since he would have to answer for
kings' souls at the Day of Judgment, William must render him
immediate obedience. But the great Pope pleaded in vain; and his
pleas were at the best half-hearted, since William shared his own
interest in reform. The king would appoint and control his
bishops, but the men whom he appointed were on the whole
wisely chosen. Particularly was this the case with Lanfranc, whom
he brought over from Caen in 1070 to succeed the deposed
Stigand as Archbishop of Canterbury. Having left Rome before
the real revival of the papacy, Lanfranc belonged to the older
generation of reformers, and he was therefore perfectly willing to
work under a virtually royal supremacy. However, he did bring
with him an abridged version of the False Decretals, together
with more recent decrees against simony, and a copy of the profession made by Berengarius at the Roman council of 1059; and
although Lanfranc did not himself emphasize the papal leanings
of these documents, they were put into circulation in England,
with the result that William of St. Carileph, Bishop of Durham,
when accused of treason, conceived the idea of appealing beyond
Lanfranc to the Pope. To the monks of Canterbury, Lanfranc
gave a constitution based on the customs of Cluny, which became
normative for all English Benedictines; and the monks repaid him
by secretly forging some papal letters to support the primacy of
Canterbury as against the rival pretensions of York. Along with
Norman prelates, Norman architecture was imported; for polite
purposes the English language was replaced by Norman French;
and the old Anglo-Saxon culture was utterly submerged, apart
from the remnants of it that were taken to Scotland by Queen

Margaret. Some of the bishoprics were rearranged, archdeacons were appointed to enforce discipline, and a mild beginning was made in promoting clerical celibacy. By the time of the Conqueror's death in 1087, the English Church had seen great changes. Two years later, Lanfranc followed his royal master to the grave.

The new king, William Rufus, was fully as autocratic as the Conqueror, but lacked his father's interest in Church reform; under him, the royal supremacy was openly used to benefit the Crown and not the Church. When an episcopal vacancy occurred, Rufus kept the see unfilled for as long as possible in order to appropriate its revenues. Canterbury remained vacant for four years, until an illness frightened the king into appointing an archbishop; he then chose Anselm, already popular among the English, and the only churchman whom he himself respected. But the candidate, knowing the tensions that he would have to face, was most unwilling; "What would be the use," he asked "of yoking a feeble old sheep like myself to an unmanageable bull?" The monks of Bec made difficulties about parting with their abbot, and Anselm was not slow to indicate the principles for which he felt obliged to stand. Eventually, he accepted on three conditions: first, he must enjoy the rights and properties of Canterbury as fully as his predecessors, second, in matters of religion the king must treat him as a spiritual father, and third, he must continue to acknowledge Urban as the rightful Pope. In the schism inherited from Hildebrand there was still an imperial anti-pope, Guibert of Ravenna, who did not die until September 1100, and in the meanwhile England had not declared its ecclesiastical allegiance; but Anselm, with his strongly papal sympathies, insisted that the existence of a rival claimant must not be used to impair his relations with the papacy. None the less he was obliged to accept investiture from Rufus, a transaction which he later regarded as invalid since it had been forced on him against his will. On 5th September, 1093, he was enthroned at Canterbury, to the accompaniment of an ominous suit lodged by the king's agent Flambard against a tenant of the Archbishopric; and three months later at his consecration by the Archbishop of York, when the Book of the Gospels was laid according to custom on his shoulders, it opened ominously at the text "they all with one consent began to make excuse." Disagreement at once followed over Anselm's proposal to visit Rome for his pallium; the journey, had he been allowed to undertake it, would have symbolized the primary direction of his loyalties, while the king's refusal was an equally firm reminder that bishops must regard themselves as civil servants. Thus England joined the struggle, already raging on the Continent, between the rival powers of Church and State.

In 1095 a council met by Anselm's request at Rockingham; it was composed of both bishops and barons, and its purpose was to reach a compromise on the vexed question of England's ecclesiastical allegiance. The bishops were mostly royal nominees, who longed for a return to Lanfranc's methods; they regarded Anselm as a trouble-maker, and he knew that in the last resort they would not oppose an open rupture with the papacy. But the barons, impressed by his courage, hoped to use him as an ally in curbing the dictatorial king, and among the commons his popularity had never wavered; during the sessions of the council a soldier came forward, urging him to be brave and patient and to "remember how holy Job on his dunghill vanquished the devil." Of patience Anselm had an adequate supply, and at one point, while king, bishops and barons were engaged in furious discussion, he was discovered placidly asleep. He parried a personal attack upon himself by pointing out that, under canon law, an archbishop could be judged only by the Pope; and when the bishops threatened to disown him, the barons replied that for them, as Christian laymen, it would be impossible to renounce obedience to their primate, since religious ties, unlike those of feudalism, were not reciprocal. But although the Council had witnessed the emergence of what might become a papal party under Anselm's leadership, it decided nothing, and for the next two years it was followed by an uneasy truce. With great audacity Rufus asked Pope Urban to send a pallium to England, where it would be bestowed on Anselm by the king himself; thus the royal supremacy would be exemplified in a manner outrageous to any papalist; but at the same time Urban's title to the papacy was tacitly admitted in the request, and he was therefore weak enough to comply. Anselm, however, was saved by a threat of rebellion in the Welsh marches and the North, and he was finally allowed to take the pallium directly from the altar, where it had been laid by a papal legate. Other charges were fabricated against him, of a petty but vexatious character, and by 1097 his position had become so untenable that he decided to leave for Rome; he parted amicably from Rufus, crossed the Channel to spend the winter in France, and after keeping Christmas at Cluny, he reached Rome in the spring of 1098.

Urban welcomed him with ungrudging respect and secret embarrassment. His visit might well serve to forge a closer link between the papacy and the English Church; but too hasty a decision would only drive Rufus to support the anti-pope. For months Urban procrastinated, while Anselm gladly escaped from the summer heats of Rome to the hill monastery of St. Saviour's, where a former monk of Bec was now the abbot. Here in the mountains between Capua and Benevento, he was able to return to his quiet routine of prayer and study. He had brought with him an unfinished treatise on the Incarnation and Atonement, of which a pirated edition had just been published; it seems that on the first stages of his journey, while he stopped for five days in the neighbourhood of St. Omer, one of the monks who entertained him had copied out the draft without his knowledge. He was therefore anxious to produce a properly revised edition as rapidly as possible; by September he had given to the world his major work, entitled *Cur Deus Homo?* or "The Reason for the God-man." His first draft had apparently been a short theological meditation; the final version is a vigorous piece of apologetics, cast in the form of a dialogue, where Anselm meets and answers objections to the central doctrines of the faith. Few books, perhaps none of comparable length, have had so great an influence on the development of dogma. Its new and epoch-making feature is the idea that, on the cross, Christ offered a satisfaction to His Father and not a ransom to the devil. Previously most theologians had followed Origen in believing that the cross represents a cosmic drama, in which Satan is beaten by his own devices. It was recognized that mercy and justice must somehow be reconciled, but the claims of justice were regarded as claims of the devil, who had acquired proprietary rights over mankind when Adam sold himself into the power of evil. God could not justly redeem man, unless the devil could be persuaded to exceed his own just dues. And so the flesh of Christ was offered as a sort of bait; the devil claimed it as his rightful possession, only to be caught on the concealed hook of Christ's divinity. For when Satan took Christ, he took One who alone among men did not rightly belong to his jurisdiction; and when he had thus broken the rules of strict justice, it was only just for him to be deprived of those others whom he held in bondage.

Apart from a few dissenting voices, such was the generally accepted doctrine of Atonement, until Anselm worked out a more acceptable alternative, by showing that the claims of justice which must be satisfied are the claims of God and not the devil. He pours scorn on the older theory, declaring that neither God nor man owes Satan anything except defiance; the idea that the divine wisdom was exhibited in a piscatorial trick to cheat the devil seems to him unworthy and repulsive. And so he turns from the metaphor of ransom to that of satisfaction. God's honour must be satisfied, since it has been outraged by human sin. Anselm here speaks the language of feudalism, in terms natural to contemporaries who were familiar with the *Wergild* or compensation paid for murder; but in speaking of sin as an affront to the divine dignity, he at least recognizes that it is an offence against a person rather than against a principle. In satisfaction for so vile an insult, God demands the free offering of something greater than all that is not God, a gift which in fact He Himself alone can make; but by making it in the person of man, by becoming incarnate so as to render up His divine life, He allows its benefits to be communicated to men who are mercifully, and at the same time justly, saved. For although on the human level Anselm utterly rejects the possibility of supererogation, declaring that everything a man can do is no more than his bounden duty, yet in the case of Christ, His death in perfect obedience goes beyond what could be required of Him and therefore deserves to be rewarded; having no need of the reward Himself, He transfers it to those for whom He died, an elect company of human souls from every generation, sufficient not only to replace the fallen angels but also to make up to its perfect number the citizenship of the heavenly Jerusalem. Anselm claims that, although his argument is in full accord with the teaching of Scripture, it does not depend for its validity on any appeal to scriptural proof-texts; it is put forward as a purely logical demonstration of the reasonable character of Christian doctrine. However, it presupposes the following assumptions: the existence of a divine purpose for humanity, which must be fulfilled if God's acts are to be self-consistent; the inescapable duty of man to obey God, which renders disobedience a sin of infinite gravity; God's inexorable demand for satisfaction to His wounded honour; and man's total inability to redeem himself. Granted these assumptions, the rest does logically follow, and belief in an objective act of Atonement has been shown to be entirely rational. Anselm's use of feudal terminology need not obscure the permanent value of his conviction that, even in showing mercy, God must uphold the moral order of the universe; such, rather than the "celestial etiquette" to which some critics have reduced his notion of the divine honour, is the meaning of his cardinal ideas. He wrote at a time when epic poetry was giving place to romance in literature, and when the crucifix, hitherto a figure of triumphant majesty, was becoming a much more realistic representation of the Passion. Sensitive to these current trends, his treatise is, by contrast with its predecessors, a romance of love incarnate in redemptive agony, and even in his lifetime he was criticized for excessive pathos. But his work is timeless. It could

lead easily to a doctrine of the appropriation of Christ's benefits
by faith alone; with equal ease, it could be used to emphasize the
sacrificial value of the mass. The tender quality of his romantic
approach comes out in his devotion to the Virgin, a devotion
which his nephew was later to help in popularizing. Mary, he
says, was rendered sinless through faith in her Son's future sacrifice; but this, as he is quick to point out, does not mean that
Christ was under the necessity of dying in order to be born.
Elsewhere, in the fifth of his collected prayers, he addresses the
Virgin as "Holy Mary, next to God among all the saints in holiness . . . bearer of life, mother of salvation, temple of piety and
mercy," and he beseeches her to heal his wretched soul by her
"potent merits and pious intercession." But such exuberant language is out of keeping with his strict doctrinal position; and
although, out of nineteen prayers in the collection, three are
addressed to Mary, ten to other saints, and one to the Holy Cross,
none the less his theology is clearly based on the principle that
Christ is the sole author of salvation, even for those who lived
before His coming. In the chivalrous atmosphere of the eleventh
century, homage to the Virgin was increasing, along with a
revived interest in the humanity of Christ; but despite this growing tendency, the attitude of Anselm remains Christocentric, and
the most typical example of his ardent faith is provided by the
third of his Meditations, on the preciousness of Christ's redemptive work.

As soon as he had completed his *Cur Deus Homo?*, Anselm was
sent by the Pope to the Council of Bari in October 1098, where
he impressed the Greek delegates by his arguments in favour of
the double procession of the Holy Spirit. Next year he took part
in a council at Rome, which renewed the prohibition of simony
and clerical marriage, and decreed the penalty of excommunication against both donors and recipients of lay investiture. In 1100
William Rufus died in the New Forest, to be succeeded by his
younger brother Henry I, an equally strong-minded but at the
same time more law-abiding monarch. Anselm was immediately
recalled to England, where he helped to arrange the marriage
between Henry and Matilda; by this the union between Normans
and English was cemented, for Matilda, the daughter of Queen
Margaret and the Scots King Malcolm, belonged to the old royal
family of Wessex, whose blood she transmitted to the Angevin,
Scottish and Hanoverian dynasties of England. But although
Henry united the nation under a compact central government, he
failed to obtain from Anselm the full submission he demanded.
When he required an oath of homage he was met with a blunt

refusal. For Anselm, confirmed by the Roman Council in his opposition to lay investiture, did not believe, as Cranmer was later to believe, that his episcopal powers required renewal at the start of a fresh reign. On the contrary, he maintained that he owed allegiance solely to the Pope. To Urban's successor, Paschal II, he wrote early in 1101: "I have recourse to the guidance and advice of Your Paternity, because the sons of the Church depend for their guiding directives on the authority of the Holy See." A few minor reforms were introduced. But as Anselm refused to consecrate bishops whom Henry had invested, the major cause of deadlock remained, and by 1103 Anselm had again exiled himself to Rome. Paschal proved more willing than his predecessors to seek a compromise, exempting the English King from the penalty of excommunication which his actions had incurred. For his own part, Anselm was ready to be reconciled, provided that this could be achieved with papal sanction; he assured Queen Matilda that he bore no personal rancour against her husband, and in writing to Henry he regularly sent his "prayers and loyal duty." At last agreement was reached, on the lines later to be followed in the Concordat of Worms: the king gave up investiture by ring and staff, while the bishops were allowed to do him homage for their lands. When this compromise had been accepted by the papacy, Anselm returned to England in 1107. Two years later, on 21st April, 1109, he died in sack-cloth and ashes, lamenting that his many political preoccupations had prevented him from completing a treatise on the origin of the human soul.

The effect of his life's work had been to secure for the English Church a relative freedom from secular control, at the price of increasing dependence on the papacy. With a high sense of papal prerogative, he believed that St. Peter is constantly present in the person of his vicar, and in letters he repeatedly stressed the duty of obedience to Rome. The trend which he began was consolidated by the posthumous victory of Becket, who declared, as Anselm had done, that he was fighting for the liberties of the Church of England; in both men's minds liberty meant liberty to serve the Pope, and for both of them a Free Church was synonymous with a papal one. Paradoxically, it was the papacy and not the Crown which made the Church of England a united national institution; for the separate convocations of Canterbury and York could only meet together when summoned by a papal legate, and the very phrase *Ecclesia Anglicana* first appears, about the year 1165, in the correspondence of a Pope.

Anselm's place in the history of thought is less easy to determine. He inaugurated a new method of free philosophical inquiry, which would place him with the thinkers of the modern world, if it were not that his speculations are always controlled by a basic acceptance of the Christian faith. Unlike most medieval schoolmen, of whom he is sometimes called the first, he made no clear distinction between natural and revealed theology; that distinction only became essential in the thirteenth century, after the rediscovery of the pagan Aristotle. But he is undoubtedly linked to the Middle Ages by his Marian devotion. The Virgin was in a special sense the Lady of the scholar as well as of the knight, and it became customary to invoke her patronage at the commencement of an academic exercise; even Calvin, before his breach with Rome, introduced this customary invocation in the otherwise evangelical address, which he composed for his friend Nicholas Cop to deliver as Rector of Paris University. What distinguishes Anselm from the later schoolmen is his lack of the academic atmosphere; for him, as for the earlier Fathers, philosophy is a way of life rather than a specialized, professional technique; and although he seldom quotes Augustine, he is deeply imbued with the Platonism of the African saint. In him, almost for the last time in the Latin West, a strain of Greek mysticism appears. He stands at a watershed, from one point of view the earliest of the scholastics, and from another the last of the Fathers.

CHAPTER VIII

ABELARD AND BERNARD OF CLAIRVAUX

IF THE THIRTEENTH CENTURY WAS TO BE THE GREAT AGE OF scholasticism, the twelfth provided a fitting prelude. For it was then that the medieval universities had their first obscure beginnings, so obscure that in many cases it is impossible to give even an approximate foundation date, and yet so important that they were soon being described as a "third force" in European politics, comparable to that of Papacy or Empire. In Italy the study of law had survived, while in Northern Europe there were the cathedral and monastic schools; what turned a local school into a *studium generale* was the appearance of a teacher, or group of teachers, sufficiently famous to attract an international audience; and although the curriculum, like the membership, of a university was supposed to be all-embracing, none the less Italy remained the great centre for legal studies, with its distinguished law-school at Bologna, while Paris in the North, under the shadow of the cathedral of Notre Dame, became the home above all others of theology. Salerno, south of Naples, had for some time been a centre for medical training; a health resort, situated at the meeting-point of Greek, Arabic and Latin culture, it provided that strange blend of astrology with ancient medicine and philosophy which was the education of the medieval doctor, and it is said to have been sufficiently modern in outlook to admit women professors to its teaching staff. But Salerno originated nothing new; with a rigid ban on practical anatomy, its pseudo-science was at the best antique. The ferment of fresh thought was to be found farther north, where that familiar spectacle, the wandering scholar, tramped with his few books from the feet of one distinguished master to another, and the guilds, of students or of teachers or of both, banded themselves together in pursuit of learning. Something of the craft guilds, with their different grades of apprentice and master, entered into the constitution of medieval universities; something too came from chivalry, with its corporate loyalties and its ceremonies of inauguration. The scholar's search for knowledge seemed at this romantic period to be like the knight's quest of the Holy Grail; it could be fully as exacting and protracted, for when courses of study came to be organized, a preliminary six years were demanded in Arts, with a further twelve or thirteen before graduation in Divinity. For the final part of his course, the scholar, now with the degree of Bachelor, acted as an assistant lecturer; but unless they had a good benefice coupled with leave of absence, few men could afford to stay the entire length and obtain the mastership or doctorate which, by conferring the licence to teach, was equivalent to a professorship. None the less, a smattering of Latin and logic, a thin stream of general education, was diffused widely enough to justify the term "twelfth-century Renaissance."

The primitive university was completely mobile. With neither buildings nor endowments, it hired a room for lectures, or borrowed a church for faculty meetings; and if relations between town and gown became, as they sometimes did, too strained, masters and scholars might simply pick up their books and migrate elsewhere. Such a migration from Paris, towards the close of the twelfth century, seems to have produced the new University of Oxford; and a generation later, a fresh movement from Oxford gave birth in turn to Cambridge. But some control of studies and of graduation was required. At Bologna, the guild consisted of students, mostly mature and beneficed men, who studied law with the hope of preferment in Church or State. They formed a corporation, hired professors to teach them, and subjected these teachers to a minute and searching supervision; the professor was fined if he was late for lectures, if he overran his time, or if he skipped a difficult passage in the prescribed textbook; and although the city fathers eventually ended this remarkable system by founding salaried chairs, a relic of the student's paradise at Bologna survives in the constitution of the Scottish Universities, with their Rectors elected by the student body. At Paris, however, and at her daughter Oxford, the guild consisted of the teaching staff, who both enforced discipline and regulated admission. There were various schools, conducted by several masters, in different parts of the city, but the nucleus consisted of the cathedral school, controlled by the Chancellor of the diocese, with whom lay the ultimate right of granting academic degrees. This full-fledged system took time to develop. Alongside the formal lecture expounding a set book, there was also the university sermon, and the more informal disputation, by which wits were sharpened and the candidates for degrees were tested. But though development took time the seeds were planted early in the twelfth century, when the lawyer Irnerius laid the foundations of Bologna University, and the fame of Paris was blazed abroad by the turbulent career of Peter Abelard.

Northern universities, unlike their more secular Italian counter-parts, grew up under patronage of the Church; all higher educa-tion was provided through the international medium of the Latin language; scholars and masters ranked as clerks, wearing the clerical gown. This did not prevent them from indulging in a great deal of rough horse-play, ribald parodies, and riotous drinking-songs. But scholarship none the less remained so much of an ecclesiastical occupation that it was largely disdained by knight and noble. The Bible was the most widely read book of any throughout the Middle Ages. Vernacular translations were scarce and incomplete, but for all who could read Latin the Vulgate was basic at almost every stage of education; it was used for teaching grammar in the primary schools, it provided the staple diet for monks, and along with the *Sentences* of Peter Lom-bard it was the sole prescribed textbook for the academic study of theology. Overlaid with the venerable dust of gloss and com-ment, its meaning wrested into the strange shapes of allegorical interpretation, the Bible still retained its place as the supreme fountain-head of knowledge. Consequently the period was a pro-lific one in sermons. Several thousand survive from the thirteenth century, when the friars had come to add their popular appeal as preachers; but from the twelfth century several hundred survive, together with a few works, like that by Alain of Lille, on the science of homiletics.

Moreover, in this predominantly religious atmosphere, the rise of the universities was accompanied by the growth of fresh monastic institutions. In the parlance of the time, "conversion" was equated with taking monastic vows, "religion" with the monastic life; increasingly the monks claimed to be "the poor," to whom the blessings of the Gospel were vouchsafed, and on whom the alms of the rich should be expended. But Cluny had lost its first reforming fervour, and the Cluniac monks, bounti-fully endowed as landlords, were settling down to a comfortable collegiate existence; they drew their tithes, patronized the arts and beautified their churches, but despite the efforts of Peter the Venerable, who became Abbot of Cluny in 1122, they had slipped into an irreversible decline. It was other sources that now pro-vided the impetus to a reformed monasticism, by returning to an austere simplicity in obedience to the primitive Benedictine Rule. Weary of the world, a teacher from the cathedral school of Rheims called Bruno retired, in 1084, with six companions to a mountainous retreat in the snows above Grenoble; here, in con-ditions of extreme poverty, they lived almost as hermits, giving up their time to contemplation; the name of their retreat was La

Grande Chartreuse (anglicized as Charterhouse), from which they were known as Carthusians, and although not numerous, they formed the one Order which never declined from its original strictness. In 1098 a friend of Bruno called Robert of Molesme founded at Cîteaux the mother-house of the Cistercian Order; aiming at a less inhuman pitch of asceticism, the Cistercians none the less cultivated a puritanical simplicity in life and worship; and after the first struggles of their early years, they acquired a glorious recruit in the person of Bernard of Clairvaux.

Both men, Abelard and Bernard, despite their obvious dissimilarities, were strangely linked together. Even in appearance they were not unlike—fair-haired, handsome, and of medium height. Abelard was under no illusions about his personal good looks; Bernard was noted for the almost womanish delicacy of his complexion, the brilliant purity of his blue eyes. If the intellectual interests of the one contrasted strongly with the mystical devotion of the other, none the less both were loyal sons of the Church, reared in religious homes, dedicating their great gifts to God's glory. Abelard, beginning as a scholar, was forced into the cloister where, almost against his will, he developed a deep sense of monastic vocation; Bernard, joyfully becoming a monk in his early twenties, was obliged to leave his solitude, to play the part of an ecclesiastical statesman and to engage in theological debate. Above all, the *leitmotiv* in both their lives was love. Abelard's more earthly passion for Heloise was sublimated through his sufferings; Bernard's soul burnt with a divine charity, which he none the less interpreted in the human symbols of the Song of Songs.

Of the two, Abelard was about eleven years the elder. The correct form of his name, now unknown, may perhaps have been Abaielardus. Of Breton stock, he was born in 1079 at Le Pallet not far from Nantes. His father, a knight with a small landed estate, was sufficiently well educated to insist on a proper schooling for the family, of which Abelard was the eldest; mother and father were both devout enough to end their days in the cloister, so that religion as well as learning played a prominent part in the home. Hence, as he himself tells us in his *Historia Calamitatum*, the young Abelard scorned the military obligations of his primogeniture, and devoted his life to Minerva rather than to Mars. But even as a man of letters he retained the fighting spirit of his race; quarrelling in turn with all his teachers, he became an *enfant terrible* of the schools. His first master was Roscelin, a nominalist philosopher who had once been accused of heresy, and was now lecturing at Loches. Thinkers of the period were sharply divided over the problem of universals, the status of such general concepts as "humanity." Do these exist, apart and by themselves, as the real prototypes of individual things? Or are they merely names, convenient labels applied to the members of a class? Realist philosophers accepted the first alternative, regarding universals as distinct and concrete entities; the nominalist school, of which Roscelin was perhaps the founder, believed that individuals alone exist. The debate had pressing theological implications. For Christian doctrine insisted on the solidarity of the human race in Adam, and it therefore welcomed the realist conception of humanity, as an organic whole infected by original sin rather than a mere class of unrelated individuals. Moreover, nominalism quickly led to heresy when applied to the doctrine of the Trinity. If deity is no more than a name, attached to the three separate and individual Persons of Father, Son and Holy Ghost, then monotheism becomes impossible and there are in fact three distinct Gods. This was the precise accusation that had been made against Roscelin at the Council of Soissons in 1092; but he repudiated tritheism, and was allowed to continue teaching. Abelard studied under him for a period, but soon left and later attacked his master. His thirst for knowledge quickly took him to other schools, perhaps to Chartres, where he seems to have made a fruitless attempt to learn mathematics from the celebrated Thierry, and certainly to Paris, where William of Champeaux had been lecturing in the cathedral school since 1095. William was an extreme realist, standing at the opposite pole to Roscelin; but realism also had its pitfalls for the unwary theologian, for if the individual is merged and lost in the universal, then Father, Son and Holy Ghost are identified, and the ancient heresy of Sabellius results. Abelard himself, as appears from his glosses on Porphyry, took a sensible, mediating position, which was largely adopted by the later schoolmen: universals are admittedly names, not things, but a name has meaning, derived from the natural resemblance which really exists between members of a class. William of Champeaux was baffled and annoyed by the brilliant dialectic of his pupil; and Abelard, in the flush of youthful self-confidence, set up his own rival school at Melun, from where he moved it to Corbeil, still nearer Paris, with the purpose of attracting all the students to himself. His lectures were immensely popular, not least because they attacked the established masters, and a generation of angry young men flocked to listen. But the effort had overstrained his physical resources; he was obliged to spend the next two or three years, a sick man, in his Breton home.

On returning to Paris, soon after 1108, he found that William had withdrawn from the world to become a canon regular at the Abbey of St. Victor. Perhaps he too had suffered from the strain, perhaps he felt a genuine vocation; Abelard rather unkindly suggests that he had entered St. Victor simply as a step to a bishopric. The canons regular were professed as monks, but their rule allowed them to undertake parochial responsibilities. St. Victor became a sort of chaplaincy centre for the University, developing a school of devotional philosophy, in which mysticism and scholarship were combined. Run like a well-appointed college, it had waiters to wipe the dishes before they were laid upon the table-cloth; with a library enriched from royal benefactions, it attracted men from many nations to its staff. Among the more notable of William's successors were Hugh the Saxon who, in his *De Sacramentis Christianae Fidei*, worked out a sacramental conception of the entire universe; Richard the Scot, who wrote on contemplation and sought to prove the doctrine of the Trinity from a psychological analysis of love; Adam the Breton, author of many poetical sequences to be sung in Church; Walter, a vigorous opponent of dialectic, who treated the work of Abelard and his fellow-logicians as labyrinths of error; and Andrew the commentator, who learnt Hebrew from the Rabbis, ventured to question the authority of Augustine and Jerome, and inaugurated a literal, scientific exegesis of the biblical text. While at St. Victor, William of Champeaux continued teaching, and Abelard attended his lectures on rhetoric; but the old antagonism remained, and after he had forced his master more and more to abandon the extremes of realism, Abelard again established his own school, this time on Mont St. Geneviève. In 1112 William delightedly accepted the bishopric of Châlons, and about two years later, on returning from another visit to his home, Abelard decided to embark on the study of theology. Though his age was now about thirty-five, he joined younger students in the classes conducted by Anselm of Laon, a product of the monastic school at Bec, and reputed to be the most learned divine of the period. Abelard found his lectures dull, verbose and unintelligible, filling the room with smoke instead of light. When he expressed his criticisms vocally, the other students challenged him to lecture himself, and with characteristic audacity he announced a course on that most difficult of books, Ezekiel. The course proved so successful that he was able to return to Paris as a teacher of theology, with some official position, perhaps as a minor canon of Notre Dame. "I believed," he writes, "that I was now the one philosopher in all the world;" rapid success had gone to his head, and it was now that his tragedies began.

Fulbert, one of the canons of Notre Dame, had a beloved niece called Heloise, a lovely and learned girl of seventeen. Remarkable among the women of that period in being a blue-stocking, she was still more remarkable for beauty. Abelard was entranced; it was his first love affair, but his intentions were at the start strictly dishonourable. He offered to give the girl some coaching, and in the privacy of her uncle's house she gave herself to him; "it was you alone that I desired," she later wrote, "and I kept nothing for myself." Soon a child was expected; he smuggled Heloise away to his sister's home in Brittany; and the offspring of these amorous scholars was rather pedantically christened Astrolabe. To pacify the wrathful Fulbert, Abelard now offered marriage. It would have been a lawful union, for he was at the most tonsured and certainly not ordained; but apart from the fact that he might have had to resign his benefice, it would have severely hampered his professional career. Heloise refused to hear of it; she quoted St. Paul on the distractions of the married state, she recalled the troubles that Socrates had suffered from his scolding spouse Xanthippe; the Christian Jerome was marshalled alongside the pagan Cicero to prove that no man can cultivate philosophy and marriage at the same time. In thus rejecting the conventional amends, Heloise again sacrificed herself to what she conceived to be the interests of her lover. And Abelard agreed entirely with her principles; to him as to her, the spectacle of a married professor would have been ridiculous. So he proposed a compromise. Fulbert must be pacified by a form of marriage, but to preserve his own good name the marriage would be kept secret. Unfortunately the secret was divulged; to end the scandal, Abelard placed Heloise in the convent of Argenteuil; and Fulbert, now utterly enraged, broke into his room and castrated him one night.

After this outrage, he saw no alternative to entering the rich abbey of St. Denis, where he was professed a monk about 1118, and some years later was ordained. Accepting the justice of his punishment, he threw himself into the pursuit of monastic sanctity. But his own sufferings had made him severe on others, and he rebuked the lax living of his fellow-monks: a laxity for which, ten years later, the same abbey was reproved by Bernard. Still worse, he tactlessly applied his keen critical sense to demolishing the legend of the abbey's patron saint. And to crown his offences, he wrote a book *On the Divine Unity and Trinity*, in which two former pupils of Anselm of Laon, still smarting from their master's defeat, professed to find traces of Sabellian heresy. In the first edition of that work, Abelard had written "God in three Persons means that the divine substance is at once powerful, wise and good;" by thus treating the Persons as mere attributes of the one Godhead, he virtually identified them, and the obnoxious phrase was omitted from subsequent editions. It was undoubtedly a careless slip, which gave his opponents their eagerly awaited opportunity; and they seem also to have accused him of teaching theology without proper ecclesiastical licence. At the Council of Soissons in 1121 he was condemned unheard, by a papal legate who so far forgot his Athanasian Creed as to declare: "Of course we believe in three Almighties." After being forced to burn his book, Abelard was imprisoned in the penitentiary of St. Médard, but when the legate came to his senses, he was allowed to return to St. Denis; and from there, with the help of powerful friends, he managed to migrate to a little hermitage in the parish of Quincey, which he built with his own hands and named the Paraclete. Here students still crowded to listen to him in the wilderness, surrounding the hermitage with their wattle huts. But he was afraid of further persecution; he said that the watch-dogs of orthodoxy were on his trail; and although he did not name him, it is probable that he already had Bernard in his mind.

He was therefore glad when the monks of St. Gildas de Ruys, a remote Breton monastery, invited him to become their abbot about the year 1125; here he felt that he would at last find peace to work out his vocation, but he was sadly deceived, for the monks developed homicidal tendencies. And only three years later, he heard that Heloise and her nuns had been dispossessed of their house at Argenteuil. To provide them with a home, he gave them the now deserted Paraclete; and then there began that most poignant of medieval documents, the correspondence of the lovers. Heloise, though utterly devoted to her husband, rebelled against her seclusion in the cloister. "I am still young," she wrote, "and full of vigour; my love for you is greater than before, and this life to which I feel no calling is a bitter cup." Abelard tried patiently to convert her, writing: "Sister, once dear to me in the world, and now most dear to me in Christ;" but Heloise, insisting on the permanence of their secular relationship, replied: "To her only one after Christ, she who is his only one in Christ." Abelard reminded her that, as a nun, she was now wedded to Another than himself; his letter must go "To the spouse of Christ from His servant;" but in a phrase of crystalline logic that defies trans-lation, she answered: "In species the Lord's, but in person yours." To ease the tension that had become unbearable, she con-tented herself now with asking his advice in the guidance of her sisters, to which Abelard sent an erudite and lengthy answer. But even here, the attitude of Heloise is notable. She refuses to

I

see anything of special merit in monasticism, insisting that it adds nothing but celibacy to the already high demands of ordinary Christian living, and her remark that we cannot aim at being more than Christians to some extent anticipates the Reformation. And so she passes from the scene, unreconciled to the tragedy that love has brought upon her; surviving her husband for some twenty years, she arranged for his burial at the Paraclete, and at the last was laid to her long rest by his side.

Meanwhile Abelard had found his Breton monks incapable of discipline; they were married, living on individual prebends, and when he attempted to reform them, one of them put poison in his sacramental wine. Ten years were enough of this dangerous and uncongenial abbacy; by 1134 he was back lecturing in Paris, where John of Salisbury attended his classes at St. Geneviève. His most famous book, *Sic et Non*, consists of a series of apparently contradictory pronouncements from the Bible and the Fathers, on a variety of moral and doctrinal topics which include: whether anything is impossible to God, whether Adam was saved, whether a man can be saved without the sacrament of baptism, whether marriage is equally permissible for all, whether works of mercy avail if they are performed without faith, whether lying can ever be allowed. The method of contrasting parallel authorities was not original; it had been used for some time by the canonists, and Anselm of Laon had already applied it to theology. But Abelard gave it a much wider vogue, so that it was quickly followed not only by the lawyer Gratian, in his monumental *Concordantia Discordantium Canonum*, but also by Peter Lombard, whose *Sentences* with their wealth of patristic quotations became a standard textbook in the schools. These later writers were careful to harmonize the apparent conflict in their sources; Abelard placed discrepant statements side by side, without normally troubling to suggest a reconciliation. His object was to stimulate independent thought. Like Descartes at a much later date, he wrote in the Prologue to his *Sic et Non*: "By doubting we come to enquire, and by enquiry we reach truth." Only in the Bible did he recognize an infallible authority, derived from an inward illumination of the sacred writers by the Holy Spirit; anything in Scripture which appears to us untrue must be attributed to a fault of the copyist, an error of the translator, or our own failure to understand. But outside the canon, no writing is exempt from criticism, and when the Fathers disagree we must decide the question for ourselves. This is not arrogant rationalism; it is a plea for the rights of sanctified common sense. Abelard was well aware that unaided reason cannot penetrate the heights of faith, and in a treatise on dialectics he wrote: "However long you practise dialectic you will spend your time in vain, unless your mind is rendered capable of such great mysteries by grace from heaven." Moreover, he accepted the value of tradition provided that it agreed with Scripture; "after the Gospels were written, many things essential to faith, but not clearly mentioned in the Gospel record, were added by Apostles and apostolic men." Apostolic inspiration is thus his criterion of authority; the later the source, the weaker it becomes. For this reason he attacks the claim of contemporary bishops to exercise the power of the keys; such power, he holds, had been bestowed on the Apostles but not on their successors; and in his book on ethics, *Scito Te Ipsum*, he quotes Origen, Jerome, Augustine and Gregory the Great to prove that a bishop's judgment may frequently fail to coincide with that of God. Absolution is no more than declaratory, like the Jewish priest's certificate that a leper has been healed; guilt is immediately removed by penitence, and the father confessor is merely a spiritual guide. For the morality of an action is determined by the intention of the agent, which God alone can truly judge. Believing that the Gospel precepts are simply a republication of natural law, Abelard is sympathetic to the ancient pagan philosophers, of whom he thought that some had actually adumbrated the doctrine of the Trinity. His approach to theology is thus highly intellectual; Christ to him is the eternal Word of God, rather than the warm human personality to whom Bernard offered the devotion of his heart.

None the less, Abelard insists more than once on the necessity of grace, both actual and prevenient; in his commentary on Romans, he says that we are like sick men, who require to be lifted up by God before we can even drink the medicine that we need. At the same time he allows considerable scope to human free-will, denying that any sort of constraint is imposed by divine providence or predestination. Once we have received the gift of grace, he says, we do not require a fresh supply to enable us to do each separate good deed; and to his opponents this statement seemed to savour of Pelagian heresy. Justification comes by faith working through love; commenting on Romans 4 : 3, Abelard writes that "it is only the faith of a loving heart which suffices to justify a man with God." The great purpose of the cross was to demonstrate the love of God, and so to evoke an answering love in man. "Thus our redemption is that supreme love to us-ward shown in the passion of Christ, which not only frees us from the bondage of sin, but wins for us the true liberty of the sons of God, so that we obey all the commandments through love rather than through fear of Him. . . ." (*Commentary on Romans*, 3 : 23–6.) Such is Abelard's doctrine of Atonement. It has been called the Moral Influence Theory, and criticized for treating Calvary as nothing more than a divine example. But elsewhere he maintains that it has a real, objective effect; Christ, he says on Romans 5 : 15, actually imparts to us from His own merits whatever good we have. The consequence of faith is union with Christ in His Church, opening all the channels of abundant grace. On the question of the sacraments, Abelard is not himself entirely clear, and he tells us that the great eucharistic controversy had not yet ended in his day; he says in the fourth book of his *Theologia Christiana* that while some regarded the communion elements as bare symbols, others believed them to be the true substance of the Lord. For his own part, he seems to have accepted a real presence, though he tends to identify the sacramental Body of Christ with the Church; and he adds that the original forms of the elements remain in such a way that, if a mouse were to eat the reserved sacrament, as apparently sometimes happened through carelessness, it would eat only bread and wine.

Abelard was not a modernist in the sense of wishing to change the accepted doctrines of the Church; he was merely a thinker who demanded liberty to think. But to conservatives like Bernard his ideas seemed highly dangerous. His neglect of Christ's human nature, his fellow-feeling for the pagan philosophers, his attenuated doctrine of Atonement, his emphasis on free-will, his denial of the priestly power of absolution were alike intolerable, and Bernard went so far as to write, "when he speaks of the Trinity he has the taint of Arianism, on grace he stinks of Pelagius, and on the Person of Christ he is Nestorian." The two men had met in 1131, if not before, and the Abbot of Clairvaux, prompted by zealous friends, had been keeping a watchful eye on the activities of the Parisian scholar. According to Bernard, learned explanations could only destroy the merit of simple faith; "Peter, Andrew and their fellow-apostles were not chosen in a school of logic or philosophy;" and to counteract what he regarded as the baneful influence of rationalism Bernard willingly accepted an invitation to preach before the students of Paris University. Abelard's disciples responded by asking the Archbishop of Sens to arrange a public disputation between the two protagonists, and the Archbishop, who had been planning an exhibition of relics in his church at Whitsuntide, felt that the debate would provide an added holiday attraction. The result was a formal council, held at Sens in either 1140 or 1141—the precise year is unfortunately not

known. Abelard entered into the proposal with zest, summoning
some of his students to join the argument. But Bernard was too
wary to expose himself to attack from the best logician in the
country. His own strength lay not in intellect, but in a knowledge
of the Bible, of which he could quote almost any part from
memory. Unable to convert his opponent in a private interview,
and convinced that Abelard, "a monk in habit and name alone,"
was in reality a precursor of Anti-Christ, he spoke to the assembled
bishops on the eve of the Council's meeting; and when, according
to one account, they were deep in their wine-cups, they agreed in
advance that Abelard should be condemned. The victim, realizing
that he had no prospect of a hearing, appealed to Rome. He disdained giving a profession of his faith to Bernard, whom he
accused of "ignorance, falsification and frenzy;" but to Heloise
he sent a perfectly orthodox profession, adding "I would not be
a philosopher if that should mean spurning Paul, I would not be
Aristotle if that should separate me from Christ, for there is no
other name under heaven in which I must be saved."

While the bishops sent the Pope an account of their proceedings, Abelard set out for Rome in person. But he was now a
tired traveller of over sixty, and when he had reached Cluny,
Peter the Venerable persuaded him to stop. The great abbey
might now be luxurious and decadent, but it at least provided a
kind-hearted refuge for the weary scholar. Peter arranged an
interview with Bernard, who then gave Abelard the kiss of peace;
when news arrived that the Pope had condemned him, he accepted
the papal judgment, was welcomed into the ranks of the Cluniac
monks, and in a spirit of humility and gentleness prepared himself for death. He passed away in 1142, at a pleasant daughter-
house of Cluny, where his hosts had sent him for the sake of his
health. And Peter, courteous to the last, wrote to tell Heloise of
his edifying end. "Venerable sister, the husband with whom you
were first joined in marriage and then united by the better and
more lasting bond of holy charity, he whose companionship and
guidance have helped you in your service of the Saviour, is now
sheltered in the arms of Jesus. Christ now guards him in your
place, instead of you, and will give him back to you on that day
when He returns from heaven with the voice of the archangel
and the sound of trump." The good Abbot could give her no
stronger assurance that her beloved had attained to that "vision of
peace," in the true Jerusalem, of whose endless Sabbaths he had
sung in his most famous hymn.

Bernard was emboldened by his success to measure swords
with another philosopher some eight years later. Gilbert de la

Porrée had spoken as if the concept of deity was something distinct from God, for which he was attacked unsuccessfully by Bernard at the synod of Rheims in 1148. Hunting heretics was only one of the many activities pursued by the Abbot of Clairvaux, but it was in keeping with the character expected of him; before his birth, his mother had dreamt that she was bearing a white dog-pup which barked furiously, and a discerning monk had explained the dream by predicting that her son would be a good watch-dog for the Church. Both of his parents are said to have been religious people. The father, Tescelin, was an upright, generous and valiant noble, who played a distinguished part, both as soldier and as councillor, in the service of the Dukes of Burgundy. The mother, Aleth, had been intended for the cloister; after her marriage, she cared in person for the poor and infirm of the neighbourhood; and her seven children were religiously brought up, each of them being dedicated to God at birth. Bernard, the third of the family, was born about 1090 at Fontaines-lès-Dijon, a hill town near the ancient capital of Burgundy from which, on a clear day, the snows of Mont Blanc can be discerned. Educated by the canons at Châtillon-sur-Seine, where his family possessed a mansion, he seems to have rebelled against the study of secular literature; at all events, his precocious talents were directed by preference to reading the Bible, and in his boyhood he was described as shy, obedient, with a "heart given to God." His mother died when he was about sixteen years of age, and although he accompanied his family in their knightly occupations, he was pondering the choice of a career. Conversion overtook him in thoroughly evangelical fashion, amid a storm of tears, as he prayed by himself at a wayside church. It was during the autumn of 1111, while he rode to join the Burgundian levies at the siege of Grancey; next spring found him riding to the gate of Cîteaux, with twenty-nine well-born relatives and friends, all of them fired by his own enthusiasm and begging the privilege of admission to the Cistercian novitiate. They had deliberately chosen a life very different from that to which they were accustomed, in an Order which prided itself on bare walls, plain churches, patched garments and meagre food.

Such recruits proved a godsend to the poor and struggling monastery. Bernard buried himself in the pursuit of his new vocation; he was overheard saying to himself that he had come "to perish from the hearts and memory of men, to lie hid and unnoticed like a lost vessel;" and he kept his eyes so carefully upon the ground, that after a year he could not tell how many windows there were in the chancel of the abbey church. Overcoming his physical weakness, taking his turn of all the drudgery, and becoming in time a good farm-labourer, he underwent additional fasts and vigils, though distressed by snoring in the dormitory, which he described as a thoroughly "carnal" way to sleep. We are told that although he studied the Latin Fathers, he "more often and more willingly read the canonical Scriptures in their simple meaning and due sequence." The Bible was in fact his one great book, from which he quoted almost exclusively, and with which his familiarity rivalled that of Luther or of Bunyan. A dedicated monk, Bernard never thereafter left the cloister, except under obedience to the Pope or his superiors; and when he did, from time to time, take part in the wider business of the Church, his purpose, pursued in a spirit analogous to that of Hildebrand, was always to instil in all men the same monastic virtue of obedience.

After only three years of probation and training, and while still in his early twenties, he was appointed abbot of a new monastery. In 1115 he led a small colony from the mother-house to a bleak spot called the Vale of Absinth, which his *Vita Prima* describes as "a place of terror and deep loneliness, a veritable den of thieves." But by the faith and labours of the monks, it was turned into a smiling valley and renamed Clairvaux. Bernard himself was not yet in orders. As the local diocesan was absent, he travelled to Châlons where Abelard's old master, William of Champeaux, was now the bishop; and William not only ordained and blessed him, but treated him with such evident marks of respect that his stature in the Church was assured. The desperate poverty of the new foundation was alleviated from time to time by friendly gifts, which appeared as regular answers to the abbot's prayers. He had no anxiety about material things, but the mere physical strain proved too much for his feeble constitution; his own cell was like a prison, open to the cold, without room to stretch; and when his health broke down in 1118, William of Champeaux insisted that he should spend a year, resting from responsibility, in slightly better quarters. But of luxury every trace was rigorously banished from Clairvaux. When the monks, in 1131, entertained Pope Innocent II and his suite, their visitors "saw bare walls only in the church . . . everyone rejoiced in the Lord, feasting on virtues, not on viands . . . if a piece of fish appeared, it was placed before the Lord Pope, while the community enjoyed the sight of it, but not the taste." All this was in stark contrast to the comfortable amenities of Cluny, which Bernard roundly criticized; "they bring you dish after dish," he wrote in his *Apologia*, "and double helpings of enormous fish . . .

of serving eggs there are ten different ways." On one occasion, when his own sister came to visit him, richly dressed and attended, he sent a monk to tell her that her appearance was offensive; refusing to see her till she promised to submit to his direction, he so worked upon her feelings that in two years' time she had become a nun. Bernard made no parade of his personal austerities; on hearing that his use of a hair shirt had brought him a reputation for sanctity, he at once discarded it; and when offered a bishopric, he refused saying "the monk's habit does not make men holy . . . no one knows me better than I know myself." Yet in spite of his humility, he was treated with the profoundest veneration; at Milan, which he visited in 1135, the crowds surged forward to touch his garments, bringing the sick for him to heal. His preaching was so powerful that a single sermon often brought in twenty or thirty converts to monasticism; he persuaded a young brother of the French King to take the cowl and wash dishes at Clairvaux; and mothers were so terrified of his magnetic attraction that they hid their sons from his approach. With a constant growth in the number of his disciples, fresh houses were established to accommodate them; in the year 1131 alone, he founded no less than three monasteries during the space of four months; and by the time of his death in 1153, the daughter-houses of Clairvaux numbered sixty-seven, situated in Belgium, Britain, Denmark, France, Germany, Italy, Portugal, Sardinia, Sicily, Spain and Sweden. Partly through these fresh foundations, and partly through the affiliation of existing monasteries, the spread of the Cistercian Order was phenomenal; it possessed a total of 350 houses in 1153, and the influence of Bernard is indicated by the fact that 160 of these attached themselves to Clairvaux.

Although he was twice pressed to accept a mitre, first at Langres, and then at the important archiepiscopal see of Rheims, Bernard steadily refused preferment. Had he been bent on a career, he might have worn the papal tiara. Instead, he was content to remain a simple abbot; but his forceful character made him the leading personality in the Church, especially after one of his own disciples had become Pope Eugenius III in 1145, and he was deeply involved in all the main transactions of the time. He helped to draw up a Rule for the Templars, giving it a few Cistercian touches such as the white robe which the knights wore above their armour, and to encourage recruitment he wrote a stirring tract *In Praise of the New Militia*. He played a prominent part in healing the schism between Innocent II and the anti-pope Anacletus; neither of them had been elected in a strictly legal way, but Bernard was convinced of the moral superiority of Innocent, and in supporting him, his methods were nothing if not direct. To win the allegiance of Duke William of Aquitaine, he brought the consecrated Host to the church door, saying "here is the Virgin's Son, the Head and Lord of that Church which you are persecuting; your Judge has come to you . . . do you disdain Him?" After the capture of Edessa by the Moslems in 1144, it was Bernard's preaching that inspired the Second Crusade, for which he enlisted the hesitant Emperor Conrad by a direct personal appeal from the pulpit. The disastrous failure of the expedition was a sore disappointment, and it impaired Bernard's popularity; but despite his warlike zeal, it was he, and he almost alone, who protested against the massacres of Jews by which it had been accompanied. A vigorous hammer of the heretics, he attacked not only philosophers, but also popular preachers whose views appeared to be unorthodox; here his attacks were successful through the known holiness of his life rather than through profundity of intellect, and it is notable that he approved the use of force only as a last resort. Troubled by a chronic gastric disorder, his closing years were spent in great vexation of body.

Even more significant than his opposition to Abelard and Gilbert de la Porrée was his constant criticism of the Church's growing worldliness and wealth. Against lax monks and luxurious prelates he fulminated without ceasing, and the shafts of his denunciation proved all the more telling because of the unimpeachable orthodoxy of their source. In one of his sermons he says: "The goods of the Church are dissipated in vanity and superfluity," and in another he declares: "We can no longer be content with the proverb *Like people, like priest*, for the corruption of priests is far greater than that of the people." In his treatise *De Moribus et Officio Episcoporum*, he attacks pride rather than unchastity, since the Hildebrandine reforms had by now taken some effect, but pride, extravagance and mounting ambition had combined, in his view, to produce a catastrophic situation. He tells the bishops

> You should be distinguished by your works, not by your embroideries and furs. . . . You may shut my mouth by saying that it is not for a monk to judge bishops; please God you would also shut my eyes, so that I could not see what you forbid me to condemn. . . . But if I kept silence, the poor, the naked, the starving would rise up to cry with a pagan poet, "Tell me, pontiffs, why the gold on your horses' bridles?" While we suffer wretchedly from cold and hunger, why have you so many changes of raiment folded away in your cupboards? We are your brothers, and it is from your brothers' portion

that you thus delight your eyes; it is our livelihood which provides
your superfluity, and all that adds to your vanities is a theft from our
indigence. . . .

In his attitude to clerical pomp, Bernard was a thorough-going
puritan, following the tradition of that pristine Roman simplicity
which, in the fifth century, had prompted Pope Celestine I to
write to the bishops of Gaul, "we clerics should be distinguished
from other men by preaching, not by vestments, by our lives and
not our dress." But in the interval there had been a vast growth
of ostentation. Badges of rank and other ornaments were bestowed
upon such churchmen as the papacy delighted to honour; the
mitre, in origin a Phrygian cap adopted by the Popes as part of
their imperial heritage from Constantine, was in the twelfth century for the first time widely worn by bishops. Against such
clerical display there was a strong popular reaction. Men began
to debate the famous question, whether an archdeacon can be
saved; and by the thirteenth century, it was a commonly received
opinion that the majority of bishops would be damned. Indeed
the popular feeling became so vehement, that when a Dominican
scholar like Albert the Great accepted a bishopric, it was regarded
as a serious fall from grace. Bernard had no objection to the
spiritual power of the episcopate; what vexed him was its mere
outward pomp, combined with idleness and neglect of preaching.
And so in his exasperation he cried out "On unbounded ambition, how many of the clergy, young and old, high and low,
learned and ignorant, thrust themselves into ecclesiastical cures,
as if, when once they obtain a cure, they need thereafter care for
nothing more!"

But his puritan censures were directed also against light
amusements and idle conversation by the laity. "There is pleasure,"
he says in one of his sermons, "in talking to pass the time. To
pass the time! To lose an hour—this hour which God's mercy
gives you for repentance, for gaining pardon, for growth in
grace, for pressing on toward the promised glory! . . . God grant
that in light talk you lose only the period of your earthly life.
Too often it is the life eternal which thus is miserably lost."
Knights and nobles are castigated for luxurious habits, rich ladies
for the dress and jewellery in which they walk "adorned like
temples." Nor are the poor spared from general denunciation by
the preacher; Bernard tells them that their besetting sin is avarice,
that they must share their bread with one another, and pay their
lawful debts. But his preaching also had a gentler side. For married people, he paints the ideal of "an affection so chaste and

charitable that the love of Jesus has always the first place in their hearts." The Countess of Blois, who was having trouble with a difficult son, was advised to "win his heart by kindness." To Bernard himself the ties of family affection were so strong that, when his brother died as a monk at Clairvaux, his sermon was almost choked by tears. And at the start of his treatise *De Diligendo Deo*, he penned words which might have been echoed by Abelard in his old age: "the cause of our loving God is God Himself, the measure of it is to love immeasurably."

For the whole of society, Bernard envisaged a new order based on the principles of Christian ethics. And in attaining his ideal he looked for leadership to the papacy. His views, closely following the *Dictatus Papae* of Hildebrand, were expressed in a letter to the turbulent citizens of Milan: "plenitude of power over all the churches of the world has been conferred by a special privilege on the Apostolic See, so that he who resists this power resists the ordinance of God." Still more emphatic were the statements of his treatise *De Consideratione*, written for his own disciple Pope Eugenius III; the Pope, with "no equal upon earth," is "the high priest, supreme pontiff, prince of bishops, successor of the Apostles, in authority Peter and in unction Christ." Such language was the most extravagant yet used to describe the papal office. And just because of his high conception of the office, Bernard could be extremely critical of an individual Pope. He advised Eugenius to remember that even as supreme pontiff he was still "the vilest dust." Surrounded by the selfish and parochially-minded Roman clergy, it would be difficult to maintain impartial justice; hence the Pope would do well to make the membership of his curia more international, so that "those who are to judge the whole should be chosen from the whole." But even so, the centralized administration of papal government, the hungry horde of ecclesiastical bureaucrats, the multitude of time-wasting appeals appeared so perilous a distraction from spiritual concerns, that Bernard did not shrink from describing the Church, "filled with ambitious men," as being now no more than "a robbers' cave where the spoils of travellers are heaped." The very treatise, which had so highly extolled the stature of the papal office, at the same time painted a dismal picture of the actual situation of the papal Church; Bernard believed that drastic remedies were needed, and with a characteristic touch, he urged his pupil to take refuge from the unenviable burden of the papacy in the practice of humility and prayer.

In his own devotional life, Bernard gave a great impetus to the cult of Mary. Preaching on her assumption, he declared "It is

God's will that we should have everything through Mary," since she is "a mediatrix in whom you have no cause to doubt." "Praise her whom angels revere," he wrote in one of his epistles, "praise her whom Gentiles desired, whom patriarchs and prophets foretold, who was chosen from among all creatures and is superior to all; glorify the discoverer of grace, the mediatrix of our salvation, the restorer of the world." It was at this very moment that medieval architecture was making its significant change, from the sombre masculinity of Norman to the more flamboyant and more feminine beauty of the Gothic style; when churches, now flooded with light from the delicate tracery of pointed windows, began to be expressly designed for the purpose of a Lady's bower. Bernard was in full sympathy with the ideas represented by this change, but he refused to advance too quickly. About the year 1140 the Canons of Lyons, without papal sanction, instituted a Feast of the Conception of the Blessed Virgin; and Bernard wrote them a strongly-worded letter of protest, describing the proposed Feast as "a novelty unknown to the practice of the Church, without sanction from tradition or support from reason."

Indeed, however vigorous might be his devotion to the Virgin, Bernard's deepest thoughts always centred on her Son. For him, the name of Jesus is "honey in the mouth, music to the ear, and joy to the heart." In one of his occasional sermons he spoke as follows: "Thou art good, O Lord, to the soul that seeks Thee— if to the seeker, how much more to the finder? if the memory of Thee is so sweet, how shall we describe Thy presence?" Such language immediately recalls the Rosy Sequence, parts of which are familiar as "Jesus, the very thought of Thee," "Jesus Thou joy of loving hearts," and other hymns usually attributed to Bernard. The attribution is almost certainly false, since the few undoubted pieces of verse which the saint has left us are extremely unpoetical; but the Rosy Sequence, even if written by a disciple, breathes the genuine spirit of the master. So does another hymn, "O sacred Head sore wounded," the original of which dates from Bernard's time; but here again the attribution sometimes made to him is undoubtedly inaccurate.

It was above all as a mystic and a preacher that Bernard excelled. His sermons were usually delivered extempore, but after profound meditation, and he thought that preachers should be men of deep and constant prayer. The spiritual ecstasies which he described have some affinity to the quietism of Madame Guyon, with this difference that, for Bernard, they are always transitory transports and not a permanent passivity of soul. He says, in his sermons on the Song of Songs, "I declare, fool though I be, that the Word has entered into me more than once, coming and going like the wind." For the experience of such heavenly communion, the best and only preparation is the childlike heart. Bernard indeed addresses the Child Jesus as the Desire of children—*O parvule, parvulis desiderate*—and it was this touching simplicity which made his sermons so popular that even those intended for monks were soon translated into the vernacular. His great series on the Song of Songs, planned during a time of illness, was begun in Advent 1135; it was continued at intervals throughout the remainder of his life, and he found so much material that, although by then he had preached 86 sermons, he had only reached the first verse of chapter three. He insists on the divine inspiration of the book—"we must agree that this work was written, not by human genius, but through the Spirit's art." Hence the allegorical interpretation is alone acceptable, for the literal meaning would be "inept and unworthy" of Scripture. It is indeed a love-song, but it is sung to the divine Bridegroom by the human soul. "This is the canticle of love, and none knows how to sing it if he is untaught by grace . . . none understands it save she who chants and He to whom she chants it, the bride and Bridegroom." For a love-song needs a lover, and "to him who loves not, the language of love is a foreign tongue." Much of Bernard's nuptial mysticism may be strange and even repulsive to the modern mind, though in the seventeenth century it commended itself to a puritan like Samuel Rutherford. But in the forty-third of these glowing sermons he has left a Credo which can stand the test of time. "At the beginning of my conversion," Bernard says, "instead of merits which I had not, I took pains to gather a bouquet of myrrh and to lay it on my heart. I made it of all the agonies and sorrows of my Lord. . . . Never would I forget those sufferings, for in them I have found life. . . . To know Jesus and Him crucified is the sum of my philosophy."

CHAPTER IX

THE WALDENSIANS

BERNARD WAS THE MOST ORTHODOX, BUT BY NO MEANS THE only, outspoken critic of the twelfth-century Church. Puritanism was in fact characteristic of many preachers who, throughout the Middle Ages, denounced idle amusements, inculcated Sabbatarianism, and even began a movement to ban the use of organs from public worship. Hell-fire became a prime ingredient of medieval sermons; even the most optimistic announced that four men out of five would probably be damned. Visionary souls beheld a procession, not only of knights, judges and fair ladies, but also of monks, priests and prelates going down to hell. The effect produced by such strictures was on the whole extremely slight; despite the preachers, maypoles and music, drinking and dancing, continued to solace the rather cheerless atmosphere of medieval life. In the Provençal novel *Aucassin and Nicolette*, the hero tells his beloved that he prefers not to go to heaven, with the ragged old cripples who spend their days and nights in prayer—hell is the place for him, since there he will see all the fine churchmen, the gallant knights and amorous ladies, the sable and ermine, the harpers and the minstrels and the kings. But such bravado was apt to disappear at the time when men came to die. Then, the suppressed fears of a lifetime impelled them to a late repentance, and by gifts to some monastery they would buy the privilege of dying in the habit of a monk; or, if their wealth allowed them, they would endow masses to be said for their soul's repose. The preaching of hell at least encouraged an interest in purgatory, and purgatory became a profitable source of revenue to priests. By 1244, the monks of Durham had received endowments pledging them to say 7,332 masses every year, and when the task became impossible, the monks both there and elsewhere defaulted on their obligations. But the tendency had begun much earlier, adding fresh fuel to the criticisms of clerical greed. Already in the tenth century, Odo of Cluny had complained that the multiplication of masses bred irreverence; in the twelfth, Petrus Cantor of Notre Dame advised a radical reduction in the number of altars, and with a typically puritan appeal to Old

Testament precedent, he suggested having no more than about three celebrations a year. His contemporary, Abbot Philip of Harvengt, writing about 1160, complained that "our priests often sacrifice Christ on the altar for a penny," while Petrus Cantor himself declared that this was to "crucify Christ afresh." Such ideas could quickly lead to an attack on the very doctrine of purgatory, and in fact they did so in circles which were regarded as heretical; but amongst the more orthodox, the main complaint was the insatiable greed of clergymen for money. Walter Map, the garrulous Welsh canon of St. Paul's, had a neat acrostic on the text "Avarice is the root of all evils;" put into Latin as *Radix Omnium Malorum Avaritia*, its initial letters spelt the name Roma. Even so staunch a churchman as John of Salisbury could not refrain from criticism. When his friend Hadrian IV, the only Englishman ever to have been Pope, asked him to write frankly in his *Policraticus*, John stated that in the opinion of the people, the papacy was imposing burdens like the Pharisees, amassing wealth, selling justice and living luxuriously, while the churches lay in ruin; and although he was careful to testify his own respect for Rome, he added, "I confess that it would be better to follow your precepts than to imitate your works . . . give freely what you have freely received, for justice is queen of the virtues, but she blushes at being sold."

Criticism came from a wide variety of sources. Scholars attacked the authenticity of relics, and students parodied the services of the Church. Mysticism produced prophetic revolutionaries, some of whom were content to predict the imminence of doom, while others acted to hasten the fulfilment of their dreams. Isolated individuals condemned every feature of institutional religion. But there was also a fully organized dissenting Church, with its own ministers and congregations, claiming to represent the pure form of Christianity, and teaching the dualist doctrine of the Cathars. Above all, the Waldensians expounded a simple, Biblical type of piety, going out two by two to preach, and despite some remnants of medievalism, these in fact constituted the first Protestants. Very different in their beliefs and practices from the undoubtedly heretical Cathars, the Waldensians often suffered with them under persecution; for the hierarchy could tolerate no attack upon its privileges, and all these varied forms of dissent at least united in being strongly anti-clerical. The priestly monopoly in sacramental grace, coupled with its sordid financial operations, provoked a full-blown storm of protest, at the very time when the papacy was advancing to the climax of its earthly power. And if Waldo's followers alone survived into the future, it is none the

less desirable to place them in their historical context by some
account of the other dissident groups and movements that have
perished.

Typical of much satire that was written in the twelfth century
is the self-styled *Gospel according to the Mark of Silver*. In ribald
parody of the gospel narrative, this describes how a poor man
came to the Pope's door, only to be told, "Get thee behind me,
Satan, for thou savourest not of money; thou shalt not enter into
the joy of thy Lord till thou hast paid the uttermost farthing." So
he sold his cloak and tunic, and gave to the door-keepers and
cardinals; but they said, "What is this among so many?" and
they cast him out. Next came a rich clerk, "who had grown fat
and stout, and had committed murder in the insurrection;" his
handsome gifts to all the appropriate officers threw the Pope into
an almost mortal fit of envy, from which His Holiness was only
cured by a "medicine of gold and silver." Calling the cardinals
together, the Pope then delivered himself of an allocution in the
following terms: "Brethren, see to it that no man deceive you
with vain words, for I have given you an example, that ye also
should receive gifts, even as I have received them. . . . Blessed are
the rich, for theirs is the Curia of Rome." The unknown author
of this skit was perhaps an impoverished scholar, almost certainly a clerk; his touch is light-hearted, but there is obviously a
target for his shafts. A similar note is struck in some of the
Goliardic poems, that riotous collection of student songs, sometimes poignant, often immersed in the perennial themes of wine,
women and song, but occasionally rising to a pitch of genuine
moral indignation. From the same circles came a long Office of
Gamblers; a Drinkers' Mass, with *potatores* substituted for *pastores*
in the text; outrageous parodies set to sacred music; even the
alleged minutes of an assembly of nuns, to whom a "cardinaless"
expounded Ovid on the mysteries of love. Little of all this was
intended to be taken seriously, but it was always pointed: Ovid,
in his more erotic portions, was a strangely popular author in
monastic libraries. A strain of wild buffoonery ran like comic
relief through the observances of medieval religion. The ceremony of the Boy Bishop, when aged canons knelt to receive a
choirboy's blessing, might be a harmless expression of Christmas
as the children's festival; but the orgies conducted at the same
season by the Abbot of Misrule were more licentious; and when
the flight into Egypt was celebrated by a Feast of Asses, for which
the rubric instructed priest and people to bray loudly, religious
drama had lost its due decorum. Like the hideous grotesques
which decorated the exterior of churches, these ribaldries were

the obverse side of faith; while helping to justify reproof of a Church which tolerated them, they were at the same time in themselves a part of that reproof.

More serious was the attack on relics delivered by so respectable an abbot as Guibert of Nogent. Spiritually-minded men were becoming distressed by the extravagance of popular superstition; Bernard's successor actually besought the saint to stop working posthumous miracles, in order that his monks might be left in peace from the visits of the curious. But such self-abnegation was unusual. Most monasteries found their relics a profitable source of income, and opportune discoveries were often made when the convent was in need of funds. Pious thefts were not uncommon or else, to share the benefits more widely, fraud might produce a remarkable reduplication. Guibert wrote his treatise on the subject about 1119, and he wrote it in a vein of extreme scepticism. Saint-Jean d'Angely had a head of John the Baptist; so had Constantinople; and unless the saint was two-headed, one or other must be false. Soissons claimed to possess a tooth of Christ; if the claim is true, Christ is not fully risen, and the doctrine of the Resurrection is invalidated. Such arguments and a host of others were later repeated by a fellow-countryman of Guibert's called Calvin. But they failed to check the popular appetite for wonders, the belief in the potency of bones. An old woman, vexed by tax collectors, and finding her prayers unanswered by the saints, ran into the church at Fleury, where Benedict's body, stolen from Monte Cassino, was supposed to lie; she tucked up the altar-cloths and beat the altar, crying: "Decrepit old Benedict, why are you taking a rest?" What answer she received is not recorded; but there was a more instant response on the occasion of a visit by Pope Alexander III to Paris in 1159. When the monks of St. Denis showed him the body of Hippolytus, the Pope expressed a doubt as to whether that holy object had ever been removed from Rome. At once the saint's bones began to rumble like thunder in their shrine, and Alexander was reduced to exclaiming: "I believe, my lord Hippolytus, but please be quiet."

The cult of relics, like the sale of masses, at once enriched and secularized the Church. It indicated a gross materialism abhorrent to mystics, several of whom were moved to protest. Hildegard, Abbess of Rupertsberg and popularly known as the "Sibyl of the Rhine," had experienced abnormal psychic manifestations from her childhood; believing herself to be the subject of direct prophetic inspiration, she published an account of twenty-six visions in her *Scivias*, which castigated the contemporary vices of both Church and society in no uncertain terms; and when Bernard gave them a somewhat guarded approval, she was able to enter into correspondence with no less than four Popes and two Emperors, writing as a self-styled "agent of the living Light" to denounce clerical worldliness and wealth. Her fellow-mystic, Joachim of Fiore, turned his studies of the Apocalypse into a prophetic interpretation of history. Born about 1132, he made a pilgrimage to Palestine in his youth. Though he regarded Islam as the seventh head of the apocalyptic Beast, he disapproved of the Crusades, saying that Christians should preach and not fight their foes; and his sympathies for the East were deepened when some Saracens nursed him through a period of sickness. In consequence, he came to some extent under the spell of Eastern religious dreams, accepting from the Moslems the idea of a progressive revelation, which made him look, not backward into an ideal past, but forward to a future climax. While he spent a solitary Lent on Mount Tabor, strange visions of |the night filled him with a sense of inspiration; returning to Italy he entered the Cistercian Order, and was later elected Abbot of Corazzo; but with a burning desire to write the message of his visions, he obtained a papal dispensation from his other duties, and ended by founding his own monastery at Fiore in Calabria. In his commentary on the Apocalypse and other writings, he divided history into three successive ages. The first, the age of the Father, covered the period of the Old Testament dispensation, when men lived under the law in the characteristically married state of the patriarchs. The second, the age of the Son, was the time of New Testament grace, characterized by the discipline of clerical life. The third would be the age of the Holy Ghost, when mysticism would spread over the whole world, ministry and sacraments would disappear, and a new spiritual Church would arise. Joachim allowed forty-two generations to each period, and he therefore expected the age of the Spirit to begin about the year 1260. He himself died in 1202, widely respected for his sanctity, and submitting his novel theories to the judgment of the Church authorities. Radical criticism of the existing institution was implied by his prophecy that it would soon be superseded; but so long as his visions were safely located in an unknown future, the Church to whose verdict he had submitted them made little attempt at censorship. Fifty years later, the Spiritual Franciscans, that radical left wing among the followers of Francis, claimed to be in their own persons the spiritual Church whose advent Joachim had predicted. Although he never himself intended that his writings should supersede the Bible, excerpts from them were published under the title of the

"Everlasting Gospel;" and in 1256 the papacy was obliged to issue a partial and reluctant condemnation.

A mystic like Joachim might be allowed to pursue his meditations in comparative peace; but it was very different when men ventured to translate the dream into reality. Arnold of Brescia had been a pupil of Abelard at Paris. With a passionate and practical interest in the Bible, he became a fiery preacher of ascetic self-discipline. "That man," wrote Bernard, "neither eats nor drinks. . . . I wish his beliefs were as sound as his life is strict." Coming from such a pen, this was an impressive tribute to Arnold's conduct, if not to his theology; and it was confirmed by John of Salisbury, who described him as "a forceful exponent of contempt for the world, accustomed to mortify his flesh by fasts and horse-hair, gifted with an acute mind, diligent in studying the Scriptures, but said to have been seditious." His sedition consisted in a violent attempt to rescue the Church from its preoccupation with politics and wealth, by returning to the poverty and other-worldliness of the early Christians. Becoming a canon regular in his native city, he declared, like the Donatists of old, that sacraments ministered by an unworthy priest were valueless; on this point he was certainly heretical, but something very similar had been said by Cardinal Humbert and others of the reforming party. Arnold urged the clergy to renounce their earthly goods and temporal dominion, meanwhile advising the people to confess their sins, not to the priests, but to one another. Expelled from Brescia by an indignant bishop, he fled to France, where he was condemned along with his old teacher Abelard at the Council of Sens. He submitted to the Pope in 1146, but finding a republican party at Rome, he there led a revolt against the temporal jurisdiction of the papacy. Excommunicated and largely deserted by his followers, he was finally arrested and hanged by the Emperor Frederick Barbarossa in 1155.

So ended an abortive attempt to remedy the morals of the Church. On its doctrine, a more radical attack had already been launched from a variety of sources. Eudes de l'Etoile, a religious maniac, changed his name to Eon, and believed himself to be either an aeon of the deity or else He who should come to judge the quick and the dead; ordaining bishops and archbishops from among the credulous who accepted his fantastic claims, he repudiated the Church's sacraments, especially the baptism of infants. Tanchelin, who seems also to have suffered from mental derangement, began preaching in the neighbourhood of Utrecht. Like Arnold of Brescia, he denied the value of ministrations by unworthy priests, from which he went on to denounce all sacraments, including marriage; he took extreme liberties with his female adherents, and betrothed himself to the Virgin by joining hands with her image. So libertine a reaction against the strictness of the Hildebrandine reforms was clearly due to psychological disorder; but Tanchelin won a tremendous following, which at least indicates a latent opposition to the sacramental system of the Church. Peter de Bruys, a much less unbalanced character, was apparently a priest who preached on his own after being deposed from office. Believing that faith and personal righteousness were alone needful, he rejected infant baptism and the eucharistic sacrifice; prayers for the dead were profitless, since only faith can save, and church buildings were superfluous, since all places are equally sacred; each individual should interpret Scripture for himself, and the cross, so far from being venerated, should be loathed by good Christians as the instrument of Christ's death. Acting on these principles, Peter made a bonfire of all the cruci-fixes that he could find. But his doctrines were repeatedly con-demned by the authorities; and he himself was burnt, about 1140, by a Catholic mob infuriated at his burning of their crosses. Another preacher, who like Peter laboured in southern France, was a vagrant monk called Henry of Lausanne. At first he had had episcopal licence for his preaching, but when he began to insist on the binding obligation of clerical poverty, and to teach that the effect of the sacraments depended on the character of the officiating priest, he was disowned and imprisoned by the Church. Shrinking from a public debate with Bernard, he died soon after 1145; in several respects his teaching foreshadowed that of the Waldensians.

Such isolated individuals produced no more than a momentary impression, and were quickly disposed of either by mob violence or by the ecclesiastical authorities. A better organized and more permanent form of dissent was found amongst the group who styled themselves Humiliati. Sometimes supposed to have been banded together under a rule given them by Bernard, these seem in fact to have originated as a trade union, in the guise of a religious guild, for the protection of unemployed workmen. Whatever its origin, the group consisted almost entirely of laymen who lived simply on the proceeds of their own work as weavers. Centred in Lombardy, they spread through the mercantile connexions of the wool trade. As a token of simplicity they wore undyed clothing, thereby unconsciously copying the more puritan members of the early Church. When they met in fellowship, some of their number preached and heard confessions, which set them on the fringe of institutional religion rather than in deliberate opposition to it.

They appear to have insisted on the need for spiritual baptism and communion, to have accepted the doctrine of predestination, and to have taught salvation through the imputed righteousness of Christ. For a time they joined forces with the Waldensians, but later separated, and a section of them was reconciled to the Church by Innocent III under the name of Poor Catholics. Again, there is the characteristic emphasis on poverty, in contrast to the wealth of the official clergy.

Older than the Humiliati and still better organized, the heretical Cathar Church was particularly strong in Lombardy and southern France, regions that were prolific of dissent. Provence had been to some extent contaminated by Moslem culture from across the Spanish border, and as the home of the troubadours, its secular atmosphere proved receptive to the spice of Eastern religion. And it was from the East that Catharism came. With gnostic and Manichaean origins, it had been professed by the Paulicians of Asia Minor, those dualists who, at the time of the iconoclastic controversy, had not only denounced images, but had also rejected sacraments, incarnation and every use of matter as a vehicle of grace. Some of these Paulicians were transported to the Balkans during the ninth and tenth centuries; by the end of the twelfth they had so far prospered as to become the national Church of Bosnia. Here they were known as Bogomils, a corrupted plural form of the name Theophilus, which had been borne by a Bulgarian priest and leader of the sect about the year 950. From Bosnia their beliefs spread so widely that Pope Urban V was to call that land "the cesspool of heresy for every part of the world." Cloth-merchants brought the false doctrine with the bales that they carried from the East; it was also spread by travelling physicians who practised faith-healing and thus obtained an easy access to the privacy of numerous homes. There was a Bogomil congregation at Constantinople, until the sack of that city by the crusaders in 1204. Greek theologians, who studied its beliefs at first hand, felt certain that they were dealing with a revival of the ancient gnostic heresy. Like the gnostics, the Bogomils believed that the material world had been created by the devil. Hence they rejected much of the Old Testament, while in the New they sought to spiritualize Christ's miracles, saying that the five loaves with which He fed the multitude were not material bread, but the Gospels and the Book of Acts. Sacraments, cross and images were repudiated for the same reason, and the Orthodox Church with its sensuous liturgy and vestments was regarded as an apostate body. Believing themselves to be the one true Church, the Bogomils had their own hierarchy of bishops; each bishop was assisted by an Elder Son and a Younger Son, who were designated in turn to succeed him; and this peculiar arrangement may have been a muddled reflection of the Bogomil doctrine of the Trinity, according to which the Father begat the Son and the Son begat the Holy Ghost. But Zigabenus, who made a report on the subject for the Emperor Alexius, records their belief that Satanael, the demonic creator of the material universe, had been the Elder Son of God before he fell; defeated by Christ, the Younger Son, he was now deposed from his divine status, with his name reduced to Satan; and this modification of the doctrine saved it from an ultimate and eternal dualism between the powers of good and evil. The Bogomils themselves are described as a quiet, meek and sober people, pacifists who practised a passive resistance to authority. In worship they used only the Lord's Prayer, which they repeated four times by day and as often again at night. Marriage was discouraged since it increased the dominion of matter over spirit. The full members of the sect, who were empowered to give absolution to one another, abstained from wine and meat.

By the eleventh century the sect was spreading into Western Europe. Several heretics were put to death at Toulouse in 1022; and since their heresy is described as Manichaean, they doubtless had affinities with the Bosnian Bogomils. Eight years later a regular congregation appears at Monteforte, describing itself by the name of Cathar; this term is derived from the Greek word for "pure," and those who bore it claimed to be puritans, uncontaminated by the worldliness of the official Church, unspotted by the evil taint of matter. In southern France they were known as Albigensians, because they had an important centre at the town of Albi; in the north the name Poplicani, a latinized form of Paulician, betrays the Eastern origin of the sect. Soon it had spread into Flanders and Germany, where seven Cathars were burnt at Cologne in 1163. But four years after this, the Albigensians were strong enough to hold a large council near Toulouse, attended by Bishop Nicetas from the Bogomil Church of Constantinople; he ordained more bishops for them, delimited their diocesan boundaries, and persuaded them to accept a completely Manichaean dualism of two separate Gods. In Italy Catharism drew its strength from among the poor, and largely escaped notice. But in southern France it was openly supported by the nobles, which forced it on the attention of the Church. Setting a rigid standard of perfection for its full members, while at the same time allowing an extreme laxity to the mere adherents, Catharism appealed simultaneously to the highest and the basest motives in human nature. Refined and well-born ladies were drawn into the

ranks of its elect. Licentious noblemen were assured of liberty to
sin on condition of a death-bed repentance. As amongst the
ancient gnostics, this double standard of morality sprang from
the contempt for matter; when material and spiritual things are
utterly divorced, the ideal life may be that of a celibate vegetarian,
but indulgence of the flesh cannot seriously harm the soul. With
such beliefs the Cathars were led to the paradoxical conclusion
that adultery is less sinful, because less permanent, than marriage;
and if a full member was unable to practise the austerity demanded
of him, he was encouraged to end his bodily struggles by commit-
ting suicide, starving himself to death in a rite which they called
the Endura. The Cathar ceremonies were few and simple. There
was the Consolamentum, a blend of spiritual baptism and ordination, which admitted to the ranks of the Perfect through laying
on of hands and of the gospel; those who received it were committed to a life of preaching, vegetarianism and celibacy, but the
lawless majority submitted to it only at the moment of their
death. There was also a simple agape or love-feast, and a monthly
confession made to the senior members. In doctrine, they identified Jehovah with the God of Evil, and regarded Jesus as no
more than the highest of the angels; His task as a teacher was to
liberate the divine spark that had become imprisoned in flesh, but
His incarnation had been only an appearance, and in reality He
had neither died nor risen. Oaths, warfare and all shedding of
blood were condemned. Purgatory was rejected, being replaced
by the theory of metempsychosis, and it was believed that after
a sufficient number of transmigrations, all souls would ultimately
be redeemed; one Cathar actually said under examination that he
would spit in the face of the Catholics' malign God, who was
supposed to damn all but one in a thousand of the men that He
had made. Believing that the Catholic Church had been corrupt
since Constantine, the Cathars repudiated its sacraments, along
with images and the cross. They had their own ministers—bishops,
elder and younger sons, and deacons—but all the Perfect, being
in some sense ordained, were required to preach on every possible
occasion, while the adherents, though free from every moral
restraint, were at least expected to venerate the Perfect and to
attend their sermons. The sect thus had a profound zeal for
evangelism. It provided vernacular translations of Scripture, but
as these were mingled with gnostic fables, the Catholics became
suspicious of all unauthorized translations. In 1163 the Council of
Tours forbade any contact between Church members and Cathars.

Such were the multiform varieties of twelfth-century dissent:
in part puritan and orthodox, in part licentious and heretical. A

detailed description of them has been necessary, in order to explain the somewhat equivocal attitude adopted by the official Church. While ready to tolerate the complaints of undoubted saints and mystics, it frowned upon unauthorized meetings of the laity, since these might often become breeding-grounds for false doctrine and immoral conduct. It was in this setting that the layman Peter Waldo began to preach an evangelical message and to practise a life of complete poverty. His poverty might be an implicit criticism of the official clergy, his preaching an attempt to make good their omissions; but without any intention of separating from the Church, he was driven out of it like the Wesleyans because he refused to be silenced by authority. In fact his aims were identical with those of Francis of Assisi. But whereas the latter became a saint and the founder of a great religious Order, Waldo was treated as a heresiarch whose followers had to be savagely suppressed. Only a generation divided the two in time, but this short interval was sufficient to open the Church's eyes; having learnt wisdom from its failure to arrest the Waldensians, it managed when dealing with Francis to control and contain this movement of evangelical revival.

Our sources of information about Peter Waldo are not numerous; they are written by opponents, who none the less admit the strict morality of his teaching; and since most of them begin in 1220, after he himself had died, it is difficult to present a detailed picture of his life. The Christian name Peter is not mentioned until 1368. The surname Waldo or Valdes is probably authentic, although it is just possible that the group was called Waldensian or Vaudois, not after its founder, but because it came to be located in the mountain valleys of the canton of Vaud. Even the date given for his conversion varies from 1161 to 1176. Whenever it happened, it began when he heard a minstrel sing the legend of St. Alexis, that rich young Roman who had left wife and family to follow Christ in utter destitution. Waldo was himself a wealthy merchant of Lyons, grown prosperous by usury, and his conscience was troubled. Next day he consulted a learned priest, who gave him the advice that would have been given by any well-instructed cleric: "if thou wilt be perfect, go and sell that thou hast . . ." (Matt. 19 : 21). After presenting his wife with sufficient for her livelihood, and providing for his daughters by making them nuns of Fontevrault, he repaid his unjust exactions and gave the rest of his property to the poor. He begged his own bread from friends, some of whom criticized while others copied his conversion. A group formed, and for their instruction Waldo persuaded two sympathetic priests to translate portions of Scripture into French. Then, according to the Dominican Etienne de Bourbon, he "usurped the apostolic office" by preaching and sending out his friends to preach. There were no regular sermons at the ordinary parish services, and even Etienne admits that these lay preachers had a good knowledge of their Bible; but it was desirable to obtain the Church's blessing, for which purpose two of the group journeyed to the Third Lateran Council in 1179.

A bishop, deputed to examine their theological attainments, passed on the irksome duty to Walter Map, who tells us in his *De Nugis Curialium* that he approached it with some diffidence, since the men were reported to be the leading members of their group. However, he began the examination on safe ground by asking: "Do you believe in God the Father? In the Son? And in the Holy Spirit?" To each question they replied with a simple affirmative. He next set them a little trap, inquiring: "Do you believe in the Mother of Christ?" In their innocence, the men again gave an affirmative answer, which involved them in a double heresy. For in order to avoid the error of Nestorius, Mary should be called the Mother of God; and although the Church paid her peculiar honour, it was not accustomed to profess its faith in her. Sharing the popular devotion to the Virgin, the Waldensians had unwittingly exalted her too high for any creature; they were in fact condemned for a degree of Mariolatry greater than that allowed by Rome. The upshot was that they were refused permission to preach, except when specially licensed by the diocesans, but Pope Alexander III seems to have approved their vow of poverty, and also their translation of the Bible. Thus the Church, while sanctioning the Waldensians' ideal in general, did not consider the group as a whole to be well enough qualified for preaching. Professional jealousy of the amateur may doubtless have influenced the decision, but however zealous, upright and devoted they might be, these simple laymen had shown a regrettable ignorance of doctrine.

None the less, they insisted on continuing to preach. It would seem that the ethics of the Sermon on the Mount provided them with the main content of their message, for when one of their hearers was interrogated, he explained that he had been taught "neither to speak nor to do evil, to treat others as he himself would wish to be treated, and not to lie or swear." All this would have been admirable, if only the preachers had been authorized. But the Church continued to withhold its favour, the Archbishop of Lyons issued a definite prohibition, and eventually, for their continued disobedience rather than for any actual error, the Waldensians were condemned and excommunicated by the Council of

Verona in 1184. Here Pope Lucius III and the Emperor Frederick I agreed on rigorous measures for the suppression of heresy and dissent. The imperial edict has not survived, but it is clear that Church and State combined to enforce religious uniformity, in a situation that threatened to become chaotic. Under the terms of the papal decretal, which is still extant, excommunication was pronounced against Cathars, Waldensians, Humiliati, Arnoldists and other sects, against all those who preached irregularly or whose sacramental beliefs differed from the official doctrine, together with their protectors and adherents. Clerics and monks, if convicted of sympathizing with the sectaries, were to be deposed and handed over to the State for punishment; laymen also were to be handed over, if they could not prove their innocence in the episcopal court; and in order to discover the guilty, bishops were to visit suspect parishes once or twice a year, where they were to hold an inquisition by putting some of the inhabitants on oath to denounce any heretics of whom they knew. The Church always confined itself to the infliction of spiritual penalties, and where violence or bloodshed might be needed it employed the services of the secular arm. At the end of the twelfth century, the normal civil punishment for heresy was banishment and confiscation of goods; burning of the impenitent, as part of the legal code, first appears in 1197, in an ordinance of Peter II of Aragon, but this extreme penalty had occasionally been used from the year 1022 onwards. The Waldensian victims, who were to suffer under these savage measures, are universally admitted to have been of blameless moral character. "They are," according to a typical inquisitor, "modest and well behaved, taking no pride in their dress, which is neat but not extravagant. Avoiding commerce, because of its inevitable lies and oaths and frauds, they live by working as artisans, with cobblers as their teachers. Content with bare necessities, they do not accumulate wealth. Chaste in their habits, temperate in eating and drinking, they keep away from taverns, dances and other vanities. They refrain from anger and are always active. They can be recognized by their modesty and precision of speech." By way of contrast, one suspect sought at his trial to prove that he must be a good Catholic, because he lied and swore and drank like other men.

Some of the specific points of difference between the Church and the Waldensians were brought out by a disputation held in 1190 at Narbonne. In the first place, the Waldensians refused obedience to Pope and prelates; secondly, following from this, they maintained that all Christians, including laymen, have the right to preach. These were their two great offences which, taken together, amounted to a doctrine of the priesthood of all believers. By way of amplification they stated, third, that God must be obeyed rather than man, and fourth, that even women can preach under the gospel dispensation. Fifth, they utterly condemned prayers, alms and masses for the dead; some went further, denying the existence of purgatory, but on this point the majority was undecided, and their opposition was chiefly directed against a financial traffic in the means of grace. Sixth and last, they rejected the idea of any special sanctity attached to places, declaring that prayer in Church is no more acceptable than prayer offered in bed, in a chamber or a stable. To prove their contentions, the Waldensians appealed to Scripture, the sole authority of which soon became for them an explicit tenet. From the Sermon on the Mount, they had already derived an objection to taking oaths or telling lies; military service and capital punishment were now opposed on the same authority (Matt. 5 : 21, 25). Against prayers and masses for the dead they quoted a number of texts: John 12 : 35 ("Walk while ye have the light, lest darkness come upon you"), II Cor. 5 : 10 and 6 : 2 ("We must all appear before the judgment seat of Christ . . . behold, now is the accepted time, now is the day of salvation"), and Gal. 6 : 10 ("While we have opportunity, let us do good unto all men"). In defence of lay preaching, they quoted: Num. 11 : 29 ("Would God that all the Lord's people were prophets"), Mark 9 : 38–40 ("He that is not against us is on our part"), Phil. 1 : 15 ("Some indeed preach Christ even of envy and strife, and some also of good will"), Jas. 4 : 17 ("To him that knoweth to do good and doeth it not, it is sin"), Rev. 22 : 17 ("And let him that heareth say, Come"). And with particular reference to women preachers, they appealed to the texts: Luke 2 : 38 (Anna the prophetess) and Tit. 2 : 3 (the aged women to be "teachers of good things"). With this careful searching of the Scriptures, the Waldensians multiplied their vernacular translations, some of which were said to be inaccurate; but they acquired a very extensive knowledge of the Bible, so that even illiterates among them could sometimes recite all four Gospels by heart.

Expelled from the Church by the Council of Verona, Peter Waldo proceeded to organize his numerous followers into a separate institution. Regarding himself as a bishop directly commissioned by God, he ordained priests and deacons with the assent and assistance of the assembly of the brethren. The clergy thus ordained were sent out two by two on preaching circuits, while others were consecrated by Waldo to the episcopate for the purpose of more general supervision. In theory, all believers could preach, absolve and celebrate, but in practice celebration of the Lord's Supper was a function restricted to the bishops. There was an annual communion service, held on the evening of Maundy Thursday, at which fish was sometimes eaten as well as bread and wine; this peculiar feature, which appears in ancient representations of the eucharist, was copied from the loaves and fishes with which Christ fed the multitude. The doctrine of transubstantiation was denied, and although adherents of the Waldensians might attend Catholic services, they were forbidden to communicate there; for the ministrations of clergymen, whose lives did not conform to the apostolic standard of poverty, were treated as invalid. All these arrangements had the effect of constituting a distinct Church or denomination. But in other respects the Waldensians were organized rather more on the lines of a religious Order. Full membership was limited to those who, by formal vows, accepted a definite and stringent rule of life. Like the monks they vowed poverty, chastity and obedience to the law of Christ, promising that they would renounce the world and follow the example of the apostles. There was a period of novitiate, lasting for one or two years in Lombardy, and up to six years in France, during which large parts of Scripture were memorized. The vow of chastity dissolved any prior marriage, so that in fact only celibates were admitted. Their dress, which they called the apostolic habit, consisted of a plain woollen garment, and although at first they went barefoot, they later adopted the use of sandals. Later still, persecution obliged them to discard this conspicuous attire, and from the same cause preaching by women was discontinued. The membership seems to have been drawn almost exclusively from the lower classes.

The Humiliati, whose headquarters were situated at Milan, had been condemned at the same time as the Waldensians. Both groups united for a period under Waldo's leadership, which extended his already wide influence into Lombardy. But the union proved uneasy and impermanent, since Waldo was criticized, like Wesley, for using dictatorial methods, and when he insisted on the rule of celibacy for full members, the Lombards replied that a married couple should only separate by mutual consent. In consequence of the disagreement, some of the Humiliati rejoined the Catholic Church in 1201, and during the following ten years most of the remainder repudiated their connexion with Waldo. This separate Lombard branch continued until the fifteenth century to have its own Primate or Archbishop, who presided over the supreme governing body or chapter, whereas the French branch, after the death of Waldo, had no permanent head. In Lombardy, the preachers were called *barbes* ("uncles"), and like monks they changed their personal names on entering the movement.

By the time of Waldo's death, which occurred about 1218, persecution had already touched his followers. Some of the executions mentioned may have been of Cathars, but in 1211 there was a particularly large massacre, when about eighty Waldensians, both men and women, perished at the stake in Strassburg. The Church, however, was handicapped by a lack of adequate instruments for suppression. Previous heretics had mostly been isolated priests, who were subject to the regular discipline of the ordinary Church courts; a widespread lay movement was more difficult to combat, and although the bishops had been urged to visit suspect areas, it was soon found that some centralized machinery was needed. The papacy sent special legates and preachers, of whom Dominic was one, to attempt the conversion of the Cathars, and when persuasion failed, it employed Simon of Montfort to exterminate them by fire and sword; such operations were reckoned as a Crusade, in return for which the combatants received a plenary indulgence, and after about a generation the Albigensians of southern France had ceased to exist. But the other groups of humbler, less heretical noncomformists continued to flourish and expand. In 1232 the Emperor Frederick II issued an edict for the suppression of heresy by government officials throughout his dominions; Pope Gregory IX, though willing to use the secular power as an ally, insisted that the judicial process must be entrusted to the Church, and for this purpose he established the Papal Inquisition as a court of universal jurisdiction. Its members were chiefly drawn from the Dominican and Franciscan friars, whose theological learning and devotion to the papacy proved useful qualifications for the work. Zealous and high-minded men, they believed themselves to be engaged in the salvation of souls, and they therefore made it their primary object to secure a confession from the accused. Aquinas indeed says that since corrupting the faith is a worse offence than counterfeiting the coinage, the Church must use every possible endeavour to reclaim the heretic and protect his neighbours. The result was a form of process so heavily weighted against the accused that it would have been illegal in any other court. Arrest could be made on mere suspicion, which was itself sufficient to create a presumption of guilt; the judge was at the same time the prosecutor, and as it was highly dangerous to defend a heretic, the accused was normally unable to obtain legal aid; the evidence of witnesses, whose names were withheld, could only be rebutted by proving malice; the witnesses themselves might be young children or persons otherwise incapable of giving evidence in an ordinary court, and yet only two were needed to secure a condemnation. When they visited a district, the inquisitors did allow a period of one month's grace, during which all heretics who confessed voluntarily were dismissed with a comparatively mild penance. But after this there was no more leniency, and the suspects, who were normally at least known to have absented themselves from public worship, were subjected to an elaborate technique of brain-washing by solitary confinement, on a miserable diet, for a completely indefinite term, under examination by expert interrogators. The use of physical torture was authorized in 1252; and although the papal bull directed that it should not be applied more than once, this handicap was circumvented by the fiction that torture was not being repeated but continued. Even worse perhaps was the mere fact of hopeless and apparently unending imprisonment; one man, arrested in 1301, was not finally sentenced until eighteen years later, and this was by no means an isolated instance. If the suspect at last confessed, the inquisitor rejoiced that he had saved a soul; and the sentence, technically a penance, would normally be life imprisonment on bread and water in a monastery. The obstinate, the impenitent, and still more those who relapsed into a former heresy, were handed over to the civil power; and although the Church theoretically avoided the guilt of bloodshed, such relaxation always meant burning at the stake.

Such were the methods by which undoubtedly honest and devoted men considered themselves to be serving God. Despite it all, a remnant of the Waldensians survived. Indeed their congregation at Turin was so flourishing in 1352 that it met without any attempt at concealment. By this time they had definitely come to regard themselves as the one true Church, dismissing the Roman communion as the *Ecclesia malignantium*. For themselves they retained certain medieval practices until the Reformation; clerical celibacy, the cult of the Virgin, regular fast-days and a compulsory annual confession of sins were features that they did not discard before merging in the wider movement of the Protestant revolt. Before then, their Bohemian branch had fused with the Hussites, finding that the doctrines of Wycliffe which the latter professed were extraordinarily similar to their own; there is no evidence that Wycliffe borrowed from Waldo, but both of them rejected papacy and transubstantiation, appealed to Scripture, criticized clerical wealth and sent out a group of poor preachers. With such antecedents, the Waldensians naturally welcomed the teaching of Luther and Calvin when it came, while on their own part the Reformers respected them as venerable witnesses to evangelical truth. A legend even appeared, to the effect that the Waldensians were directly descended from the primitive Church, having existed as a separate group since the time of Constantine. For this there is no shred of proof. It was only the Cathars who could claim so ancient a lineage, and they were the descendants, not of early Christians, but of early heretics. None the less, even if they date from no earlier than the twelfth century, the followers of Waldo have some right to be regarded as the first Protestants; and their small community, today of some 20,000 members, has an honoured place in the history of religious dissent.

CHAPTER X

THE PONTIFICATE OF INNOCENT III

MORE OF A STATESMAN THAN A SAINT, INNOCENT III WAS the first great Pope whom the Church did not canonize. Of his real greatness there can be no doubt, for to a very large extent he made good those claims to ultimate and universal authority which Hildebrand had only been able to enunciate as an ideal. Under him the medieval papacy reached the climax of its power, thereafter to enter on a slow and lingering decline. And the cause both of its present power and of its subsequent decay was identical: a lack of saintliness, a growing secularization of purpose, which Innocent imported into the papal policies. Calm, energetic, far-sighted and efficient, he was capable of writing sermons and treatises which show some depth of devotional feeling; but he was also desperately ambitious, and although he continued to act ostensibly in the cause of international righteousness, his programme was more and more dominated by the methods of power politics. Rome became a secular principality, using spiritual weapons for temporal ends, and nowhere is this more clearly evident than in Innocent's use of the Crusade as a political instrument. He was sadly lacking in the Christian virtue of humility. Where previous Popes had been content to be regarded as the successors of St. Peter, Innocent was the first officially to describe himself as the Vicar of Christ; the idea was not entirely new—Bernard of Clairvaux had already made it current—but by its regular employment Innocent claimed to be the direct representative not merely of the Chief Apostle, but of God Himself. Using the old metaphor of Hildebrand, he declared that "priesthood is the sun, and monarchy the moon; kings rule their individual kingdoms, but Peter reigns over the whole earth . . . and the Lord Jesus Christ has established one sovereign over all as His universal Vicar, whom all things in heaven, earth and hell should obey even as they bow the knee to Christ." Such words betokened something much more than the old demand for the spiritual independence of the Church; they implied a complete theocracy, with the Pope, as near as man might dare to be, set upon the throne of God.

None of these claims was essentially an innovation. The novel fact was that Innocent could so largely put them into practice. Profiting from a temporary eclipse in the imperial power, he made himself master of the Papal States and cleared the Germans out of Italy, placed the French and English kingdoms under interdict, forced the rulers of England, Aragon and Portugal to become vassals of the Holy See, crushed the formidable revolt of the Albigensians in Languedoc, encouraged a long civil war in Germany, and made and unmade Emperors to suit the convenience of the Church. Such is the catalogue of his political achievements. In the spiritual sphere, he obtained establishment of the Latin rite in Constantinople as a fruit of the Fourth Crusade; while at the Fourth Lateran Council in 1215, he completed the Hildebrandine programme of reform, and by making transubstantiation the official creed, he set the corner-stone to the edifice of priestly power. Though he was aware of the administrative dangers pointed out by Bernard, there was during his reign a marked expansion in the appellate jurisdiction of the Roman See, together with a careful codification of canon law and chancery procedure. By patronizing the new orders of Dominicans and Franciscans he captured a sort of evangelical revival for the Roman obedience. By promoting the foundation and endowment of schools he ushered in the great century of scholasticism. His vision of a united Christian community of Europe was both genuine and lofty, but the attempt to achieve it under papal leadership was of necessity short-lived. For the lay element was coming more into its own, not only in politics, but also in literature and society as a whole. It was the age of the troubadours and minnesingers, when a brilliant vernacular poetry was developing in Germany and France, when *Parsifal*, the *Niebelungenlied*, *Tristan and Isolde* were composed; and the minnesingers were not ecclesiastically minded —the best of them, Walter von der Vogelweide, called Innocent's code of canon law "the blackest book hell ever gave." This lay spirit was equally prominent in the evangelical revival as typified by Francis of Assisi, and it was fortunate for the Church that Francis did not choose to set himself in opposition. None the less, Europe had become more thoughtful, more critical, more disturbed in its beliefs, as a result of the Crusades; and in this wide enrichment of human experience, this tumultuous proliferation of lay interests, the papacy had to hold the reins with a firm hand.

Innocent was born in 1160 or 1161. His father, Count Trasimund of Segni, belonged to one of the four oldest families in Italy, while his mother Clarissa came from the aristocratic Roman house of the Scotti. They gave him the baptismal name of

L

Lothario, which had more of an imperial than a churchly ring. But he studied at Rome, Paris and Bologna, thus acquiring the best theological and legal education of the day. From Paris he made a pilgrimage to Becket's shrine at Canterbury, and this youthful admiration for the martyred Archbishop may serve to indicate his own views on the right relation between Church and State. After a brilliant career in the law school at Bologna, he became a Cardinal Deacon at the early age of twenty-nine; the church assigned to him in Rome was that of St. Sergius and St. Bacchus, which he repaired at his own expense; and his talents, no less than his social position, seemed to assure him of a distinguished future. But in 1191 the death of Pope Clement III, who may have been his uncle, set a temporary check to his ambitions. He remained at Rome, but in semi-retirement, and employed his time in writing. It was at this period that he composed a treatise *On Contempt of the World*, in the conventional tones of pious resignation, but with a forthright attack on pride and sensuality such as would have gratified a puritan like Bernard; accepting the Augustinian doctrine of total depravity, he described mankind as "a mass of corruption, stinking and unspeakably foul," and with the powerful rhetoric of which he was a master, he demonstrated in abundant detail how the whole of life is infected by original sin. His little *Dialogue between God and the Sinner* is written in a similar vein; but with a highly characteristic touch, it invokes the assistance of papal indulgences to ease the sinner's burden. Of his other early works, the most important is devoted to *The Sacred Mystery of the Altar*. Much of this is concerned with the allegorical meaning of ceremonies and vestments. In the sphere of doctrine, Innocent declares that the mass is a threefold sacrifice, of repentance, righteousness and praise. By virtue of the words "This is My Body," he states that bread and wine are converted into Christ's Body and Blood. But transubstantiation means no more than that the reality of the sacrament is Christ. The forms of the elements remain in such a way that what the priest breaks, or what a mouse might chance to eat, is bread; what is received in the communion is Christ, but after reception His presence in the communicant becomes spiritual and not corporeal, since "this is food not for the body but for the soul."

The aged and vacillating Pope Celestine III had vainly tried to nominate his own successor. But on the very day of his death, 8th January 1198, the cardinals unanimously elected Lothario of Segni under the name of Innocent III. Young, learned, vigorous, and popular, he had the advantage of not being committed to any party in the curia, and his elevation was vociferously welcomed

by the Roman populace. Celestine had reached his ninety-second
year, but Innocent, the youngest member of the Sacred College,
was no more than thirty-seven, and it was obvious that his pontificate would mark a fresh beginning. We possess a sermon which
he may well have delivered on the day of his consecration, and
which, combined with others on the same subject, clearly indicates his exalted conception of the papal office. Taking his text
from Matt. 24 : 45 ("Who then is a faithful and wise servant whom
his lord hath made ruler over his household, to give them meat
in due season?") Innocent remarks that a Pope is required to
show fidelity, prudence and pastoral zeal, feeding the flock by
personal example, by teaching and by dispensation of the sacraments, with godly wisdom and unshaken loyalty to the apostolic
faith. "It is impossible," he said, "to please God without faith,
since what is not done in faith is sin. If I did not myself firmly
believe, how could I strengthen others? . . . But I have a faith
which is firm because it is apostolic, and I am convinced that my
faith will save me, according to the promise of Him who said,
Thy faith hath saved thee, go and sin no more." As a preacher,
Innocent was dignified and scriptural, but brilliant rather than
profound. None the less he regarded preaching as so essential a
part of pastoral duty, that in 1213 he deposed a Bishop of Brixen
simply because the man was too aged and infirm to preach.
Realizing the greatness of his own task, Innocent took comfort in
the thought of God's ever-present help: the Church is founded
on rock, Christ is always borne in Peter's bark, and the Pope, like
a new Noah, pilots the one Ark in which men can be saved. Soon
after his consecration, in a letter written to the Archbishop of
Monreale, he quoted the text "Thou art Peter" and continued:
"we must infer from this that, just as there is a single mediator
between God and men, the man Christ Jesus, so in the Church by
God's will there is a single head for all . . . The Holy Roman
Church, founded by Peter at Our Lord's command, has been
given authority over all the churches." A year later, Innocent
wrote to the Patriarch of Constantinople that St. Peter received
the government, not only of the Church, but also of the whole
world. And in another of his sermons on the meaning of pontifical consecration, he declared: "I have obtained from Peter the
mitre for my priesthood and the crown for my royalty; he has
made me Vicar of Him upon whose vesture is written, King of
kings and Lord of lords, Priest for ever after the order of
Melchizedek." It has been pointed out that much of this language
is traditional, derived from such sources as the liturgy for the
Feast of St. Peter's Chair. But although in practice Innocent

limited his political interventions to cases in which morality was involved, it remains true that in theory he laid claim to a sovereignty which knew no bounds.

The situation when he became Pope was menacing. Jerusalem had fallen to Saladin in 1187, and although Acre was recovered four years later by the gallantry of Richard Cœur-de-Lion, the Third Crusade proved largely ineffective through the mutual strife of France and England. Abroad, Islam was still a dangerous threat, while at home, heresy was growing; and as an even greater menace to papal independence, the Emperor Henry VI had united the crowns of Germany and Sicily, only to die four months before Innocent's accession. Rome was thus providentially delivered from encirclement, since Henry's heir, Frederick II, was then an infant too young to be accepted as Emperor by the German princes, and although Sicily descended to him by right of inheritance, his widowed mother quickly made him a ward of the papacy and his kingdom a vassal of the Holy See. In Italy, Innocent was opposed by a number of German governors installed by Henry, but acting as the champion of local patriotism, and aided by the Frenchman Walter of Brienne, he acquired control of the Papal States by 1207, and a year later he removed the last trace of German influence from the south. He thus provided himself with a temporal dominion which could offer a secure base for further operations; but it had been a hard struggle, and even at Rome itself his authority was not unquestioned until 1208. The first act of his pontificate had been to demand an oath of loyalty from the city prefect, who up till then had been an imperial nominee; and by controlling elections to the Roman Senate, he gradually quelled the strife of the various factions, from whose violence he was more than once compelled to take flight. Meanwhile he attended to the administrative problems of the Church, banishing the greedy young nobles from his court, reducing the expenses of the papal household, and insisting that the curial officials must accept no gratuities apart from a recognized scale of fees for secretarial work. How far these reforms were effective is uncertain, for complaints of corrupt practices continued; but Innocent did take a very personal interest in the details of administration, restricting pluralities, trying to ensure that every curate got a reasonable living wage, and restraining frivolous appeals to Rome. At Montpellier he created four or five new parishes to provide for the needs of a rapidly increasing population. Both there and at Rome he patronized the work of the Order of the Holy Ghost, in nursing the sick and caring for orphans and abandoned children, while he made determined efforts to encourage the reclaiming of prostitutes. When faced by the spread of heresy in southern France, he organized preaching missions, first by the Cistercians and then by the followers of Dominic. And in all his administration, he based his actions explicitly on the papal plenitude of power, asserting for example that, since a bishop is spiritually married to his diocese, only a "divine authority" such as the Pope possesses can dissolve the union by deposing the bishop or translating him to another see.

In Germany, the vacant throne was contested between two adult relatives of the dead Emperor, who had failed in his attempt to establish a hereditary succession. No one took serious notice of the infant Frederick in his far-off Sicilian kingdom. His uncle Philip of Swabia was chosen Emperor on 8th March, 1198, by a majority of the electoral princes; but three months later a minority elected Otto of Brunswick, the English king's nephew, who was promptly crowned by the Archbishop of Cologne at the traditional locality of Aix. Philip's coronation was delayed until September; it was slightly more spectacular, since he had managed to possess himself of the German regalia, but it suffered from the fatal defect that at the time Philip was an excommunicated person. Both sides appealed to Innocent for recognition of their candidate, though without intending that he should act as arbiter between them. But the Pope asserted a right of decision that was both original and final: original since Charlemagne's Empire had been instituted by the papacy, and final since the imperial crown, as distinct from that of Germany, is always bestowed by Rome. In 1201 he issued his judicial decision, setting aside the claims of Philip because of his excommunication, and recognizing Otto as the lawful Emperor. The verdict, ostensibly based on considerations of morality, was intended to serve the best interests of the Church; but it at once embroiled the papacy in the internal politics of Germany, and by 1206, when Otto was decisively defeated, it had become apparent that Innocent was on the losing side. Having prolonged the struggle for as long as possible, he was on the point of changing over, when Philip was unexpectedly assassinated in 1208, and next year Otto at last received his crown at Rome. To Innocent he promised his grateful obedience. He would protect the Papal States, allow unhampered appeals to the Roman Curia in all ecclesiastical causes, surrender his right to the revenues of vacant churches, and permit free elections to the German bishoprics; in a word, he resigned much that had been won for the Empire at the Concordat of Worms in 1122, reversing the ecclesiastical policy of Barbarossa and his son Henry VI. But once securely seated on the throne Otto showed no disposition to

fulfil his promises; indeed, though he belonged by birth to the
Guelf or papal party, and was descended from Hildebrand's old
ally, Countess Matilda of Tuscany, under pressure of circumstances he was now fast becoming a Ghibelline or imperialist. In
1210 Innocent started his intrigues with the French King Philip
Augustus, leading to the replacement of Otto by young Frederick
II, who had come of age four years before; but Frederick had
to fight his way to the throne, and he did not finally defeat Otto
until French support had won the battle of Bouvines in 1214.
Meanwhile, to satisfy Innocent, he had been obliged to renew all
the promises once made by Otto, with more substantial guaran-
tees for their performance, by the Golden Bull of Eger issued in
1213. So long as Innocent lived he was more or less obedient to
the Church, but after the Pope's death in 1216, he began to
attack the papacy, and was actually excommunicated at the time
when he led the sixth and most successful of the Crusades. Papal
writers described him as an atheist, and he was certainly an
advanced free-thinker, half oriental sultan, half renaissance
despot; but with his brilliant mind, his knowledge of half a dozen
languages, his skill in poetry, his devotion to the arts and sciences,
he was more charitably described by friends as the Wonder of the
World; and in the vastness of his ambition for a universal sovereignty, Frederick became the perfect secular counterpart to
Innocent III.

In France, the Pope measured swords with a capable, devout
and resolute monarch in the person of Philip Augustus, who had
entered into a rash but tempting matrimonial alliance during the
year 1193. Canute VI of Denmark was nephew to the English
Richard and cousin to the German Otto, both enemies of France;
in order to detach him from his relatives, and at the same time to
take over his possible claim to the English throne, Philip agreed
to marry his sister Ingeborg, then a beautiful young girl of eighteen. But no sooner were they married than he conceived an in-
explicable repugnance for his bride; shutting her up in a convent,
he forced the French bishops to dissolve the marriage on grounds
of alleged consanguinity, and although Pope Celestine III
annulled the dissolution, he proceeded to wed a lady called Agnes
of Meran. Such was the situation when Innocent became Pope.
While the unfortunate Ingeborg in her solitary confinement continued to demand justice from Rome, Innocent determined to
teach the bigamous monarch that even kings are not exempt from
the moral law; he went so far as to legitimize the children of
Agnes, who tactfully died soon after, but by placing France under
interdict he at last obliged Philip to take back his lawful spouse,

just twenty years after their original marriage. Equally firm in protecting ecclesiastical property, he compelled the king to restore certain Church lands which he had confiscated. But in 1207 when Peter of Castelnau, the Pope's legate to southern France, was murdered after threatening Count Raymond of Toulouse with excommunication, Philip refused to lead the Crusade launched by Innocent against the Albigensians. Having reconquered Normandy three years before, the French king was preoccupied with plans for the invasion of England, and in his absence the Crusade degenerated into a process of undisciplined savagery; Simon of Montfort, the actual leader, ravaged lands claimed by Aragon in defiance of the Pope's effort to restrain him, but none the less won for himself the dukedom of Narbonne; and even after the Albigensians had been annihilated, the bloody war continued until 1229 in order that Languedoc might be incorporated under the French Crown.

In England, Thomas à Becket had championed the Church's independence, and in particular the right of clergy to be tried in ecclesiastical courts. He won his case by dying for it; benefit of clergy remained on the statute book until 1827, and the saint himself remained in his shrine until 1538, when Henry VIII not unnaturally had his bones removed and scattered. But despite the appalling set-back to royal authority when the king was compelled to do public penance for the archbishop's murder, Henry II was able to bequeath a strong monarchy to his son Richard Cœur-de-Lion, who became King of England, Duke of Normandy and Count of Anjou in 1189. During the ten years of his reign, Richard took more interest in the Third Crusade than in his kingdom, where he only spent a very few months; the government was carried on by great officers of state, many of them churchmen like Archbishop Hubert Walter of Canterbury, despite a protest from Innocent that prelates should not be diverted to such tasks. The result was a decline in the authority of the Crown, coupled with a steady drain on the country's finances for foreign wars, so that a clash with the nobility became inevitable when the mean, astute and autocratic John succeeded his brother upon the throne. On Walter's death in 1205, some of the younger monks at Canterbury rushed through the election of their sub-prior Reginald, an unsuitable and precipitate choice which infuriated the rest of the chapter, the bishops and the king; at once John appointed his own nominee, the Bishop of Norwich, but when all parties appealed to Rome Innocent quashed both elections and provided a candidate of his own choosing. This was Stephen Langton, an English Cardinal, formerly a student friend of

Innocent's at Paris, and now distinguished by a European reputation for scholarship which made him well fitted to continue the
learned succession of Lanfranc and Anselm. But John refused
to let him land, and in 1208 the Pope placed England under interdict. At once the normal Church services were stopped, many of
the clergy fled to the continent, and the king retaliated by imposing heavy taxes on the remainder who stayed at home. This
crippling taxation, which affected all classes of the people, rendered John still more unpopular; he had already lost most of the
English possessions in France, he refused the advice of sensible
councillors, and the land was wretchedly misgoverned. Innocent
excommunicated him in 1209, but he replied by a propaganda
appeal to national sentiment, declaring that he was protecting the
ancient liberties of England against papal intervention. In 1212
the Pope resorted to his ultimate weapon; he declared John
deposed and invited Philip Augustus to invade England at the
head of a Crusade. Next year John tardily submitted to the combined threat of spiritual and military attack; promising full resti-
tution, he handed over his kingdom to Innocent and received it
back as a vassal of the papacy. From then onwards he was treated
by Rome as a beloved son, while Langton, who landed and took
up office in 1213, was actually suspended by Innocent for ventur-
ing to side with the rebellious barons against their king. None the
less, archbishop and nobles succeeded in extracting the royal
assent to Magna Carta; and when John complained that it had
been extorted from him by force and without consulting his
Roman overlord, Innocent annulled the charter and sentenced the
barons to excommunication. This sentence Langton refused to
publish until he had discussed matters with the Pope at the
Lateran Council; the dispute ended when John died, only three
months after Innocent, from a surfeit of peaches and new cider.

    The rivalry between France and England, coupled with the
state of civil war in Germany, hampered Innocent's dearest ambition of dispatching a Crusade to Palestine. From the start of his
pontificate he had prepared the way for a joint effort by East and
West, which might at the same time serve to promote reunion of
the Churches. But the Greeks were cool in their response, insisting that the differences could only be composed by an Ecumenical
Council, and the Pope was therefore obliged to rely on Western
support. He ordered all beneficed clergy to contribute one-
fortieth of their income, thus levying what was the first direct
papal tax upon the Church. He sent Fulk of Neuilly to preach the
Crusade. But when Fulk urged King Richard to dispose of his
three daughters, pride, avarice and incontinence, the king replied

that he would bestow them on those best able to employ the gift —pride on the Templars, avarice on the Cistercians, and incontinence on the bishops. Since the monarchs of Europe showed no interest in the papal project, leadership devolved upon the barons, who chose Boniface of Montferrat as their chief; and Boniface, the cousin and confidant of Philip of Swabia, had inherited the old Norman plan for an initial attack on Constantinople. His plan was shared by the Venetians, because their trading privileges had been restricted by the Eastern Empire, and both in 1171 and 1182 their quarter at Constantinople had been sacked. Dandolo, the blind but alert Doge of Venice, agreed to transport the crusading army and to feed it for twelve months, in return for a sum of 85,000 marks, which in modern currency would equal about half a million pounds; he further promised to maintain a fleet of fifty armed galleys, in return for a half share of any conquests that might be made. Innocent had given precise instructions that the crusaders were to make no attack on any fellow-Christians, but when they were unable to raise more than two-thirds of the money demanded by Venice, the Doge suggested that the deficit might be made good by plunder.

At the same moment a young Greek refugee called Alexius appeared in Italy, soliciting Western help to reinstate his father, the Emperor Isaac Angelus, who had been blinded and deposed from the Byzantine throne. Receiving scant sympathy from the Pope, Alexius applied to his brother-in-law, Philip of Swabia, for whom his appeal offered a legitimate opportunity of subjugating the Eastern Empire. Boniface and Dandolo were taken into their confidence, and despite protests from some of the crusaders, reinforced by a second papal prohibition, the flotilla set sail for the Adriatic town of Zara, which was sacked and pillaged at the end of 1202. Innocent promptly excommunicated everyone concerned in the assault, but later absolved all except the Venetians, who did not trouble to seek pardon. Alexius now made a definite and tempting offer: if his family was restored, he would himself pay the Venetians and contribute reinforcements for the Crusade to Palestine. This satisfied the scruples of all but a small minority. Constantinople was odious for schism and heresy, but attractive for its riches, and in such circumstances to attack it seemed a just and pious deed. The resistance was half-hearted; Alexius and his father were restored; but very soon they proved utterly unable to fulfil their promises, or even to maintain themselves against a hostile Greek population. In April 1204, after a revolution in the city, the crusaders stepped in to take possession. Its wealth surpassed their most extravagant dreams; "no man," wrote the chronicler Villehardouin, "could believe that so rich a city existed anywhere in the world;" and amid scenes of rapine and debauch the army of the Cross appropriated all the plunder. The actual bloodshed has sometimes been exaggerated, for it seems that not more than two hundred people were slaughtered in cold blood. But nuns were ravished, churches desecrated, and a vast store of artistic treasures ruthlessly despoiled. The remnants of the Greek government installed themselves in Asia Minor, nursing a hatred for the West that was now implacable. In Constantinople Count Baldwin of Flanders was elected Latin Emperor and a Venetian, Thomas Morosini, was appointed Patriarch. The imperial territory in Europe was divided into fiefs, of which Venice took the most lucrative share. And when the papal legates had incredibly absolved the crusaders from their vows of proceeding on to Palestine, they settled down to enjoy the delights of their new-won territory. But the Greek population remained stubbornly hostile, and the Latin Empire, always a precarious institution, lasted only until 1261.

Before the savage onslaught on the Eastern capital, Innocent had written plainly to Boniface: "let none of you imagine that he is free to occupy or plunder Greek territory . . . we positively forbid you to invade or try to injure the lands of Christians, unless they themselves oppose your journey to the Holy Land." But after hearing of the capture, the Pope was transported with delight. "We read in Daniel the prophet," he declared, "that it is God on high who reveals mysteries, changes times and removes kingdoms. These words have been fulfilled in the realm of the Greeks, as we now rejoice to see. For He who rules over the kingdom of men and gives it to whomsoever He will, has transferred the kingdom of Constantinople from the proud to the humble, from the disobedient to the devout, from schismatics to catholics. . . . This is the Lord's doing and it is wondrous in our eyes." When he made this comment, Innocent was not aware of the brutality of the attack, which he subsequently condemned, but it would still be difficult to find a more complete *volte-face* than his cynical acceptance of the *fait accompli*. It was not for nothing that his courtiers called him Solomon III; he knew his Old Testament well enough to find a precedent for almost anything, and he seems to have convinced himself that the sack of Constantinople was the divinely appointed means to ecclesiastical reunion. Its result was in fact the opposite. For although a Latin hierarchy might be nominally installed, although Morosini might be confirmed in office as soon as he had sworn obedience to the Pope, and although Roman missionaries might invade Greece with their breviaries and their doctrinal arguments, the Greeks now had juster cause than before for resentment, and their ancestral opposition to the papacy was renewed with unquenchable vigour. However, if in the East the increase of papal government was no more than a temporary occupation, in northern Europe its frontiers were advanced partly by missions to the Baltic and partly by the Knights of the Sword, while in Spain the Moslems were decisively defeated in 1212 on the battlefield of Las Navas de Tolosa.

Fortified by these successes, in April 1213 Innocent summoned the great Council which was to be the climax of his reign. More than two years were allowed for preparation, in order that the whole Church might give careful thought to its agenda, composed of the three main objectives which the Pope had consistently pursued: a renewal of the Crusade, a reform of the Church and the repression of heresy. This fourth assembly at the Lateran, reckoned by Rome as the Twelfth Ecumenical Council, was to be as widely representative as possible, and orders were therefore issued that all bishops must attend, with the exception of two in each province who might remain behind for urgent duties. The Greek clergy refused to participate, and the attendance from Germany was thin; but when the council opened on 11th November, 1215, there were 412 bishops, including the Latin Patriarchs of Constantinople and Jerusalem, more than 800 abbots and priors, ambassadors from all the great secular monarchs, and deputies from the Italian towns. It was the most spectacular of medieval gatherings, and it enacted a larger amount of legislation than any council prior to Trent. In honour of the Trinity, only three public sessions were held, for the purpose of ratifying decisions that had been already reached in private. At the solemn opening Innocent preached on Luke 22 : 15: "with desire I have desired to eat this passover with you before I suffer." Though no more than fifty-five years old, he seems to have had a premonition that his life would soon be done; he said that he desired a triple passover—materially to the reconquest of Jerusalem, spiritually to a Church purified of abuses, and for himself eternally to heaven. A fresh Crusade was arranged to meet, under papal direction, in June of 1217; to finance it, clerks were to give one-twentieth of their incomes for three years, the Pope and cardinals a tenth. In opposition to Greek and Western heretics, various dogmatic definitions were adopted. According to the first of the Council's seventy canons, "The Universal Church of the faithful is one, outside of which no man can be saved. In it Christ is both Priest and Sacrifice. His Body and Blood are truly contained in the sacrament of the altar under the appearance of bread and wine; there is a substantial change, by the power of God, of bread into His Body and of wine into His Blood. . . . None can perform this sacrament except a properly ordained priest. . . . The sacrament of baptism, which can be performed by anyone, confers salvation if properly administered. For sin committed after baptism true penance can atone. . . . Not only celibates, but also married persons can merit eternal bliss, if they please God by right belief and good works." The last sentence is a salutary protest against the Cathar insistence on celibacy for all of the elect, while in the previous clauses the Church's sacramental system was defined. Transubstantiation was explicitly named in canon 21, which enjoined the faithful to communicate at Easter and to confess to their parish priests at least once a year. The seal of confession was imposed, on pain of deposition and perpetual penance in a monastery. With a slight anticipation of modern ideas on psychosomatic medicine, doctors were bidden to collaborate with priests "since bodily sickness is often caused by sin." By another touch of modernity, clerks were forbidden to participate in any form of trial by ordeal. Jews on the other hand were ordered to wear a distinctive dress, and there was a severe prohibition of usury. New regulations were issued in the matter of marriage: whereas the forbidden degrees of affinity had previously been extended back for seven generations, now the restriction applied only to those who had a great-grand-parent in common. False relics were to be suppressed by the bishops, and no new ones exhibited without papal permission, while the issue of indulgences at the dedication of a church was to be kept within moderate limits. No new religious Orders might be founded, and the existing ones were to subject themselves to a triennial chapter with regular visitations. Metropolitans must hold annual synods for the discipline of disorderly clerics; preaching by bishops or suitable deputies was encouraged; cathedrals were to provide improved facilities for theological education; clerks should dress soberly, avoiding taverns and hunting-parties; and in general there was a detailed attempt to raise both moral and academic standards.

His great work completed, Innocent died of a fever at Perugia on 16th July, 1216. By a strange reversal of fortune, thieves stripped the once-powerful pontiff of his vestments while his body lay unguarded. In him, sincere idealism and vast practical ability were corrupted by the use of questionable methods, which enhanced the material splendour of the papacy but at the same time weakened its spiritual resources. After listening to one of his sermons, John Capocci, his bitterest enemy at Rome, is said to have exclaimed: "your words are the words of God, but your actions are those of the devil." By persecution, by the use of force, by excessive dogmatization and by incessant recourse to the weapon of the interdict, he cheapened the currency of the Church. Under his successors the process of secularization was continued; Innocent IV, in the course of a protracted and mortal combat with Frederick II, sold every grace and privilege that he could put upon the market; and men discovered that, by a slight mis-spelling, the name *Innocenscius Papa* could be added up to the bestial number of six hundred and sixty-six.

CHAPTER XI

FRANCIS AND HIS FOLLOWERS

THE SO-CALLED AGE OF FAITH WAS IN FACT A PERIOD OF mounting crisis. On the one hand, popular dissent rebelled against the whole system of the hierarchy; on the other, popular superstition used the consecrated Host as a love-philtre or even as a garden insecticide. Robert Grosseteste was soon to tell Innocent IV that corruption of the priesthood was the main cause of heresy, a truth which had already impressed itself upon the mind of Innocent III. For at the time when Catharism was rampant in Languedoc, Archbishop Berengarius of Narbonne proved utterly indolent, never visiting his diocese and sometimes absenting himself from church for weeks on end; and although threatened with fulminations that would have brought a monarch to his knees, he defied the Pope for over twenty years, being deposed only a few months before his death in 1212. Academic theology was fast becoming the preserve of secular masters, whose temper was rationalist or even sceptical; two Parisian teachers, Amalric of Bena and David of Dinant, were condemned by the Fourth Lateran Council for a pantheism more outrageous than that of Erigena. Tithes were remorselessly extracted, even from the wages of day-labourers and maidservants, but the proceeds went for the most part into the pocket of an absentee incumbent, and Innocent III complained that the wretched curates often received no more than a sixteenth of their due. But surviving accounts prove that a vast amount of wine was frequently consumed at mass, although the priest alone communicated; and Giraldus Cambrensis explains with learned wit how wine, even after the miracle of transubstantiation, can retain its power to intoxicate. For many offences the bishops imposed a monetary fine, sometimes taking a regular tax from their clergy in return for the privilege of keeping concubines. And in all this riot of flagrant vice or slothful indifference, the common people were neglected and oppressed; in the year 1200 more than half the population of Europe was unfree, and of these unhappy serfs an enormous number belonged to the Church. Surveying so dismal a prospect, the Cistercian Caesarius of Heisterbach declared: "the

Church has now sunk to such a level that it is only fit to be ruled by bishops who are doomed to damnation." To this disparaging judgment there were of course notable exceptions, like the saintly Bishop Hugh of Lincoln; but the fact that it was made, by an intelligent and spiritually-minded observer, suffices to show the general attitude to the episcopate.

Whenever their spiritual life was ebbing, men had been accustomed to look for salvation to the monks. But apart from the Carthusians, too few and too secluded to be widely influential, the older Orders had entered on a serious decline. Still regarding themselves as "Christ's poor," with a promised blessing and a right to gifts, they had by now abandoned poverty and joined the ranks of the oppressors. Exemption from tolls and customs, such as had at first been given to starving monks who worked with their own hands, enabled their now opulent communities to sell produce at a cheaper rate than was possible for ordinary tradesmen. Tithes from benefices were appropriated to improve monastic standards of living. In the early years of the thirteenth century, the Abbot of St. Albans made an arrangement which Matthew Paris thus records: "I have been pleased to assign the church of St. Stephen in this town for the support of the monastery kitchen, which I have always embraced in the bowels of spiritual affection." A generation later, the Bishop of Durham gave to the same monastery "the church of Egglingham for the improvement of our beer." At Kelso the monks drove a brisk trade in ale; in some places they held a virtual monopoly of the trade. Acting as bankers they profited from the crusaders' need of ready cash, and although their financial operations involved them in unedifying lawsuits, they were the first to enter the insurance business, selling "corrodies" or pensions to their benefactors as a sort of speculative life annuity. Apart from nobles and rich merchants, only the monks at this period lived in comfortable stone houses, with absolute security, opulent furnishings and a train of serfs and servants. Some monasteries would accept none but aristocrats as members; it was always unusual for a poor man to be admitted to any higher rank than that of a humble lay-brother. The great abbots had become barons, the monks a squirearchy, and with their widely scattered estates they were absentee landlords of a sometimes hard and cruel type. A lay proprietor might emancipate serfs as a charitable deed at his death; but the abbey never died and its serfs were never freed. Even the Cistercians succumbed to the temptation of keeping serfs like the others, and with their large sheep-farms they became capitalists on an extensive scale. Free tenants also were subjected to burdensome obligations. The "heriot" was originally a weapon lent by the lord to his tenant and restored on the latter's decease, but by 1200 it had come to mean that when the bread-winner of a poor family died, the landlord could claim his best animal or other personal possession; the parson was entitled to the second best, and cases are on record where an abbot claimed both, the heriot in his capacity of landlord and the mortuary gift as absentee incumbent. Communal mills and ovens, built for the benefit of the neighbourhood, became grievous monopolies no less resented when their owners were the monks. Towards the middle of the thirteenth century, Cardinal Hugh of St. Cher stated roundly that the monastic Orders "oppress the poor and fleece the naked by rapine and extortion." Monasticism of the older type had in fact outlived its usefulness; Innocent III tried to revive its ardour by means of legislation; but what the times required was not the republication of old laws so much as a radically new approach. With the papacy enmeshed in the nexus of power politics, with theology inclining towards an arid scholasticism, with corruption among the clergy and avarice among the monks, the gospel had to be recovered in its stark simplicity; and if this could not be done inside the Church, it would be achieved for the masses outside it by the dissenting sects.

There was a rich cloth-merchant of Assisi, Peter Bernardone by name, married to a pious and perhaps aristocratic wife called Pica. His business often took him among the troubadours of France, and it was during an absence on one of these expeditions, about 1182, that his eldest son was born. The boy was christened John, but his father renamed him Francis, "the little Frenchman," in remembrance of the gay land that he had visited. While some saints have taken a new name from their religion, it might almost be said that Francis derived a religion from his name, with the gaiety of a minstrel as its outstanding feature. As a boy he was mirthful and open-handed, a leader of the town's wild revels. But his generosity showed traces of devotion, prompting Pica to tell her neighbours: "this son of mine is going to be a child of God." Poverty or unhappiness moved him to a spontaneous sympathy. When he was taken captive after a battle between the troops of Assisi and Perugia, he noticed that one of his fellow-prisoners was morose and lonely, and took pains to befriend him: later, when he joined a contingent that was to fight in the papal army under Walter of Brienne, he bestowed the splendid armour provided by his parents on an impoverished knight. Dreams of chivalrous loyalty had captured his generous young mind, and he was accustomed to throw his money about with the prodigality

of one who never had the slightest understanding of its value.
But on the very first night of his journey to join the papal forces,
he felt obscurely called to a more exalted service. Lying half-
awake when the contingent had halted at Spoleto, he heard a
mysterious voice asking whether it was better to obey the servant
or the lord, and when he answered "Lord, what wouldst Thou have
me do?" the voice told him to return to Assisi for further orders.
To desert the army meant abandoning his dreams, but Francis
went. It was the first of a series of divine encounters that were to
change his life, or rather to bring out its latent qualities. At home
in Assisi he became more silent and collected, and when his
friends concluded that he must have fallen in love, he told them
that he had plighted his troth to a lady "nobler, richer and fairer
than you have ever seen." They imagined that this bourgeois
youth was dreaming again of some fairy princess; but in truth it
was the Lady Poverty, the spouse of Christ, who alone remained
with Him upon the cross.

Still in doubt of his exact vocation, Francis made a pilgrimage
to Rome. Shocked by the meanness of the gifts offered by the
pilgrims, he threw his purse bodily into the Apostle's shrine, and
then solved the problem of paying for his dinner by changing
clothes with a tramp and begging on St. Peter's steps. The experience confirmed him in the conviction that the poor are
closest to God's kingdom, that the wealth which most men covet
is a crippling bondage for the soul. But on his return to Assisi he
was faced by a sterner challenge. Leprosy, spread by crusading
contacts with the East, was the most dread disease of the Middle
Ages, mysteriously loathsome and utterly incurable. Francis suddenly met a leper, in a narrow place where there was no turning
back. He gave the man money, but realizing that money without
love means little, he summoned all his courage and kissed the
leprous hand. Legend has it that when he looked again there was
no man to be seen; and although this may be a touch of pious
embroidery, it remains true that henceforward Francis devoted
his life to loving Christ in the persons of the poor and the unfortunate. In his last Testament he described this encounter as the
beginning of his penance; "for when I was in my sins, I could not
bear to look at lepers, but the Lord Himself led me among them
... and what had seemed bitter to me was turned into delight ...
and then after a little while I forsook the world."

So far, the calling of Francis had been negative; he felt the urge
to renounce ambition, delicacy, riches; but he was waiting for
some specific work to do. While he prayed in the lonely, half-
derelict church of St. Damian, a voice spoke to him from the

M

crucifix: "Go and repair My house." So he loaded his own horse with bales of his father's cloth, sold both beast and merchandise, and brought the proceeds to St. Damian's as a contribution for the fabric fund. But the priest, uncertain of the paternal attitude to this act of pious appropriation, refused to accept the money; and Peter Bernardone, long grieved by his son's unbusinesslike behaviour, exploded in a fit of indignation. Francis fled from home, and after some months' struggle, was haled before the bishop's court on a charge of theft. Bishop Guido, a sympathetic soul, had more than an inkling of what was passing in the young man's mind, and he felt little taste for the tactics of the father, but he told Francis plainly that the Church could not accept stolen money. In reply, Francis stripped stark naked, gave his father every rag that he possessed, renounced his family and declared that for the future he would depend only on his Father in heaven. In the past he had dazzled Assisi by his gorgeous garments; now he astonished the town still further by his nakedness, and while Peter made an undignified exit with the pile of clothing, a wave of sympathy for his son swept round the court. The bishop robed him in the cast-off tunic of a footman, and Francis went out into the cold singing a gay French song.

He had been told to repair God's house, and with his amazing gift for simplification, he realized that the way to rebuild is not to borrow money but to gather stones. He begged them from everyone he met, and with his own hands built them into the ruinous church walls. The priest of St. Damian's looked after him, and he extended his care to other forsaken churches of the neighbourhood; notably to St. Mary of the Angels, a remote and ancient building whose very name, the Portiuncula or Little Portion, appealed to his sense of lowliness. It was here that he received his definite vocation. The date is disputed, but it was probably in 1206, when he was twenty-four, and certainly on St. Matthias's Day, the 24th of February, that he heard mass from a visiting priest and listened to the gospel words: "As ye go, preach, saying The kingdom of heaven is at hand. Heal the sick, cleanse the lepers, raise the dead, cast out devils: freely ye have received, freely give. Provide neither gold nor silver nor brass in your purses, nor scrip for your journey, neither two coats, neither shoes nor yet staves: for the workman is worthy of his meat." These are uncomfortable words, which most Christians in all ages have attempted to gloss over; but Francis determined to adopt them quite literally, as his marching orders for a new apostolate. They came to him as a direct, personal call from God, a clue to the way of life he had been seeking; in nakedness he would follow the naked Christ—*nudum Christum nudus sequere*—a phrase borrowed from Jerome by Bernard of Clairvaux, and later to be echoed by John Wesley at the start of his Savannah ministry.

For some time he remained alone in his remarkable purpose of living literally by the gospel. Bishop Guido and a few others continued to be sympathetic; Peter Bernardone continued to curse in baffled humiliation. Most people felt that Francis was either a saint or a madman, but they were quite unable to determine which. But one rich man of Assisi, a middle-aged town councillor called Bernard of Quintavalle, had watched the experiment with interest, and after about three years decided to put the sincerity of Francis to the test. Inviting him to spend the night at his magnificent *palazzo*, he arranged a bed for Francis in his own room, so that while pretending to be asleep he might watch what happened. Francis rose as soon as he thought that he was unobserved, and spent the night on his knees, repeating the words "My God and my all" with rapturous devotion. Next morning Bernard offered to join him permanently in his discipleship. They opened the gospel at random after hearing mass together, and the three texts which met their eyes were these: "If thou wilt be perfect, go and sell that thou hast," "Take nothing for your journey" and "If any man will come after me, let him deny himself and take up his cross and follow me." So Bernard sold his great possessions, gave to the poor and joined Francis in the ragged garments of a beggar. The ideal had at last been understood, and the years of loneliness were over; more disciples were recruited, the first of them Peter of Cataneo, a learned canon of Assisi; and when their number had reached seven, they divided into small groups for mission preaching, in which Francis himself set the example by going with Brother Giles into the Marches of Ancona. Whenever they reached a church the brothers stopped to pray: "We adore Thee, O Christ, and we bless Thee in all Thy churches that are in every place, for by Thy holy cross Thou hast redeemed the world." This with the Lord's Prayer was their only form of devotion, used in place of the long monastic offices, and it shows how firmly their thoughts were centred on Christ's Passion. Always rejoicing, they were never ribald and their gaiety was seldom far removed from tears; Francis would sometimes make a toy fiddle from two sticks and sing one of his gladsome songs, only to dissolve in weeping at the thought of the agonies of Christ.

But freelance evangelism was a dangerous occupation. Francis was too loyal to the Church to risk being expelled like Peter Waldo, and as soon as his disciples numbered twelve he deter-

mined to seek authority from Rome. To indicate the purpose of
the fraternity, he composed a simple Rule, couched for the most
part in those gospel precepts which had marked the stages of his
own conversion. No copy of this *Regula Primitiva* has survived;
but its contents can be disentangled from later documents with a
fair degree of certainty; and two points of capital importance are
disclosed. In the first place the "Penitents of Assisi," as they liked
to call themselves, were in no circumstances to degenerate into a
heretical or non-conformist sect; "all the brothers shall be
Catholics," and the Rule opens with a profession of obedience to
Pope Innocent and his successors. Throughout his life Francis
showed a marked reverence for the Church's ministry and sacraments, and at the end, in his closing Testament, he wrote as
follows: "The Lord gave and still gives me such faith, because of
their office, in priests who live under the discipline of the Holy
Roman Church, that if they persecuted me I would none the less
submit. And though I had as much wisdom as Solomon, if I
found poor and humble priests of this world, I would never
preach against their will in the parishes where they reside. These
and all others I wish to fear, love and honour as my lords . . .
because in this world the sole corporeal manifestation of God's
Son is His most holy Body and Blood . . . which they alone
administer." In the second place, Francis intended to found a
brotherhood, not of mendicants, but of labourers. The brothers
were to ply whatever honest trade they knew, or else to learn one
if they were unskilled; they were to earn their bread by casual
labour, and only in the last resort were they to have recourse to
the "table of the Lord" by begging. To Francis there was an
almost sacramental value in food given for charity, but he was
remorselessly opposed to indolence, and one of the great things
he did was to make honest poverty respectable. On the other
hand he refused to burden his disciples with detailed rules of
fasting; they were to eat whatever was set before them, whether
a dry crust or a sumptuous banquet; and to encourage sick
brothers he would himself sometimes eat beside them with a
hearty appetite. Only in one respect was his prohibition absolute:
the friars must never on any account touch money. Wages were
to be paid in kind, as they normally were to labouring men, and
anything not needed for immediate consumption was to be given
to the poor. Money in the eyes of Francis was a tainted object,
inextricably involved in the devilish process of laying up super-
fluities for the morrow, and on one occasion when a friar negli-
gently touched a coin that had been offered by someone at the
Portiuncula, he was told to take it in his mouth like a dog and

throw it on the dung-heap. For wealth was a positive hindrance
to the spirit, and if the friars were to reach the unchurched masses
they must themselves be the poorest of the poor. Every candidate
for admission must sell all his property; none was to hold
dominion over the others; and as they went they were to preach
saying: "Repent and bring forth fruits worthy of repentance, for
we shall shortly die." Shabby clothes patched with sackcloth were
to be the livery of the new Order; preaching must be demonstrated
in life. To sum up his intentions, Francis named his little band the
Friars Minor or Lesser Brethren; for "he that is greatest among
you, let him be as the younger." But in more light-hearted mood
he would call them his "knights of the round table" and "minstrels of the Lord."

Armed with what was an idealist manifesto rather than a
monastic constitution, Francis in 1210 betook himself to Rome.
Bursting unannounced into the Lateran Palace, he thrust his Rule
before the face of Innocent, who not unnaturally told him to go
away; Matthew Paris adds that the Pope told him to roll in the
mud with swine, and Francis obediently wallowed. But he had
the good fortune to meet Bishop Guido, who introduced him to
the saintliest member of the Curia, Cardinal John of St. Paul, and
a little conversation convinced the Cardinal that here was a
movement of immense spiritual value to the Church. Objections
were raised at a second and more formal meeting with the Pope:
to live without possessions was a fantastic and impossible ideal.
But Cardinal John replied: "If anyone says that a vow to observe
the gospel precepts contains something new or irrational or impossible of fulfilment, it is blasphemy against Christ the Author
of the gospel." Innocent took a closer look at the ragged creature
in front of him; it was the sort of man that he might himself have
become if he had followed out the teaching of his own treatise
On Contempt of the World. He told Francis to go and pray for
guidance, and in the meanwhile remembered a dream that he had
once had, of how the Lateran Church was tottering and a little
poor man came and propped it with his shoulder. For the great
Pope was in his own way a visionary, and his discernment was
quick to recognize that the witness of Francis could support a
decaying Church. He therefore granted a verbal sanction to the
Rule, authorizing the friars to preach repentance, which meant
that they were allowed to give moral exhortations, while doctrinal sermons were left to the ordained clergy; the orthodox
Humiliati had received similar permission nine years before, and
it was a faculty not infrequently bestowed on laymen. As a sign
of their authority, and also to place them under the Church's

formal discipline, Innocent ordered them to receive the lesser ton
sure; Francis, who was probably ordained deacon at the same time,
told the barber to make him an extremely small one, as he wanted
his brothers to have a share of his head; and it was understood
that Cardinal John would give them protection and advice.

Returning to Assisi, the little band settled at Rivo Torto near
the leper colony, whose inmates they tended in the intervals of
prayer, work and preaching. With a steady intake of recruits,
their cramped quarters grew embarrassingly crowded. But the
worst embarrassment came in 1212 when Clare, a rich heiress of
seventeen, eloped by night from her family mansion and asked
leave to join the brotherhood. Francis was accustomed to speak
to women with modestly averted eyes, and he once declared that
he knew only two feminine faces by sight; but in the small hours
of that hectic morning he usurped the bishop's privilege of
receiving Clare's profession as a nun. She was temporarily placed
with some Benedictine sisters, until a special convent could be
established for herself and a few companions at St. Damian's, and
thus the Franciscan "second order," the Order of Poor Ladies,
was begun. To be immured in a convent was the last thing that
Clare desired; she had wanted to wander with the brethren and to
nurse the sick; but such a life was impossible for women in the
conditions of the thirteenth century. Attempts were constantly
made to turn the Poor Ladies into regular Benedictine nuns,
owning communal property for their support; but in her own
convent Clare resisted these attempts, and until her death in 1253
she maintained a rigidly Franciscan standard. She persuaded
Innocent III to grant her the "privilege" of owning nothing, a
grant so unprecedented for women that the Pope drew up the
minute with his own hand. About the same time, Francis too was
in attendance on the Pope, having come to Rome for the Fourth
Lateran Council. He was deeply impressed by Innocent's opening
sermon, particularly by a passage where the preacher, after speaking of the threefold Passover that would cleanse the Church,
turned to expound the ninth chapter of Ezekiel; applying that
prophecy to the present situation, Innocent declared that his
audience were the men charged to smite the rebellious city, while
he himself was the writer with the ink-horn, whose duty it was
to mark the foreheads of those that grieved for the abominations
of Jerusalem; and the saving mark set upon them was to be the
letter Tau, the last and lowliest letter of the Hebrew alphabet,
shaped in the pattern of a cross. This mark, said Innocent, is worn
by those that have crucified the flesh; and Francis thenceforward
took it as the sign-manual of his Order.

Many others besides Clare wished to associate themselves with the new movement, but were prevented by social or family ties from adopting the full Franciscan life. Francis had no objection to marriage with its consequent responsibilities, and he understood that absolute poverty could only be practised by a few men with a highly specialized vocation. When adherents were attracted by his preaching, he had to provide them with some simple guidance, which would enable them to live as far as possible by his ideals while remaining at their stations in the world. About 1214 he wrote an *Open Letter to all the Faithful*, urging them to practise frequent communion, almsgiving, abstinence, simplicity and love; it might almost have been the rule for an early Methodist society, and it was prompted by the same need that drove Wesley to organize his followers in fellowship. And so, alongside the Friars and the Poor Ladies, vowed to complete poverty in their itinerant preaching or secluded prayer, there arose a "third order" of Franciscan Tertiaries, lay people who would apply the gospel ethic in politics or trade. Among its earliest members were Giacoma, a wealthy Roman widow, and Orlando of Chiusi, who gave Francis the unusual present of a mountain; it was one of the few gifts that Francis accepted, and Mount La Verna became his holiest retreat. Later, the Tertiaries were to include sovereigns like Louis of France and Elizabeth of Hungary, together with the missionary Raymond Lull and the poet Dante. Elizabeth took the sick poor to her castle for nursing, and when released from State duties, she retired to a cottage where she worked with her own hands. Always fruitful in good works, the Tertiaries at Florence made it their first care to found a hospital, in which they could themselves attend the sick and unemployed. Their earliest surviving Rule dates from the year 1228, but this seems to have been based on a still more primitive version, with features strangely reminiscent of the Society of Friends: drab garments, no taking of oaths or bearing arms, no attendance at banquets or stage-plays, only two meals a day, with extra fasts and regular times of prayer. It was these lay followers who swelled the enormous numbers at the early chapter meetings, so that in 1221 no less than 5,000 persons attended.

Meanwhile, Francis continued preaching, often in the open air but always by permission of the local clergy, and sometimes visiting as many as four or five different places in a single day. His sermons were described as "penetrating the heart like fire," but so utterly spontaneous that people afterwards found difficulty in remembering the words that he had used. No respecter of persons, he chose to speak on clerical indiscipline when asked to address an assembly of prelates, and on this subject "said so much so plainly that he was enabled to bring them a very salutary confusion and edification." When preaching before the Pope and Cardinals, he grew so excited that he began to dance; his adviser at the Curia had prepared a suitable sermon for him to deliver, but he scrapped it in favour of a straight talk on the shortcomings of the hierarchy, opening the Psalter at random to pick out the text: "My confusion is continually before me." No one objected to his plain speaking, for the preacher was so obviously humble and sincere; "more than a saint among saints," writes his biographer Thomas of Celano, "he was among sinners as one of themselves." It was for this reason that he had a strong objection to book-learning for the friars; he did allow Brother Antony of Padua to teach theology at Bologna, "provided that studies do not extinguish the spirit of holy prayer," and his Testament pays honour to "all theologians and those who minister to us the Word of God;" but scholarship implied the possession of books and the enjoyment of leisure, neither of which was compatible with the Franciscan ideal, and worst of all, it was hard for a scholar to mix on equal terms with tramps. On one occasion, Francis gave a poor woman the New Testament in which the friars read their lessons, when there was nothing else at hand to give her; and he frequently had to be restrained from parting with his tunic to someone who seemed poorer than himself. Impulsive and free as the wind, he took his guidance from the momentary promptings of the Spirit; coming to a cross-road on one of his missionary journeys, he prayed and told Brother Masseo to twirl like a top in order to determine their direction. When he felt a pang of regret for the sort of family life that he had denied himself, his consolation was to make a wife and children out of snowmen. Games were almost a part of the Franciscan practice; Brother Juniper, greeted by a pompous procession on his arrival at Rome, played see-saw with some local urchins until the disillusioned cavalcade departed. "Let the friars take care," Francis said, "not to appear gloomy and downcast like hypocrites, but let them be joyous and mirthful, as those that rejoice in the Lord, and let them be becomingly courteous; for courtesy is an attribute of God Himself . . . and is the sister of charity." In summer-time Francis often slept out in the open, and in winter his usual abode was a hut of clay and wattle; he lived close to nature, and once asked for a law to provide extra food at Christmas for the birds and beasts of burden. This was not the sort of sentimentality for which it is frequently mistaken; the love of Francis was expended on unlovely creatures like worms, because they reminded him of the lowliness of Christ; and it sprang, as did everything else in his life, from love of the God who had created them. It was thus that he tamed a ravenous wolf at Gubbio, and turned it into the town's pet animal; thus, in his most familiar act of apparent folly, that he preached to his sisters the birds.

Year by year the friars foregathered at Whitsun for their annual chapter meeting in the Portiuncula. Dominic, who knew and respected Francis, attended the chapter of 1218, only to be appalled at the lack of any arrangements to supply food for a gathering of thousands; but he was obliged to pay a reluctant tribute to Franciscan optimism, when the local farmers turned out with a steady stream of food-waggons. At the same chapter, strong pressure was brought upon Francis to assimilate his following to more conventional societies by adopting one of the older monastic Rules. Several of the friars desired the greater security of a settled life, and in this they were supported by Cardinal Ugolino, who had become adviser to the Order after the death of Cardinal John. A relative of Pope Innocent, an able lawyer and theologian, handsome in appearance and about sixty years of age, Ugolino was a warm admirer of Francis but at the same time a clear-sighted churchman, wishing to use the Order for a reform of clerical life and theological education. He made the amazing suggestion that the friars should take the lead by accepting bishoprics; to which Francis replied that his brethren were called Minors in order to remind them that they were the least of all men, and that if they were to bear fruit for the Church, they must not forsake the humility of Christ. But they were by now an international fraternity, and already in 1217 the chapter had had to adopt a rudimentary organization by dividing itself into provinces and appointing officers. These were called ministers, since Francis objected to the title of master or prior as savouring of pride. Some of the brethren were sent on missions north of the Alps, where their ignorance of the language and their weird appearance caused them to be mistaken for heretics. Francis himself had for long desired to evangelize the Moslems, but two previous attempts to reach them had been frustrated by storm and illness. Now in 1219 he set out with a dozen companions to join the crusading army at Damietta on the Nile. Shocked by the troops' morality he prophesied defeat, but although he knew that there a price on every Christian head, he left for the Sultan's camp, singing as he crossed from one army to the other, "Though I walk through the valley of the shadow of death I will fear no evil." Melek-el-Kamil, Sultan of Egypt, was more impressed than the crusaders had been by the eloquence of Francis; forbidding him to undergo a trial by ordeal, he offered presents which were refused, and a free pass to Palestine which was accepted; and although remaining unconverted he asked Francis at parting for his prayers. This result was a bitter disappointment, ending neither in conversion nor in martyrdom. But news arrived that five of the friars had been martyred in Morocco, and heartened by their courage Francis spent some time in visiting the Holy Land. From there he was recalled by an urgent message, brought by Brother Stephen, that at home the affairs of the Order were in a state of crisis.

During his absence the vicars, aided and abetted by Ugolino, had imposed regular fast-days, threatening the spontaneity of the movement; the Poor Ladies had been subjected to a strict form of Benedictine claustration, and Brother Philip, placed in charge of them, had obtained a papal privilege which allowed him to excommunicate their enemies. Slight in themselves, the changes indicated a radical reorientation of purpose, for what had begun as a glorified picnic was becoming too much of an ecclesiastical institution. Still worse the holy vagabonds, no longer content to be wandering minstrels, were trying to settle down in occupation of permanent dwellings. When he reached Bologna early in 1220, Francis found some of them in possession of a house, and at once ordered them to quit. But outvoted at the annual chapter, he resigned the leadership; it was a sad but wise decision, for he lacked the administrative gifts that were needed to control his now enormous following; and henceforward he devoted himself to showing by personal example what he conceived to be the Christian ideal. Meanwhile a papal bull imposed one year's novitiate on would-be members, and prohibited those who were formally professed from ever abandoning the Order. In 1221 Francis was persuaded to draft a new rule, the so-called *Regula Prima*, to take account of the changed conditions; but as a compromise it pleased neither party, and was never made official. Finally in 1223 there came the *Regula Secunda*, a veritable capitulation to the new demands; it allowed a man's good-will to take the place of parting with his entire possessions; and whereas the friars had up till now gone barefoot, in a single tunic with breeches and a knotted cord, the new Rule permitted them a second tunic, sandals and a large cape. Francis was obliged to sign it with a troubled heart, after his own proposals had been conveniently lost. But at the very end of his life he published a Testament, recalling the early days of utter destitution, bidding his disciples to follow the simple gospel without gloss or abatement, and above all prohibiting the ownership of property or acceptance of papal favours.

The winter of 1223 was spent at Greccio, where Francis constructed the very first Christmas crib, and invited the villagers to see the animals gathered round the manger. He was now going blind, and although little more than forty, his sparse frame was racked by illness. But he passed the next autumn fasting on his mountain retreat of La Verna in company with Brother Leo and a few of his oldest friends, and in constant meditation on the sufferings of Christ. During the watches of a September night there came to him the vision of a crucified seraph; and when the vision left him, the five wounds of Christ were in his hands and feet and side. He attempted to conceal them, but they were observed after his death by witnesses. And it was now, tortured by pain and fever, in a tumbled-down hut where the mice ran over his body, that he composed his exultant *Canticle of the Sun*. Familiar as the English hymn, "All creatures of our God and King," its delicate phrases can never be adequately translated. There is a doubt, perhaps deliberate, whether God is to be praised by or because of His creation; and there is a childlike touch which, while calling the other creatures brother and sister, gives to the chief luminary the courteous name of "Mr. Sun." It began a literature, for it is the first great Italian poem, and it inaugurated a whole school of art. The stanza on the tenderness of those who forgive others was written after the rest, to reconcile the Bishop and Podestà of Assisi, and the concluding verse which welcomes Sister Death was written by Francis in imminent prospect of his own decease. Sung by Brother Pacifico, ex-poet-laureate and "king of verses," the Canticle expressed, more than any writing in prose, the true Franciscan spirit; it was used by the friars when they went out preaching, and it consoled their leader's closing hours.

Francis had now been taken charge of by Brother Elias, a good friend, but as the event was to show, a poor disciple; the son of an artisan, later a law student at Bologna, brilliant, charming and a good preacher, it was Elias who tried to corrupt the Order by making it into a world power. For the moment, he did what he could to alleviate his master's pain, but the best medical advice was to cauterize the eyes, an added torture which Francis bore unflinchingly. He was taken under armed escort to Assisi, and when the end seemed near, removed to his beloved Portiuncula; it was 3rd October, 1226; the brethren started to read him the Passion according to St. John, and he died just after sunset, with a multitude of larks singing.

Many years later, Brother Peter Pettignano dreamt that he saw a vast procession of apostles, saints and martyrs, their eyes all

bent upon the ground as they tried carefully to tread in the foot-
steps of the Saviour; and at the end there came a ragged little
figure, barefoot and brown-robed, who alone walked steadily and
easily in Christ's very steps. The conformity of Francis to his
Master is underlined in all the early biographies; and although
some of the Reformers were shocked at the comparison, the
sceptical Ernest Renan has called him "the one perfect Christian."
His ideal was pitched too high for anyone but a saint to follow it.
Apart from a few heroic souls, the later history of the Franciscan
Order is one of perverted purposes and declining zeal, while by a
process of almost inevitable compromise, the disciples of Francis
defied his prohibitions in their acceptance of property, privilege
and learning.

The first task was to remove his influence from earth by staging
a transcendent apotheosis. Elias left the nominal leadership for a
time to a devout nonentity called John Parenti, while he himself
advertised the stigmata and collected money to build a costly
shrine. Cardinal Ugolino became Pope Gregory IX in 1227; some
sixty years before, the authority of canonization had been formally entrusted to the Holy See, in order to avoid the chaos of
competing local cults; and in 1228 Gregory declared Francis to be
a Saint. Two years later, Gregory pronounced that the Saint's
Testament was not binding on his followers; he allowed them the
use of property including books; and he directed that they might
employ financial agents to collect and handle money for their immediate needs. In 1245, Pope Innocent IV relaxed the Rule still
further, permitting money to be spent not only for strict necessities but also for conveniences, so that the friars were relieved of
all material insecurity; a fictitious appearance of poverty was
maintained by his assertion that their goods belonged to the
papacy, unless the donor expressly kept control himself, but the
arrangement was mere legal cover for a betrayal of principle.
Meanwhile Elias had been elected Minister General of the Order
in 1232. Regarding poverty not as an end in itself, but simply as a
means to the great purpose of the Order in the conversion of
souls, he was prepared to allow considerable modification of
practice, encouraging scholarship and a university training for the
friars, providing houses and the requisite paraphernalia for settled
mission work, and if reports were true, himself devoting time to
research in alchemy. But he antagonized the Order by a dictatorial attitude, refusing to hold general chapters, superseding the
provincial ministers by sending out his own visitors, and all the
while living in luxurious state, with page-boys and a first-class
chef, as if he had been some exalted Prince of the Church. Revolt

broke out in 1239, when the chapter met on its own authority to depose him, and next year he was succeeded as Minister General by the English Haymo of Faversham. Chapter meetings became triennial events, with a membership that was partly official and partly elected, and like the Methodists, the Franciscans believed in a frequent change of office-bearers and regular movement of personnel; but Haymo made the conditions of entry so severe that laymen practically stopped joining, and as they were now prohibited from holding office, the Order became distinctly clerical. The original companions of Francis, several of whom still survived, had withdrawn into seclusion; but they wrote down their recollections of the early days, and in the mass of conflicting documents some of this eye-witness material has been preserved. Thomas of Celano, a safe and stylish author, was commissioned to write the first official life of Francis in 1228; here he omitted all account of the dissensions of the latter years, but in a second biography, composed in 1246, he incorporated fresh matter to emphasize the primitive ideal. For by then the radical wing of the movement, the "spirituals" or Fraticelli as they came to be called, had recovered the ascendancy, and in 1247 one of their number became Minister General. This was John of Parma, who had formerly lectured at Paris and Bologna, but now travelled about vigorously on foot and washed vegetables with the brethren. "You have come appropriately," said Brother Giles, "but too late." John was unfortunately sympathetic to the prophecies of Joachim of Fiore, who had predicted the rise of a new spiritual Church about the year 1260; Joachim did have a touch akin to that of Francis, for he once said that a true monk reckons nothing his own except his lute; but when his predictions were applied to themselves by the spiritual Franciscans, they were condemned by the Church as heretical, and John of Parma had to resign in 1255. He was succeeded by the moderate-minded Bonaventura, under whom the movement for scholarship and a settled life was consolidated. The new General's biography of the founder, largely derived from Celano, was approved by the chapter of 1266, which ordered all previous lives to be destroyed, so as to obliterate the memory of the primitive tradition. Bonaventura approved of large Franciscan houses in the towns, as the most efficient system of working; he defended the acceptance of papal privileges, to protect the friars from interference by the local clergy; and above all he welcomed the new attitude to learning. Francis had forbidden his disciples to have even a single book. "This," said Bonaventura, "is what has made me most to love the Franciscan life, that it resembles the rise and progress of the Church, which

began with simple fishermen, and then advanced to the most
famous and most learned doctors." "Paris, Paris," muttered
Brother Giles, "you have destroyed Assisi."

The Franciscan Order produced a number of outstanding
theologians, and however incongruous such a development
might be, they did yeoman service in rescuing academic discipline
from the rationalist attacks of sceptical secular professors. Bonaventura himself, the Seraphic Doctor, obtained his D.D. at Paris
in the teeth of opposition from the non-monastic teachers; he
commented extensively on the *Sentences* of Peter Lombard, and
expounded a mystical theory of knowledge in his *Ascent of the
Mind to God*. More conservative than his contemporary Aquinas,
he tended to resist the new Aristotelianism; but in company with
Aquinas and most of the schoolmen, he denied the doctrine of
the Virgin's Immaculate Conception. His own master, Alexander
of Hales, had been a professor at Paris before joining the Franciscans, and when he did so in 1231 he retained his chair, thus turning the Franciscan convent into one of the University's official
schools. Alexander's main achievement was to formulate a doctrine of the Treasury of Merit, comprising the surplus virtues of
Christ and the saints from which, by means of indulgence, the
Church could transfer a credit balance to more needy mortals in
remission, not of the guilt, but of the penalty for sin. Born in
Gloucestershire, Alexander was an Englishman, as was the more
famous Roger Bacon, who studied at Oxford, taught at Paris,
and became a Franciscan about 1251. One of the first to lecture
on Aristotle, Bacon developed an interest in experimental science,
which he described as queen of all the intellectual pursuits.
He is credited, though somewhat dubiously, with the invention
of gunpowder, the telescope and the thermometer. His encyclopaedic knowledge embraced not only philosophy and theology,
but also mathematics, geography, perspective, physiology and
alchemy, together with Greek and Hebrew grammar, of which he
emphasized the importance for a proper understanding of the
Bible. In constant conflict with his superiors because of an irate
temperament, Bacon's influence was not as wide as it might otherwise have been, but his scientific experiments were a remarkable
portent of modernity; in this he was typical of the Oxford Franciscan school, whose practical bent might perhaps be justified
from the Franciscan love of nature. It had already been made
famous by the teaching of Robert Grosseteste, who lectured to
the friars for ten years after their arrival at Oxford in 1224; and
Grosseteste was not only a scientist but also a teacher of homiletics, who brought new preaching methods over from Paris, and

according to Eccleston, enabled the friars to "make rapid progress in acute queries and moral tales that were suitable for sermons". To the same school belonged Duns Scotus, the Subtle Doctor, a native of Roxburgh in Scotland, whose recondite subtleties led Renaissance humanists to coin the word "dunce" in ridicule of the whole scholastic approach. Duns Scotus was the first theologian of importance to accept the Immaculate Conception of Mary, devotion to whom was popular among the friars; but the Dominicans continued to be conservatively cautious, one of them asking: "Do you want to turn her into a goddess?" In the fourteenth century, the Franciscans produced a further succession of scholars, notably Nicholas of Lyra, a Parisian master, who studied Hebrew and rabbinics, discarded allegory in favour of the plain literal sense, and wrote postils or Bible commentaries which remained in vogue until the Reformation. Above all there was William of Occam, an English friar of the Oxford school, who joined the spiritual left wing after being summoned to the papal Curia on suspicion of heresy; supporting the Empire in its renewed struggle with the Papacy, he published propaganda pamphlets against the temporal power and possessions of the Church. A distant precursor of the Reformation in doctrine as well as politics, Occam was an extreme nominalist, denying reality to universals and holding that we can acquire knowledge only of the individual, from which it follows that personal faith and not discursive reason is the way of approach to God. He tended to divorce religion from the other activities of the human mind, and while on the one hand this allowed free scope to science without theological presuppositions, on the other hand it emphasized the all-sufficiency of individual faith. Luther, who owed much to Occam, considered him the most important of the schoolmen.

All of this intellectual development had been unforeseen and unintended by the Povrello of Assisi, but it did not serve to ease the continued tension between the strict and lax interpretations of the Rule. Bonaventura, while he patronized learning, also tried without great success to check obvious abuses. The lax friars had taken to going about with a servant who carried the collecting box, and their demands had become so importunate that people said they would prefer to fall into the hands of robbers; at the same time the Order was building magnificent houses, with lands and permanent endowments, so that their poverty was reduced to a legal fiction which gave them wealth without responsibility under the technical cover of papal ownership. In 1274 the Council of Lyons suppressed or amalgamated a number of small mendicant societies, leaving only the four great Orders of Franciscans,

Dominicans, Carmelites and Austin Friars. Bonaventura died during the session of the Council, and when a rumour spread that the mendicant Orders were to be compelled to accept corporate property, the spirituals took it as a signal for revolt. Some of them were imprisoned in the Marches of Ancona, and a fierce persecution quickly spread into Tuscany and Provence. In 1279 Pope Nicholas III issued a decretal, stating that whatever was given to the friars belonged to the Church, which allowed them the use of it—the so-called *usus pauper*—for purposes of bare necessity; after long debate the decretal was reaffirmed in 1312, but the spirituals wanted the primitive discipline, and in Provence they began to resist by force. Pope John XXII ordered them to obey their superiors, handing the recalcitrants over to the Inquisition; four were burnt at Marseilles in 1318, and other executions followed. In Italy the Fraticelli simply separated from the Order and defied authority. Two crippling decretals were then issued by Pope John in the years 1322–23. The first of these withdrew from the Franciscans the privilege of holding property in the name of the Church, which deprived them of their legal cover; the second declared it heretical to believe that Christ and the apostles had no possessions, and thus made the basic Franciscan ideal a heresy. John was not particularly happy in his doctrinal definitions; in his later years he pronounced that after death the soul sleeps along with the body until the general resurrection; and when the theologians of Paris pointed out that this would make nonsense of the intercession of the saints, he retracted his views with the excuse, remarkable for a Pope, that he was only a canon lawyer and not a trained divine. In combating the spiritual Franciscans, he had contradicted his predecessors and created an entirely novel heresy. The whole Order revolted under its Minister General, Michael of Cesena; and the argument became involved in the contest between Papacy and Empire, with Occam putting out his political tracts on the imperial and Franciscan side. It was this alignment of forces which united the two demands, so urgently renewed by Wycliffe, for clerical poverty and for State control of the Church. The debate was still raging when the Black Death, a virulent bubonic plague, broke out in 1348; it destroyed well over a quarter of the population of Europe, and nearly 14,000 Franciscans are reported to have perished. With this enormous loss religious fervour declined; most of them submitted to authority and accepted the communal ownership of possessions. But a small group in remote hermitages, the Friars of the Strict Observance, kept the original discipline alive until in 1517 they were at last permitted to form a separate and distinct Order.

It was a melancholy sequel to the splendid self-denial of the founder's life. But under the strict ideal of Francis his Order could never have been numerous. With a modified and more human standard his followers, as popular preachers, learned theologians and foreign missionaries, performed a wider if less exalted service to the world.

CHAPTER XII

THE DOMINICANS; AQUINAS; AND THE GERMAN MYSTICS

INNOCENT TRIED TO SAVE THE WORLD BY VIOLENCE, FRANCIS by humility; while the one exalted justice, the other practised love. But in addition to strength of hand or heart, there was another power that might be used in the service of God's Kingdom: the power of the mind, the path of sanctified scholarship, and it was this that Dominic deliberately chose. As a result, the Dominican character has a less universal appeal than the Franciscan; it moves, not in bright Italian sunshine, but in a sombre Spanish gloom; and the Spaniard Dominic inevitably suffers by comparison with the Povrello of Assisi. Francis preached to the birds, but Dominic once plucked a sparrow alive, because he thought there was a devil in it when it hindered him from reading. His canonization, longer delayed than that of Francis, took place thirteen years after he had died, and it was then grimly celebrated by the Bishop of Toulouse with the burning of a poor woman and several heretics. But although he abhorred the devil of heresy, Dominic had a fervent love for the souls of men, including Jews and pagans; he never himself served as an inquisitor, and on the sole occasion when he attended a burning, he managed to save one of its victims from the flames. As a young student, he sold his books and other possessions to feed the starving in a famine. His personal poverty was as strict as that of Francis, but he adopted it less quixotically, and with the perfectly practical purpose of combating heretical teachers on their chosen ground. The great object of his Order was preaching and teaching; its aim was clearly understood and unanimously accepted, with the result that it was never split by those sharp dissensions which were later to divide the Franciscans; and it enjoyed so representative a form of government that the Dominican constitutions have been regarded as a model of the English Parliamentary system. As men of action, Dominic's followers had little time for contemplation, though they did produce a few outstanding mystics; as scholars, they found their crowning glory in Aquinas, whose theology has remained standard in the Catholic Church. Dominic himself possessed a strong and decisive will-power, but he was at the same time both humble and human. His humility is shown by the fact that he thrice refused a bishopric. His humanity appears in the remark made to Jordan of Saxony, but expunged in 1242 from Jordan's biography by order of the Chapter General, to the effect that he would rather talk to young women than to old ones. Above all, with his zeal for conversion, he stands in the true evangelical strain of the Middle Ages.

Born in 1170 at Calaruega in Castile, Dominic may have been related to the noble family of Guzman. After ten years' study at Palencia he became a Canon of Osma, his native diocese; here in 1199, with the encouragement of Innocent III, the bishop had turned his cathedral chapter into a community of canons regular, living under the Augustinian Rule; and thus, although his work was that of a normal priest, Dominic was subject from the outset to monastic discipline. Rapidly rising to the post of sub-prior, he accompanied his bishop on a royal embassy to the South of France, where they lodged in the house of an Albigensian at Toulouse, and were thus forcibly made aware of the need for mission preachers. In 1204 Bishop Diego, with Dominic among his companions, found himself at Rome, on returning from an embassy to Denmark; his purpose at the Curia was to resign the see of Osma, in order that he might be free to travel to South Russia and there evangelize the Cumans. But Innocent was already concerned with evangelization nearer home, having entrusted the Cistercians with the formidable task of converting the heretics of Languedoc; he strongly suggested to his visitors that their duty was to reinforce the mission there; and in order to align himself with its existing personnel, Diego took the Cistercian habit. The work was largely at a standstill, for abbots and papal legates were too lordly to appeal to simple folk whose chief complaint was the pretensions of the clergy; moreover, most of the local bishops and parsons had become notorious for their ineffective indolence, while the wealth of the Church was regarded as an offence against apostolic poverty. Dominic quickly realized that preaching must be exemplified in conduct, that missioners must surpass heretics in austere simplicity of life. He therefore not only preached with rousing fervour, but also went about barefoot, living on such alms as God might send him. On 17th November, 1206, Innocent approved this mendicant variety of faith mission. It was the first time that such a venture had been sanctioned by the papacy, for up till now priests and monks had required some visible resources, and poverty was a new type of title to an ecclesiastical post. But it was the age of great experi-

ments, and in his far-sighted vision Innocent was ahead of his
contemporaries. The Cistercians returned to their comfortable
abbeys; Diego died at Osma in the year 1207; and Dominic was
left as virtual leader of the mission.

He had already found an enthusiastic ally in Fulk, the Bishop
of Toulouse. This remarkable man was a converted troubadour,
who took his two sons with him into a monastery and then found
himself promoted to a mitre. He maintained a special interest in
both preaching and education, choosing suitable deputies to perform these essential parts of a bishop's duty. Schools had almost
been monopolized by the heretics, who attracted the lesser
nobility by providing a free education for their daughters. With
Fulk's support, Dominic opened a house at Prouille in 1206,
where girls might be taught under Catholic direction, and this
house, with a few friars attached to it, became the first Dominican
convent. Fulk appointed the learned Alexander Stavensby, later
to become Bishop of Coventry, as master of his cathedral school,
where Dominic and his companions attended theological lectures. But the most valuable thing that Fulk did was to authorize
the friars as a corps of diocesan missioners, with a commission to
preach and convert heretics, and with some tithes and churches
for their support. It was dangerous work, ever since the murder
of the papal legate in 1207 and the launching of the Albigensian
Crusade; but to those who expressed concern for his personal
safety, Dominic laughingly remarked that he had not yet earned
a martyr's crown. And in 1214 Simon of Montfort provided him
with headquarters by putting the castle of Cassanel at his disposal.

The Fourth Lateran Council took place in 1215. Here Dominic
laid before Pope Innocent III his scheme for an Order of well-
educated preaching friars, who would take the world as their
parish and be directly subject to the papacy. It was a scheme
entirely after the Pope's heart, and already to some extent
sanctioned by his blessing. The tenth canon of the Council extended Fulk's experiment to the entire Church by enjoining all
bishops to provide apt preachers, who would spread the Word of
God abroad by sermon and example. But however extensive the
effort, it was still to be carried out at the diocesan level; there was
no mention of forming a distinctive Order; and against Innocent's
wishes, as it seems, but under pressure from the existing Orders
and some of the bishops, the Council enacted in its thirteenth
canon that no new religious Order might be founded. Dominic
was therefore advised to place his brethren, now numbering
sixteen, under one of the older Rules; as a Canon of Osma he was
himself already subject to the so-called Rule of St. Augustine;

and this was sufficiently vague in its terms to allow a wide flexi-
bility of detailed interpretation. His friars thus technically became
a group of Augustinian Canons; that is to say, they were priests
under monastic discipline, with a vocation to serve the world in a
predominantly pastoral capacity. Unlike the older monks, they
were not to lead a cloistered existence, but to go out into the
parishes and preach. They did perform the monastic round of
choir offices, but in a simple and speedy fashion, so as to leave
their time free for other work. And whereas the monks had made
manual labour a staple part of their routine, the Dominicans
explicitly replaced this with scholarship and study. Their practical
objective is emphasized in the early constitutions: "our Order
was founded chiefly for the purpose of preaching and the salvation of souls." Hence a large discretion was allowed to the
conventual priors in releasing brethren from their monastic
obligations; and "all the offices in Church shall be shortened, lest
the friars lose the spirit of devotion or their studies be in any way
hindered." For the actual conduct of their services, the Dominicans borrowed much from the customs of Prémontré; here a very
similar group of canons regular had been founded, in 1120, by
the great preacher Norbert who, like Luther after him, is said to
have been converted during a thunderstorm. But the bulk of the
Dominican constitutions were peculiar to themselves, derived in
part from Dominic's own organizing genius, and in part from
the learned assistance of those of the friars who had been trained
in canon law.

Innocent's successor Honorius III expressly sanctioned the
Dominicans by papal bulls, dated December 1216 and January
1217; and taking a phrase from the festal hymn of the Apostles,
he declared that they were to be "champions of the Faith and
true lights of the world." There was an immediate and rapid
expansion of the Order, reaching to Spain, France, Italy, Germany,
Poland, Hungary and England by 1221. Dominic took particular
pains to locate his friars in the great University centres. In 1217
he sent a colony to the Rue St. Jacques at Paris, where in a few
years, by recruitment among students and teachers, their number
had grown to one hundred and twenty. Bologna was another early
citadel, as were Rome and Madrid. Distinctive constitutions for
the growing community were formulated by the chapter general
of 1220, but a courageous faith continued to be its motive power.
When the novice Buonviso of Plaisance was ordered to preach in
his native town, he pleaded that he was as yet untrained and in-
experienced: "go in faith," said Dominic, "the Lord will be with
you and will place His word upon your lips;" and the mission

proved so successful that it gained three recruits for the Order. Dominic himself was constantly engaged in travel, but worn out by many labours and frequent journeys, he fell ill on his way to preach to the Hungarian pagans; next year, when no more than fifty-one, he died at Bologna on 6th August, 1221, exhorting his followers to "show charity, maintain humility and accept voluntary poverty," and promising that he would be more useful to them after death than during his life-time. His spiritual daughter Cecilia Caesarini described him as a man "of middle stature and slender build, with a handsome face and roseate complexion, red hair and beard, and fine eyes." She continued: "his forehead and eyelashes were irradiated with a sort of splendour, which made all men respect and love him. He was ever smiling and cheerful, except when moved to pity by a neighbour's affliction. He had long, beautiful hands; his voice was full, sweet and sonorous; he never became bald, and had only a few white hairs." Friends spoke of his devout life and passion for saving souls; they said that he was always talking either to God or else about Him. His learning was almost exclusively theological, which in the language of those times means Biblical, and he knew much of St. Matthew's Gospel and the Pauline Epistles by heart. Personal holiness was combined in him with wisdom; firm faith, boundless energy and steady optimism made him a determined leader of men. Before his birth his mother, like Bernard's, is said to have dreamt that she was bearing a dog-whelp, with a lighted torch in its jaws that would enkindle the world; and by a play on words, his followers came to be known as *Domini canes*, "hounds of the Lord."

Their chapter general met annually at Whitsun, with full and final authority over the entire Order; it had power to discipline the office-bearers and even to depose the Master General, although he was elected ostensibly for life. In 1228 arrangements were made to secure a still more democratic government, by enacting that any change in the constitutions must be approved by three successive general chapters, the first composed of the provincial priors, and the two others of elected representatives. On important occasions, such as the choice of a General, both priors and elected members sat together. Unlike the General, who acted as the Order's permanent executive, the conventual priors were changed frequently, being chosen by the inmates of their convent. The provincial prior was appointed by the chapter of his province, consisting of the conventual priors accompanied by a representative from every convent, together with the Doctors of Divinity and those friars who held a roving commission as Preachers General. And in order to correct and discipline the individual convents, the provincial chapter nominated four friars as visitors each year. No other medieval body depended so much on officers elected by their constituencies; in theory all friars were equally eligible for the highest posts. This remarkably modern constitution was rearranged on more logical lines about 1240 by the third General, the great canon lawyer Raymond of Penafort, and his revision remained in force until 1924. Officially the Dominicans were known as the Order of Preachers, a title which up till then had been used collectively for the episcopate.

Within a century, the Dominicans had produced nearly 450 bishops and archbishops, a dozen cardinals and two Popes— Innocent V and Benedict XI; they were eagerly employed by the Church in a wide variety of assignments, as inquisitors, royal confessors, papal legates, missionaries. But they maintained their primary devotion to scholarship. Every convent was obliged to provide theological teaching, to which clerics from outside the Order were freely admitted. Centres of advanced study were organized for the more promising among the friars, usually but not always in connexion with an existing university, where Dominicans came to play an important part as Divinity Professors. They disliked the responsibility of spiritual oversight among the nuns who formed their Second Order, vainly trying to shelve their duties towards all the nunneries except for Prouille and one other; but although they obtained release by a papal bull of 1252, women continued to be drawn to the Dominican life, and the bull was abrogated after fifteen years. For lay associates, a Third Order analogous to that of St. Francis was formally constituted in 1285, having been in semi-official existence for some considerable time before. The duty of preaching to the laity was sedulously observed, in the parish churches or the open air when opportunity offered, and above all in the convent chapels, which were plain rectangular buildings designed explicitly for preaching. In the thirteenth century sermons for the first time became really popular, forsaking the classical models of patristic pulpit oratory, and decked out with quotations, minute divisions and illustrative anecdotes, so as to appeal to an unlettered congregation. Friction resulted with the parochial clergy, when the friars thus stole their thunder; people sought from the Dominicans, not only preaching, but also absolution and burial; and until the papacy intervened in 1300 to delimit their responsibilities, there were unedifying squabbles at funerals, when both friar and parish priest tried to collect the corpse-present for burying the body. Manuals were issued by the friars for the guidance of preachers and confessors, together with various aids to Bible study. Led by Hugh of St.

Cher, the Dominicans at Paris corrected the Vulgate in 1236, to provide what is still the basis of the present text. They also prepared the earliest concordance of the Bible, a work of minute and co-operative scholarship which was particularly congenial to their Order, and they compiled complete commentaries on all the scriptural books. They even seem to have begun translating the Bible into French, until the chapter general of 1242, for fear of the taint of heresy, prohibited vernacular translations. Nor was it merely in Europe that they concerned themselves with active propagation of the gospel. Overseas they were energetic missionaries, reaching the Holy Land in 1222, where their knowledge of Oriental languages made them highly successful among Jacobites, Maronites and Nestorians as well as Moslems. Three years later they were busy in Morocco where, like the Franciscans, they added to the roll of martyrs. In 1249 King Louis sent a Dominican embassy to the Mongol Khan at Karakorum, and although they had little success, they were followed there four years later by the Franciscan William of Rubruquis. By 1312 they had organized a Society of Pilgrim Brothers for missions to the farther East. The Orthodox communities of Greece and the Balkans, together with the pagans of Lithuania and Russia, were among their spheres of operation. And all of this evangelistic enterprise was based on serious linguistic study of Greek, Arabic and the other local vernaculars.

It was thus as a learned community that the Dominicans gave their greatest service to the Church. But here also they suffered from friction, when the older academic authorities resented their intrusion. At Paris the Chancellor of the cathedral had the technical right of conferring the *licentia docendi* or degree, but the teaching masters had limited his power by forming themselves into a corporation and refusing to admit any person of whom they disapproved. In case of disagreement they possessed the ultimate weapon of strike action, and they used it in 1229, after a tavern brawl, by decreeing a suspension of lectures and then the dispersal of the students. The Chancellor retaliated by conferring a degree on the Dominicans' theological lecturer, whose convent thus became an officially authorized school; and in 1231, after there had been a return to work, two regent masters in theology, John of St. Giles and Alexander of Hales, joined the mendicant orders, Dominican and Franciscan respectively, without resigning from their public chairs. This development was welcomed by the papacy, which in 1250 instructed the Chancellor to ignore the wishes of the other masters and grant degrees to as many friars as he himself considered qualified. It was an attempt to bring higher education more definitely under Church control. But the secular teachers resented this interference with their privileges, all the more bitterly because the friars' lectures drew larger audiences than their own; with a racy and popular approach, combined with sound learning, the friars easily filled their lecture-rooms, while the seculars were left in empty halls like sparrows alone upon the roof-tops. By 1256 feelings had become so acrimonious that for several months Paris University withheld its degrees from both Bonaventura and Aquinas. At Oxford there was similar friction from a slightly different cause. The friars were not accustomed to take an arts course, but the University statutes demanded, as they still demand in Scotland, that a graduate in theology must first become a graduate in arts. After a long struggle, it was agreed that candidates otherwise qualified could be dispensed from fulfilling this demand.

Even stronger opposition was aroused by the attempt, eventually successful, of Dominican scholars to baptize Aristotle in the service of theology. Since the time of Augustine, and indeed before it, there had been a marked strain of Platonism in Christian thought. But by the thirteenth century a steady stream of Aristotelian writings was coming into Western Europe, chiefly through translations from Arabic which emanated for the most part from the Moslem schools of Spain. To the medieval world these writings represented science in its most exact form, and there was an immediate desire to reinterpret Christianity in terms of the latest scientific thinking. It is always dangerous to link the gospel to a contemporary and perhaps passing phase of culture; the second-century gnostics had tried to combine it with the most up-to-date astronomy, only to fall into wildly heretical speculations; but because the Catholic Church has endorsed the theology of Thomism, its Aristotelian ingredients have secured a more than transitory impact on the human mind. But the result was not achieved without a struggle. Aristotle was more of a materialist than Plato, and this feature of his thought had been emphasized by his Arabic interpreters. Conservative churchmen felt that such a philosophy must be rejected as unchristian, and at first they carried the universities with them in this condemnation. In 1210 a provincial council at Sens prohibited the use of Aristotle's books on natural philosophy; in 1215 Paris University banned his Physics and Metaphysics from the curriculum. It was then suggested that a committee of experts might purge the books from pagan error, and in 1231 Gregory IX confirmed the banning of them until this should be done. None the less, only a dozen years later Roger Bacon was happily lecturing upon them in the Parisian

Faculty of Arts, and about the same time the Dominican scholar
Albert the Great began to do the same. Presumably the Church
authorities felt that no serious harm could come from such
experimental use by a competent and orthodox professor; yet the
books had never been expurgated, and one of the tasks which
both Albert and his pupil Aquinas set themselves was to recover
the real Aristotle by obtaining accurate translations direct from
the Greek originals. Albert himself was a man of encyclopaedic
knowledge, who introduced his Order to a much wider field of
studies than had been envisaged for it by Dominic. A student at
Padua, a lecturer in the German convents, a professor at Paris,
and for a time Bishop of Ratisbon, he never succeeded in reducing
his vast erudition to a logical and coherent system. But he stirred
the waters of complacent orthodoxy; and above all he was the
teacher of Thomas Aquinas.

In the late autumn of 1245, Aquinas came to Paris as a silent
young novice whom his fellows called a dumb ox; but Albert
recognized the latent genius and prophesied that the world would
hear his bellowing. As the younger man ripened quickly, the two
soon became colleagues and life-long friends, defending one
another against the attacks of hostile critics. Albert, who survived
his brilliant pupil by six years, kept pathetically repeating in old
age that Aquinas had been the flower and glory of the universe.
Under the somewhat dry lucidity of his voluminous writings,
Aquinas concealed a very human personality. He was the type of
absent-minded professor about whom innumerable tales were
told. He paid so little attention to meals that one of the friars had
to be deputed to see that he got his proper food. His great *Summa
contra Gentiles*, a textbook for missionaries to the Moslems, was
written on odd scraps of scribbling paper. On one occasion a
student, who accompanied him home from lecturing, pointed out
the beauty of Paris and expressed a wish that the fair city might
belong to his professor; to which Aquinas replied: "At the
moment I would really much rather have Chrysostom's homilies
on St. Matthew." On another occasion, when dining with King
Louis, he became lost in a fit of abstraction and, utterly oblivious
to his surroundings, suddenly banged the table with his fist,
crying: "Ha! that settles the Manichees;" but while his companions blushed for this regrettable behaviour, the King courteously sent for a secretary to note the striking idea that had just
occurred. An obscure passage in Isaiah puzzled him for many
days, but after prayer in the night he called his companion
Reginald and dictated the explanation for an hour on end;
Reginald thought that he had heard voices before being sum-

moned, and in answer to his repeated questions, Aquinas replied
that he had been conversing with St. Peter and St. Paul. Perhaps
there was a twinkle in the master's eye as he said this; perhaps he
meant no more than that he had used the New Testament as a key
to unlock the Old. But the story was solemnly repeated, at the
inquiry prior to his canonization, together with an account of how
at prayer the saint's bulky body had risen three feet from the
ground. He was indubitably a man of prayer, attending all the
routine services of his convent, spending extra time in personal
devotion, and yet he somehow crowded into a comparatively
short life the composition of about seventy-five books, several of
them monumental in character, not to mention his constant work
of teaching, travelling and debating. He had a prodigious
memory, invaluable in the days of cumbersome, unindexed books
and poor libraries, and he had the reputation of dictating to four
secretaries on different subjects at the same time. But he told his
friend Reginald that prayer and grace had been of more help to
him than intellectual power; it was his invariable custom to begin
study or any other work with prayer to God.

Born in 1225 at the castle of Roccasecca near Naples, Thomas
Aquinas was the seventh son of the Count of Aquino, a grand-
nephew on his father's side to the Emperor Frederick Barbarossa,
and on his mother's side descended from the local Norman
aristocracy. As a younger son, it was natural that his family
should design him for a career in the Church. There seems to
have been no thought of making him a soldier, though he grew
big and strong; indeed, in later life he was described as tall, stout,
erect, with a complexion the colour of ripe wheat and a large,
somewhat bald, head. So at the age of five, young Thomas was
sent to the Benedictine abbey of Monte Cassino, to learn his letters
as an upper-class pupil, and with every prospect of becoming a
princely Abbot in due course of time. From this comparatively
uninteresting future he was saved by a war between Frederick II
and the Pope, during which the monks of Monte Cassino were
expelled. He therefore continued his education at the University
of Naples, founded by the Emperor a year before his birth, where
Aristotle was already known through the work of Frederick's
court astrologer Michael Scot. More important, he fell under the
spell of Dominican scholars and preachers, who had been teaching at Naples since 1231, and when still only nineteen he joined
their Order. The family was horrified at this unthinkable alliance
with the begging friars. Pope Innocent IV was asked to intervene; he offered Thomas the abbacy of Monte Cassino, with permission to continue wearing his Dominican habit; and when this

irregular proposal was rejected, there was even some talk of offering him the archbishopric of Naples. But the friars were determined to keep their illustrious recruit, and Thomas was stubborn as a mule. While he was on the road to Paris, accompanied by the General and three other Dominicans, he was waylaid by two of his brothers, who carried him off on horseback to Roccasecca and kept him prisoner there for more than a year. Every means short of physical violence was tried to shake his resolution. A young lady of loose morals was even introduced into his room; but on seeing her, Thomas chased her out with a lighted fire-brand, and then scorched the sign of the cross upon his door. Despite such treatment, he remained on good terms with his relations, inspiring his eldest sister to become a Benedictine nun, and when his mother eventually took his side, in the autumn of 1245, he was able to escape.

It was then that he resumed his interrupted journey to the Dominican convent in the Rue St. Jacques at Paris. Here he graduated as bachelor after three years' study under Albert, and in 1248 the pair of them went to lecture in the newly opened *studium generale* of the Order at Cologne. This was not a university with power to grant degrees, but it was a centre of Dominican studies sufficiently important to employ the most brilliant teachers. For four years Aquinas acted as junior colleague to his old master, thereafter returning to the Parisian convent from which, despite opposition from the secular professors, he graduated D.D. in 1256. With a laudable feeling of unworthiness he at first shrank from professorial responsibility. He could not even think of a suitable subject for his inaugural lecture, until an aged man in the habit of St. Dominic appeared to him in a dream, bidding him speak on the text from Ps. 104 : 13, "He watereth the hills from his chambers;" and on this theme Aquinas delivered a devout homily, showing how wisdom descends like rain from God, while human teachers are no more than ministers of the Divine Word. His own attitude can best be illustrated from the scholar's prayer which is ascribed to him:

> Almighty God, who art my God, Fountain of light and Principle of being, pour, I beseech Thee, upon the darkness of my mind the bright beam of Thine enlightenment, freeing me from the double night of ignorance and sin in which I have been born; Thou who ordainest wisdom from the mouth of children, instruct my tongue and shed upon my lips Thy gracious benediction; establish my beginning, direct my going forward, and fulfil my end.

With such a spirit of devotional humility, Aquinas became a great preacher; he preached plain, powerful sermons, always in the vernacular of the people, keeping his eyes shut and his mind directed towards heaven while he spoke. His method of study may be illustrated from a letter written to a novice who asked for advice:

> By preference you should seek knowledge in small streamlets, rather than plunging at once into the full ocean. . . . Speak sparingly. . . . Guard the integrity of your conscience. Never give up praying. . . . Be charitable to everyone, without intrusiveness or undue familiarity. . . . Avoid wandering about outside your convent. . . . Make a mental note of everything good that you may hear. . . . Always try to store as much as you can in the chamber of memory.

Aquinas himself was supposed to forget nothing that he had ever read, and he regarded his work as a sort of intellectual apostolate.

Not only the members of his own convent, but students from all over the city crowded to attend his lectures. People wrote to ask his advice on everything from the simplest of private problems to the most important matters of public policy. His Order employed him to draw up new statutes for its syllabus of studies. In 1264 Urban IV entrusted him with the delicate task of composing an office for the Feast of Corpus Christi, in which he managed to incorporate most of the scriptural references to the Eucharist, making a service much admired for its liturgical perfection and the beauty of its Latin hymns. For Aquinas was by no means a dull academic pundit; he had a gift for poetry and his hymns are still regularly sung. But the Paris in which he taught was a city of amazing contrasts; only a few years after he composed this Corpus Christi office, the Parisian clerks had to be reproved for dicing on the altars; and although sacramental doctrine had become extremely high, sacramental practice left a very great deal to be desired.

Meanwhile he continued teaching at a variety of centres. From Paris he had been summoned in 1259 to act as professor of theology in the papal college, a teaching institution not of university status where he met William of Moerbeke, a fellow-Dominican and the best translator of Aristotle during the Middle Ages. This papal college migrated with the Curia, so that Aquinas was involved in frequent journeys; he spent six years at Anagni and Orvieto, two in Rome at Santa Sabina and the Dominican *studium generale*, and then moved to Viterbo, whence he was hurriedly recalled to Paris at the start of 1269. Here the gathering storm had at last broken, in a vehement onslaught on the Aristotelian philosophy, and Aquinas was urgently required to defend the very basis of his life's work as a scholar. Arabic commentators had emphasized the materialism of Aristotle's thought; in particular Averroes, who died in 1198, had taught that matter is eternal and that the human intellect is impersonal, so that there is only a common mind and no personal immortality. Did such views represent the real Aristotle, and was a scientific philosopher obliged to accept them? One of the secular masters at Paris, Siger of Brabant, had openly adopted these heresies on the eternity of matter and the impersonality of mind, defending them by the dangerous argument that something which was false in theology might yet be philosophically true. Led by Bishop Stephen Tempier of Paris, the conservatives exploded in righteous indignation. It seemed that Aristotle and all his works would be condemned. But Aquinas made a brilliant defence of his own more spiritual interpretation of the Stagirite; the teaching of Siger was censured in 1270; and although some stubborn rearguard actions remained to be fought, the place of an Aristotelian theology was now in principle secure.

When the din of battle had died down, Aquinas went in 1272 to Naples, to reorganize the course of studies in what had been his first university. For some years past he had been working on his great *Summa Theologica*, and friends urged him to continue writing; but he left it unfinished, for he was more and more absorbed in prayer and contemplation, declaring: "I cannot write —such things have been revealed to me that what I have already written seems but straw." There is a story that when he was praying before the crucifix, a Voice addressed him: "You have written well of Me, Thomas, what do you desire as a reward?"— to which he replied: "Lord, only Thyself." In 1274 the Pope summoned him to the Council of Lyons, where his help was required in promoting theological reunion with the Greeks. But on the way he fell ill and was taken to the Cistercian abbey of Fossanuova, where he began to expound the Song of Songs to the monks. When they brought him the viaticum, he said: "I receive Thee, Ransom of my soul; for love of Thee I have watched and studied, toiled and preached and taught; never have I said aught against Thee." He died on 7th March, 1274, at the early age of forty-nine.

His immense literary output included not only the famous theological treatises and the liturgical office of Corpus Christi, but also sermons and Biblical commentaries which Erasmus regarded as more careful, sane and scholarly than the work of most medieval exegetes. He commented, in whole or in part, upon Job, the Psalms, the Song of Songs, Isaiah, Jeremiah, Matthew, John and the Pauline Epistles. In the first *Quaestio* of his *Summa Theologica* he states unequivocally that God is the Author of Holy Scripture; and he quotes a letter from Augustine to Jerome, later to be quoted by Luther with equally warm approval, to the effect that unlike human writings canonical Scripture is inerrant. Augustine, whose dictum is thus accepted by Aquinas, assumes that Jerome will agree with him when he writes: "only to those Biblical books which are called canonical have I learnt to pay such honour that I most firmly believe none of their authors has made any verbal error, but when reading other writers, however distinguished for sanctity and sound learning, I do not accept anything as true simply because they thought or said it." Basically, the doctrine of Aquinas is intended to be founded on the Bible; but in practice he quotes from the Fathers, about seventy-eight of them both Latin and Greek, without indicating that he ascribes a lesser authority to these purely human sources. However, like Albert before him, he stressed the importance of taking Scripture in its literal sense, which alone is admissible for the establishment of dogma. Allegorical interpretations are too subjective to form a secure doctrinal basis; but they are not to be entirely rejected, for God, the Author of Scripture, has imparted a spiritual significance to the events which the Bible records literally, so that behind the letter there lies a deeper and eternal meaning (*Summa Theologica*, I, i, 10). Aquinas himself knew neither Greek nor Hebrew, but he took pains to obtain an accurate understanding of the text.

Thomism has been described as a Platonic Christianity made specific by Aristotle. It is a highly intellectual system, using Aristotelian categories for precise definition, but it does not entirely abandon the older Platonism which descends from Augustine. With a growing interest in foreign missions, there was a new apologetic need for the appeal to unaided human reason, and in debating with Moslems it was effective to make use of the Aristotle whom their learned men revered. Hence came the value of a book like the *Summa contra Gentiles*; but this was not a book of mere philosophy, for near the start it quotes a saying from Hilary: "I consider it the principal duty of my life that all my talk and intention should concern itself with God." Aquinas believed that the existence of God could be proved by rational arguments. The second *Quaestio* of his *Summa Theologica* poses the problem: "Does God exist?" In answer, he rejects the ontological proof of Anselm, since the human mind can form no concept of God's Being that would be adequate for the purposes of demonstration. Instead Aquinas produces the well-known *Quinque Viae*,

five proofs which argue, not deductively from concepts, but in-
ductively from the data of experience: motion implies a first
Mover, causation a primary Cause, contingent being a necessary
Being, comparisons an ultimate Standard of perfection, and design
in the universe postulates an intelligent Designer. The fifth of
these, the argument from design, is probably the strongest, since
the others are all invalid if an infinite regress should be possible.
But Aquinas was fully conscious of the limits of unaided reason.
While the existence of God may be capable of rational proof,
specific Christian verities, such as the Trinity, Incarnation and
Atonement, can only be known by revelation. These are above
but not contrary to reason, and while they cannot be logically
demonstrated, they can be shown to harmonize with other admitted
facts, or at least objections can be removed by the use of rational
processes. Aquinas is commendably ready to meet the agnostic
on his own ground, and to argue from the slightest point of
agreement he can find. At the same time he insists that faith is the
starting-point of the mind's real movement towards God, and
that God Himself is the true originator of such a movement of
conversion, so that justification is through faith (*Summa Theologica*,
Ia IIae, cxiii 4). A Calvinist would find himself in full sympathy
with much of what Aquinas has to say on the subject of predestination (I, xxiii): God elects some and reprobates others without reference to human merit, and the number of the elect is
fixed. There would be similar agreement with the parallel which
Aquinas draws between the sacraments of the Old and the New
Testaments, and in particular with his use of circumcision to
illustrate infant baptism (III, lxi 3 and lxx 1–4). In all of this he is
closely following Augustine.

But the *Summa Theologica*, which its Prologue modestly describes as a textbook for beginners, also contains a historically
inaccurate justification of the Papacy (Supplementum xl 6), and a
full-scale account of transubstantiation in the Aristotelian
categories of substance and accident (III, lxxv–lxxvii). Yet in the
hands of Aquinas, transubstantiation assumes a highly spiritual
form. He insists upon the Real Presence, but at the same time
insists that this Presence is non-material; Christ is not in the
sacrament like a body localized in space, nor can He be moved
locally with it, since He is now glorified and at rest in heaven
(III, lxxv 1 and lxxvi 6). According to Aquinas, there is a genuinely
sacrificial aspect to the Eucharist, but this arises from its mystical
identity with the one eternal sacrifice, and it is in no sense a
repetition of Calvary (III, lxxxiii 1). Again, although he is a convinced papalist, Aquinas is by no means a strong episcopalian; he

says that since the ministry is primarily ordained for the service of the altar, both priests and bishops, who alike have power to celebrate, may be considered as forming a single order in the Church (Supplementum xl 5). Indeed, at a time when the Papacy was still further exalting its pretensions, when Innocent IV was claiming that "Christ has established in the apostolic throne not only a pontifical but also a regal monarchy," Aquinas seems to have maintained that the Pope possesses no direct jurisdiction in temporal affairs. In politics he was a staunch conservative, believing with Aristotle that it is best for the lower classes to be kept in ignorance and isolation. His teaching method followed the stock scholastic line of raising objections to a thesis, giving an authoritative statement of the truth, and finally answering the objections; this was a method familiar to his students from their academic disputations, and it helped them to memorize the subject. At the Council of Trent, the Bible and the *Summa Theologica* were placed on the table side by side, as the supreme authorities for the Catholic Faith; and modern Roman canon law makes study of the Angelic Doctor obligatory for all philosophers and theologians.

There was a definite strain of mysticism in both Albert and Aquinas, another feature which links them to the Platonic trends of Augustine. In fact the mystical approach to religion, kept alive by writers like pseudo-Dionysius and Erigena, had never entirely disappeared; and although it was always in danger of falling into pantheistic heresy, Richard of St. Victor had made it intellectually respectable by his pioneer researches into the psychology of contemplation, while Bernard of Clairvaux had stamped it with his own impeccable orthodoxy. However, less sober minds, when intoxicated with excessive spirituality, were always prone to neglect the concrete manhood of the Word made flesh, and to lose the unique fact of Christ's Incarnation by treating it as the mere exemplar of a universal law. There was thus a real peril that doctrine might be dissolved in sentimentality, that a craving for direct communion with God might obliterate the sense of sin, and consequently that the need of Atonement might be denied. Medieval mystics lived on the borderland of heresy, the more so as they tended to depreciate the sacraments and to substitute personal experience for the teaching authority of the Church. Some of their fraternities, now largely unknown, may well have been ancestors of the Anabaptist enthusiasts; others, the so-called Brethren of the Free Spirit, had a reputation for outrageous immorality. The Beguines, founded about 1180 by a revivalist from Liège called Lambert le Bègue ("the Stammerer"), were intended

o

to be religious societies of women widowed by the Crusades; they did some useful work in social welfare, but they had too little discipline, too much time upon their hands, and in consequence too strong an interest in forbidden speculations. Amalric of Bena, the Parisian master condemned at the Fourth Lateran Council, pushed his pantheism to the extreme of saying that unconsecrated bread is the Body of Christ, and that God spoke through Ovid as well as through St. Augustine. And during the thirteenth century, the Spiritual Franciscans were in almost constant revolt against the Church.

To combat these disruptive tendencies, certain learned preachers sought to provide an orthodox satisfaction for the spiritual cravings to which the sects with their more personal religion ministered. This was the special task of a few Dominican friars, such as Eckhart, Tauler and Suso, who preached in the German cities where heretical mysticism was particularly rampant, and who undertook the spiritual direction of women attracted to the movement. Some of the women also were distinguished mystics, including a handful of Dominican nuns; and among the Tertiaries, Mechtild of Magdeburg castigated clerical corruption with the vigour of her predecessor Hildegard, though she is now chiefly remembered for her magnificent *Book of the Flowing Light of the Godhead*, written in Low German and containing a feast of tender lyrics, bright visions and dramatic dialogues in prose and verse.

The great teacher of the German mystics was Meister Eckhart, who was born about 1260 and became a Dominican at Erfurt when only fifteen years of age. His academic studies at Cologne and Paris were crowned with the Master's degree in 1302, after which he was appointed Provincial of Saxony and Vicar-General for his Order in Bohemia; returning to Paris for a couple of years as teacher, he divided the remainder of his life between Cologne and Strassburg, where he became one of the most celebrated preachers of the day. His sermons presuppose a high degree of spiritual discernment on the part of the congregation, but they are never divorced from the problems of ordinary life. He refuses to divide the sacred from the secular, and in an early work he rates practical service above mystical contemplation: "if one were in a rapture like St. Paul, and there was a sick man needing help, I think it would be best to throw off the rapture and show love by service to the needy." When speaking of atonement through the sacrificial death of Christ, Eckhart uses the language of traditional orthodoxy. But the idea of redemption does not really fit into his scheme of an unmediated approach to God. "Sin," he writes, "ceases to be sin as soon as one repents of it. . . . He who is truly conformed to the will of God should be glad that he has formerly sinned, because the very sin obliges him to a greater love. . . . God never dreams of making the contrite expiate his faults. . . . He does not consider what the sinner was. God is a present God." Too much interested in the "eternal now" to pay great attention to the historical incarnation of the Saviour, Eckhart's favourite themes are the present living operation of the Spirit and the consecration of daily life; he is fond of saying "God begets His Son in me," and with a certain disdain for merely sacramental communion, he writes: "when I rise above the sacrament I experience God and am actually changed into that which I experience." All of this is dangerously close to pantheism, but according to Eckhart human personality is not lost or submerged in the divine. However, "there is something in the soul which is above the soul, divine and simple, unnamed rather than named," a faculty of interior vision which he calls the "spark" or "soul's eye," acting like a mirror to reflect the light of God. "The eye with which I see God," he says, "is the same as that with which He sees me." And in a similarly pantheistic vein he declares that "nature is the lower part of the Godhead." This created universe is "the language of the Word," for "when God speaks His ideas the world of phenomena arises." But behind the God who is revealed in nature there lies an abyss of Deity, dark and formless, out of which the Trinity is somehow evolved: "the simple Ground, the still Waste, the Unity where no man dwelleth . . . itself immovable yet moving all things." It is surprising that for many years Eckhart was allowed to preach such doctrine undisturbed. The first complaint against his teaching was made by the Archbishop of Cologne in 1326, when he was accused of saying that "there is something uncreated in the human soul," and that "his little finger has created everything;" both of these are exaggerated statements of divine immanence, and although Eckhart died in 1327 pending an appeal to Rome, twenty-eight of his propositions were condemned two years later by a papal bull. As a result, his writings were forgotten and suppressed; but his influence continued in a small circle of disciples.

Amongst these, John Tauler was about forty years younger than the master, and like him, entered the Dominican Order at an early age. A noble-minded and popular preacher, Tauler distrusts the "great doctors of Paris" who read the books of men but have never studied in the Book of Life. At a time when the Church was shocked and distracted by the Avignon papacy, when Germany was racked by civil war and papal interdict, and when the Black

Death was producing hysterical excitement among the people, many of whom wandered as "flagellants" beating one another in penitential processions, Tauler for some twenty years brought hope and comfort to multitudes of hearers through preaching his doctrine of the Inner Light. Loyal to the Church and orthodox in his ideas, he insisted on the value of personal experience, declaring that "no one can teach what he has not himself lived through." With a deep sense of sin and a scorn for the empty quietism of the false mystics, he maintained a clear distinction between creature and Creator; and although he says that God's image is hidden in man like a statue in the block of marble, yet he admits that it has to be found and fashioned by the divine Artificer. Practical religion is all-important to Tauler, since "works of love are more acceptable to God than lofty contemplation." He taught men to feel a spiritual vocation in their secular work. "One can spin, another can make shoes, and these are all gifts of the Holy Ghost; if I were not a priest I should feel greatly privileged to be a shoemaker, and I would try to work so well as to be a pattern to all." Another of Eckhart's disciples and an exact contemporary of Tauler was Henry Suso, the son of a noble Swabian family who became a Dominican at the age of thirteen; liberated by Eckhart from some trouble of soul, he experienced visions and when eighteen underwent a spiritual awakening or conversion. Emotionally extravagant, Suso subjected himself to an extreme asceticism, on one occasion cutting the Name of Jesus as a "love-token" on his breast. But he was a poetic and sensitive soul; he tells us that he was heart-stricken for the sufferings of all little animals, and if he could not help them he prayed for them to God.

These German mystics were loosely associated in local groups, keeping contact by visits and correspondence. They called themselves the Friends of God and felt that they were the faithful remnant in a declining Church. Telepathy and other psychic manifestations are reported to have occurred among them, together with symptoms characteristic of revival preaching; when some unidentified master preached on the coming of the Bridegroom, there was great perturbation among his hearers and at the end of the sermon forty people lay immobile on the floor. It was such circles that produced a little anonymous book, much beloved by Luther, the *Theologia Germanica*; and in a similar way, the mystical writings of the English hermit Richard Rolle were to be used and cherished by the Lollard followers of Wycliffe.

CHAPTER XIII

THE LAST CRUSADER

IN STRIKING CONTRAST TO HIS OLDER CONTEMPORARY
Frederick II, Louis IX of France has come down in history as
a lay saint, the perfect model of a Christian gentleman. The
comparison is not entirely fair to either monarch. For the Hohenstaufen Emperor of Germany was intellectually enlightened, a
patron of learning, a crusader who succeeded by diplomacy in
recovering possession of Jerusalem; and if he is painted in the
annals of churchmen as an atheist and a despot, who was actually
excommunicated at the time of his successful Crusade, the reason
is that like so many emperors he opposed the temporal dominion
of the papacy. Yet Louis, saint though he was, rejected papal
encroachments with almost equal firmness, and although he performed works of charity and devotion with monastic fervour, his
attempt to defend Christendom against the Moslems proved an
unmitigated failure. He ruled his kingdom from a sense of duty,
and he ruled it well, acting as a peace-maker both at home and
abroad; but he would have been happier as a monk or martyr,
and his character, quaintly portrayed by his friend Joinville, is a
fascinating blend of superstitious piety with royal vigour.

Born in 1214, Louis was only twelve when his father died,
leaving the Queen-Mother Blanche of Castile as regent over a
turbulent nobility. At the boy's coronation it was remarked that
he had the blue eyes, fair complexion and yellow hair of the
family of Charlemagne, to which he was related through his
grandmother Isabel of Hainault. Under the discipline of his devout
mother, herself a Franciscan Tertiary, he was given a religious
education, from which he derived a taste for reading and a knowledge of Latin that were unusual among laymen of the time. In
memory of the late King, mother and son joined in founding the
great Abbey of Royaumont, where young Louis laboured at the
building with his own hands. But they had to face constant plot-
ting and sporadic rebellion, by nobles who resented the regency of
a Spaniard and were all too readily assisted with English gold or
troops. Blanche was a proud and fiery woman, with Plantagenet
blood in her veins; her foes called her a new Semiramis; and she

managed to put down the risings by swift action combined with politic concessions. In those troubled years of his minority, Louis learnt from his mother much of the art of government.

At the age of twenty he married Margaret, eldest daughter to Count Raymond Berengar of Provence, whose depleted fortunes could provide no more than a meagre dowry; but two years later her sister Eleanor became Queen of England, and although Margaret incurred the jealousy of Blanche, she proved a loyal wife to Louis. In the year of his marriage he received an urgent appeal from Pope Gregory IX to embark on a Crusade; too much occupied with domestic affairs, Louis was for the moment unable to respond, and in the struggle between papacy and empire he remained scrupulously neutral. But if he could not visit the scene of Christ's Passion, he collected relics of it with assiduous devotion. Baldwin, the Latin Emperor of Constantinople, had pawned the Crown of Thorns to Venice for £10,000; Louis redeemed it in 1239, and two years later paid more than twice as much for a piece of the True Cross; to house them both in fitting splendour near his palace, he built the Sainte Chapelle, a costly gem of elaborate Gothic architecture with reliquaries rich in gold and jewels.

Meanwhile Henry III of England joined the French rebels in 1242, but next year was obliged to sign a truce which left the power of Louis more firmly established than before. Frederick II, having crowned himself King of Jerusalem in 1229, had returned to Italy to embark on a long war of attrition with the papacy, and the new Pope, Innocent IV, took refuge at Lyons in 1244. On the advice of his barons Louis refused to shelter the bellicose pontiff in France, and he was soon protesting against the financial exactions levied by Innocent for the war. But an old malarial infection, contracted by Louis during his early campaigns, broke out again in Advent 1244, prostrating him with severe fever and dysentery. His mother brought the relics of the Cross and Thorns, laying them on his unconscious body, and vowing that if he recovered he would go on the Crusade to Palestine. As soon as his condition improved she changed her mind, but Louis insisted on taking the crusader's badge, a step rendered all the more imperative by news that Jerusalem had recently fallen to the Khwarismian Turks. The aid of these warriors had been invoked by the Sultan of Egypt in the course of his endemic conflict with the Sultan of Damascus; sweeping down on Palestine they defeated the Christian troops near Gaza, after defiling the Holy Places, and Jerusalem passed into paynim hands for good. In the course of preparing for his Crusade, Louis spent seven days during November 1245 in secret conference with Innocent at Cluny; that abbey was by now so magnificent that it could easily accommodate the suites of both, together with the Eastern Emperor and the Princes of Aragon and Castile; but nothing resulted except for an arrangement to meet again next year. Innocent was anxious to direct all his resources against Frederick, while the chivalrous Louis intended to relieve the Holy Land. To finance his expedition he levied extra taxes from which not even the clergy were exempt, and when the Pope continued to extort money for his private purposes, Louis joined with the French barons in a strong remonstrance. France was burdened not only with extravagant papal demands, but also with unwelcome foreigners whom the Pope nominated to benefices on his own authority. King and nobles protested in terms which Matthew Paris thus records: "It is monstrous that everywhere we should hear the threat, Give me so much, or else I will excommunicate you. . . . The Roman Church, failing to preserve her primitive simplicity, is choked with riches and thus defiled by greed." In November 1246 the French lords went so far as to sign a bond protecting one another against the exorbitant demands of Innocent, and in a significant manifesto they threatened to restore the clergy to a state of apostolic poverty.

Louis meanwhile settled the affairs of the kingdom, appointing Blanche as regent for his absence, giving large donations to the Church, and taking the pilgrim's staff and wallet on 12th June, 1248; in August he embarked for Cyprus, accompanied by Margaret his Queen, his brothers Robert of Artois and Charles of Anjou, together with a good muster of the host of France. A small English contingent followed under the Earl of Salisbury, and from Scotland there came the Earl of Dunbar, who died at Marseilles on his way. The Moslem nations were almost as divided as the Christian ones, although the Caliph of Baghdad played his part better than the Pope did in promoting unity; and the impressive array of Saracen states was already menaced by the growing Mongol power of the East. Rightly believing that Egypt was the key to Palestine, Louis was in favour of pressing on at once to the Nile Delta, but his advisers pointed out the danger of sailing during winter storms. He was therefore obliged to winter at Nicosia, where he received an embassy from one of the Mongol generals; the ambassadors were themselves Nestorian Christians, and they held out hopes not only of a military alliance against Islam, but also of the conversion of their master. Louis sent them back with a portable chapel in the form of a tent, decorated with pictures of the Annunciation and the Passion, to

which the papal legate added a letter urging the Mongols to abide
by the decrees of the first four Ecumenical Councils and to acknowledge the supremacy of the Roman See. This mission was
sadly disappointed, for the Mongols were not interested in
theology, and merely treated the gifts as a sort of tribute; but
Louis, refusing to be discouraged, sent another mission four
years later for the same purpose.

In May 1249 the great flotilla was at last able to set sail from
Cyprus: eighteen hundred vessels, of which a hundred and twenty
were of the largest size, bearing nearly three thousand knights
with their horses and followers. A violent storm scattered the
fleet when it was weighing anchor, but with a depleted squadron
Louis pushed on to Damietta in his flagship the *Montjoie*. The
troops landed in gallant order; Louis himself waded ashore behind
the oriflamme, while the Count of Jaffa ordered his three hundred
oarsmen to beach their galley with pennons flying and drums
beating. Overwhelmed by what was almost a surprise attack, the
Moslems after putting up a stiff resistance on the beaches evacu-
ated Damietta during the night. But it was impossible for the
crusaders at once to follow up their victory, for the annual flood-
ing of the Nile was due to begin at any moment; and a period of
inactivity ensued, with consequent injury to discipline. By November the march to Cairo had started, while the Queen and the legate
remained at Damietta; a Saracen offer to exchange this town for
Jerusalem was scornfully rejected; and there were high hopes of
breaking Moslem power not only in Egypt but also throughout
the East. Near Mansourah the column was held up by a broad
side-stream which Louis attempted to bridge with a mole, using
a couple of "cat-castles" or covered galleries to protect his
engineers. But the Saracens replied with catapults and Greek fire;
as each flaming barrel thundered across like a dragon, the pious
king fell on his knees to pray. Eventually a native Copt offered,
for a price, to reveal the whereabouts of a ford that was passable
by cavalry, and at dawn the crusading army set out on its flanking
march. They took their opponents by surprise—the Saracen
general was in his bath dyeing a hoary beard at the time—but the
impetuosity of Robert of Artois turned the success into a Pyrrhic
victory, so that by evening the crusaders, though in possession of
the enemy camp, were too depleted in numbers to proceed. It
was now February 1250, and they were obliged to stay in camp,
short of provisions, constantly harassed, and exposed to disease
from the multitude of rotting corpses that floated on the river.

After eight weeks of virtual siege, Louis offered on his own
part to exchange Damietta for Jerusalem; but the Saracens, con-

scious of his weakness, were no longer willing to negotiate, and
he had to extricate his army as best he could. The sick were sent
downstream in boats, while the able-bodied began to struggle
wearily towards their base, with the king bravely bringing up the
rear. There had been great feats of valour, not only by knights
but also by priests and bishops. Joinville remarks casually that at
one point the fire-darts of the Saracens only wounded him in five
places and his pony in fifteen. One of his chaplains, single-handed,
chased eight Saracens from a redoubt. And when the retreat had
begun, the Bishop of Soissons "who longed to be with God"
refused to return to his homeland, instead spurring his horse
into the Moslem ranks where "he joined the martyrs in God's
presence." Louis himself on several occasions risked death to
preserve his followers. But the retreating army was demoralized,
surrounded and at last cut off; the boats were captured, the troops
on land surrendered; and the Saracens, embarrassed by the multitude of prisoners, began to massacre those for whom they could
expect no ransom. In defeat, Louis bore himself with dignity and
courage. His illness, which had broken out again, was healed by
Arab physicians. Even when threatened with torture, he refused
to hand over the castles of Palestine, which were not his to cede.
After much bargaining, the Saracens agreed to accept a ten years'
truce, with Damietta given in exchange for the king's person, and
£500,000 as ransom for his troops. While terms were being
arranged, they showed some kindness to their captives. Lord
Ralph of Wanon, who had been hamstrung in the battle, was
carried about pick-a-back by an old Saracen knight. Joinville,
invited to dine with the chief Emir of the galleys, inadvertently
ate flesh on a Friday; but when he discovered the date, the Emir
politely assured him that it was no sin, since he had acted in
ignorance; and the papal legate later gave him exactly the same
advice. However, the terms of the truce involved a crippling payment, difficult to raise. Queen Margaret gallantly undertook the
immediate arrangements, although she had just given birth, with
an octogenarian knight as midwife, to a little son whom she
named Tristan, child of sorrow.

Released from captivity, most of the barons decided to return
to France. But Louis, accompanied by a few volunteers like Joinville, remained in the Holy Land for a further four years. His
presence did something to stabilize the situation, but despite
succour sent from home by Blanche he was short of both men and
money. Frederick had died in 1250 but Innocent, pursuing his
vendetta against the Emperor's family, gave no assistance to the
soldiers of the Cross. Louis refused an invitation to visit Jeru-

salem under safe conduct, for he could not bear to look upon the
City which he was unable to capture. He exchanged embassies
with the Old Man of the Mountains, the formidable leader of the
Assassin sect of Ismaili Moslems, and when Brother Ives reached
their mountainous retreat, he found the Old Man placidly reading
what were described as the sayings of Christ to Peter. So eclectic
was the East in its religious philosophy that Louis did not despair
of making converts, and in this he had some slight success. But
when Blanche died at the end of 1252 his presence was more
urgently required at home; in April 1254 he sailed for France.

Disappointed in his great ambition of winning a crusade, he
devoted himself the more eagerly to religious duties. One hundred
and twenty poor persons were fed from his table daily, and thrice
a week in Lent and Advent he served them in person before eating. He loved to tend the sick in hospital and to wash the feet of
beggars, giving a gentle rebuke to the more worldly-minded
Joinville who abstained from such pious but unhygienic practices. Large gifts of food, clothing and money were bestowed
upon the needy, while the friars were enriched with royal munificence; impoverished gentlefolk, fallen women, widows and the
unemployed all shared his bounty, and he built several hospitals,
including one for three hundred blind men at Paris. Abstemious
in his personal habits, Louis dressed soberly, ate without relish
and always watered his wine, informing Joinville that he considered it "a very foul thing for a gentleman to get drunk." He
did not indulge in dice or hunting, but was a good conversation-
alist, sufficiently humorous to set himself the penance of not
laughing on Fridays if he could help it. Although he considered
that a layman should defend the Faith by arms rather than arguments, he read the Vulgate and some of the Fathers after dinner,
collected a good library, and encouraged the founding of colleges,
including the Sorbonne, at Paris University, where he laboured to
compose the strife between seculars and friars. He loved sermons,
the length and frequency of which were frankly boring to his
court. When staying at Royaumont, he joined the monks in all
their services and domestic chores, expressing a strong desire to
abdicate and take the cowl. Dissuaded by his councillors from
forsaking the kingdom, he rose before dawn for matins, walking
past his somnolent courtiers, heard two masses a day, and
followed the canonical Hours and the Hours of the Virgin. It was
a time when adoration of the Blessed Sacrament was increasing,
and at mass he was often observed to be in ecstasy, while he encouraged the practice, then becoming common among religious,
of genuflecting when the words "and was made man" were

recited in the Creed. Though he prayed fervently he lamented a lack of devotional tears, and compensated for it by ordering his confessor, the Dominican Geoffrey of Beaulieu, to lash him with a scourge. A stern father to his children, he supervised their religious upbringing and urged them to follow the example of good men.

It was a period of moral decline in society, evidenced by the new edition, sceptical, licentious and anti-clerical, of the *Roman de la Rose* which John of Meung produced around 1280. In the towns a secular and materialist spirit was increasingly at large. Mounting taxes, and more frequent nomination by the Pope to benefices, moved the Archbishop of York to tell Alexander IV that Christ bade Peter feed but not shear His sheep. Robert Grosseteste declared: "the source of all the evil in the Roman Church is that by dispensations, provisions and collations it openly nominates men who are destroyers and not pastors." But by the bull *Licet ecclesiarum* of 1265, Clement IV asserted that "the entire disposition of churches, dignities and other ecclesiastical benefices belongs to the Roman Pontiff, so that he not only has the right to bestow them when vacant, but also to nominate in view of a vacancy." The result was a growing spirit of materialism in the clergy, while those with means at their disposal hunted for preferment; and a report to the Council of Lyons in 1274, prepared by Bishop Bruno of Olmütz and the Dominican General Humbert of Romans, stressed the vices of avarice and misconduct that were rampant in clerical circles.

Though generous in benefactions to the Church, Louis refused to condone the exorbitant pretensions of his prelates. When they urged him to enforce their sentences of excommunication, he replied that he must first take cognizance of the justice of the sentence, pointing out that a Count of Brittany had lain unjustly excommunicate for seven years, only to be acquitted at the end by Rome. In general, he asserted the competence of the civil courts in civil matters, the power of the Crown to supervise the prelates' use of their temporalities, and the right of lay patronage to benefices. He was himself scrupulous in appointing honest officials, whose conduct was controlled by regular commissions of inquiry, and this increase of royal jurisdiction began to change the Parlement of Paris from an assembly of magnates into a specific court of justice. Trial by combat, already illegal under canon law, was prohibited by Louis and his Parlement in 1260. He awarded severe punishments for blasphemy and foul language; but everyone obtained a fair hearing, and he loved to dispense justice personally, in patriarchal fashion, sitting beneath an

ancient oak-tree in the forest of Vincennes. Although he allowed
the local currencies to continue in circulation, he promoted a
uniform national coinage of fixed value. His reign marked a
period of prosperity and general contentment for France. The
barons were now obedient to a strong central government, and
the long-standing strife with England was settled by a peace
treaty in 1258; under this generous settlement, Henry retained
Perigord, Limousin and other fiefs, paying homage for them to
Louis, but he renounced for ever the English claim on Normandy.

Anxious to drive the Hohenstaufen out of Italy, Pope Urban IV
in 1264 gave the kingdom of Naples and Sicily to Louis's brother
Charles of Anjou. Frederick's bastard Manfred was killed at the
battle of Benevento in 1266, and two years later his grandson
Conradin, the last of the line, was captured and executed publicly
at Naples. How far Louis approved of his brother's adventures is
uncertain, but for the papacy the change of ruler hastened that
subservience to France which was to culminate, during the next
century, in the "Babylonian Captivity" of the Avignon Popes.
For the moment, Charles asserted his control by keeping the
papal see vacant for the three years 1268-71. In reply, the Council
of Lyons in 1274 formulated more stringent regulations for the
election of a Pope: the cardinals were to be actually locked up in
conclave, with a gradual reduction of their rations, should they
be unable to agree upon a candidate. The same Council achieved
an ephemeral reunion with the Greeks which, prompted by fear
of Charles's designs upon the Eastern Empire, lasted for exactly
fifteen years. Some of the smaller mendicant Orders were suppressed, and among various disciplinary measures, there was an
injunction to the people to show reverence in church by bowing
at the Name of Jesus.

Meanwhile, Louis had taken the Cross again in 1267. There
was little enthusiasm among his followers, and three years were
required for preparation. By the time that he was ready to set out
in 1270, he was physically so weak that Joinville had to carry him
in his arms. He sailed for Tunis, believing that its Sultan was ripe
for conversion, and dreaming that he might restore the ancient
glories of the North African Church; moreover, Charles of Anjou,
anxious to extend his new dominions, insinuated that Tunis
would be useful as a base. But on landing at Carthage the army
was prostrated by an epidemic, and Louis fell mortally sick. He
gave his son Philip some instructions on Christian statesmanship,
written in French with his own hand; received the Last Sacrament
with devout and repeated prayers; was heard in the night singing
the French hymn *Nous irons en Jerusalem*; and expired on 25th

August, 1270, on a bed of ashes, with his hands crossed and smiling. Posthumous miracles were quickly reported from his tomb, and he was canonized in 1297 by Boniface VIII. Prince Edward of England carried on a little desultory crusading at Acre until 1272; but with Louis's dying murmur of "Jerusalem" the old spirit of the Crusades had died.

CHAPTER XIV

THE MISSIONARY ZEAL OF RAYMOND LULL

FROM THE OUTSET THE IDEA OF A MILITARY CRUSADE HAD met with some opposition on religious grounds. As far back as 1086, Anselm of Canterbury advised a young man to seek Jerusalem in heaven rather than on earth, by enlisting not as a soldier but as a monk. Such was the negative protest of monasticism: a movement to forsake the world, with its wars and tribulations, for the secure peace of cloistered sainthood. But with the coming of the friars a new approach became possible. Francis led the way to Damietta as an unarmed preacher, and in the years that followed, both Franciscans and Dominicans sought more and more to replace fighting by missionary endeavour. As the hopes of military conquest faded, the urge to evangelism grew; and although the Crusade continued to inspire men's hearts, it was increasingly supplemented by the ideal of world-wide mission.

Raymond Lull became one of the keenest exponents of the new approach. Born about 1232 in Majorca, he grew up in an island that had been reconquered from the Moslems a bare three years before his birth. His father won a large estate in the conquered territory by fighting under King James I of Aragon; and when young Raymond was fourteen, he was appointed page and companion to the King's two sons, the younger of whom, then aged about four, was as James II to be his lifelong friend. Lull travelled widely in the royal service, and although his formal education was scanty he acquired a good knowledge of men and manners. He became an expert on chivalry, a troubadour with a gift for amorous verses, and a gay but dissolute courtier. Marriage did not reform his character; he had a son Dominic and a daughter Magdalena, of whom he appears to have been fond, but he admits that he was unfaithful to his wife. Then, at the age of thirty, when he was engaged in composing a light love-poem, he saw Christ Crucified; the vision was repeated a week later, when he tried to hide from it beneath the bed-clothes, and it returned thrice more, preventing the completion of his poem. At first he had been terrified, but he now accepted it as a divine vocation;

222

"enkindled," according to his early biographer, "and inflamed with love for the Crucified," he began to consider how best he might serve his Saviour; and remembering that the greatest act of love is to lay down one's life for his friends, he decided to risk death in converting infidels. A few months after this resolve had been taken, he heard the story of Francis told in a sermon on the feast-day of that saint. Inspired to make a like renunciation of wealth and worldly ties, Lull provided for his wife and children, sold the remainder of his property, gave the proceeds to the poor, and set off by himself, as a free-lance layman, on a lengthy pilgrimage.

His own ideal is expressed in a prayer which he later wrote: "I think that the Holy Land should only be conquered in the way that Thou and Thine Apostles conquered it—by love and prayers and by the shedding of tears and blood." He knew that the way of the cross must involve self-sacrifice, yet the cost did not appal him. "Men are wont, O Lord," as he said in his *Book of Contemplation* (cxxx 27), "to die of old age, through the failure of natural warmth and excess of cold; but . . . Thy servant . . . would rather die in the glow of love, even as Thyself." To prepare himself as a missionary he realized that he must improve his education, and his first plan was to study at the University of Paris. But friends dissuaded him, perhaps feeling that he would find its atmosphere too secular. He listened with particular respect to the Dominican Raymond of Penafort, who was already urging his Order to study Oriental languages as a part of missionary training; and on Penafort's advice, he settled at Palma to learn Latin and Arabic, while at the same time he deepened his spiritual life in prayer. People ridiculed him as a fanatical enthusiast, but he persevered in acquiring Arabic from a Moslem slave, until one day he was goaded into chastising his instructor for blasphemy; the slave replied in kind with an attempt at murder, and then committed suicide in the prison where his indignant pupil had confined him. It seems that the incident made a profound impression on Lull's mind. He was thereafter haunted by the thought of multitudes doomed to damnation for their unbelief, and he strove with all his intellectual powers to make the Faith acceptable to human reason. The result was a sort of rationalism; for despite a deeply mystical bent, Lull claimed that he could prove every Christian doctrine by logical processes alone. He argued that divine Justice should not condemn men for disbelieving what they cannot understand, and he made a sincere attempt to meet the Moslems on the common ground of philosophical debate. But in argument he lost sight of the fact of revelation, and wasted much of his missionary effort in composing innumerable books of apologetics which converted no one.

Before the incident of the slave's suicide he had already written his *Book of Contemplation*, a vast encyclopedia on God, man and nature with a chapter for every day of the year. It is divided into five volumes to commemorate the five wounds of Christ, and also into forty sections in memory of His forty days' temptation in the wilderness; each chapter has ten paragraphs to recall the ten commandments, and each paragraph has three parts in honour of the Trinity. With such a highly artificial structure, it is not surprising that the work recommends "intellectual worship by means of etymology, allegory and anagogy," or that it uses algebraical symbols to express recurrent words and phrases. Yet even here, in order to commend his argument to infidels, Lull may well have been following the more recondite methods of Mohammedan devotion. He was certainly steeped in the Koran and its expositors, so that in his account of Moslem beliefs and practices he is entirely accurate and fair. Because of the honour which they paid to Jesus and His Mother, he considered that the Saracens were nearer to Christianity than any other pagans, and he bravely declared that once they had been converted it would be an easy matter to convert the remainder of the world. Having first written his enormous *Book of Contemplation* in Arabic, he translated it into Catalan for the benefit of his own people, thus becoming a pioneer in the literature of that vernacular.

Torn between the active work of a missionary and the contemplative studies of a hermit, Lull postponed his original purpose of embarking on foreign missions in order to spend a period of retreat on Mount Randa, the most solitary part of his native isle. Here, on the eighth day of his sojourn in a cave, it is recorded that he received "divine illumination which provided him with a form and order for the books he planned against the errors of the infidels." Bursting with new ideas he betook himself to the Cistercian monastery of La Real, there to write his *Ars Magna* or general art of demonstration. To its fond author this was his major work, on which he frequently gave lecture courses, but it is of little more than antiquarian interest today. Like some modern educationalists, Lull believed in the value of diagrams as visual aids. His *Art* is therefore illustrated with a series of mathematical figures from which answers can be read off to any type of problem. The first figure (A) represents God at the centre of a circle, whose circumference is divided into sixteen sections, labelled B to R, to denote the attributes of Deity. These attributes are taken in pairs, producing one hundred and twenty permutations of the figure;

thus (BC) goodness is great, or (BD) goodness is eternal. The
second figure (S) shows the soul, in a circle with four squares of
different colours, and again with sixteen compartments, demon-
strating its faculties and their action in reference to objects. There
are thirteen of these figures in all, and if used in combination they
permit an almost endless variety. By means of them, Lull claims
to solve questions in theology, ethics and natural science: what is
thunder? do the devils sin? is celibacy better than marriage? and
so on. He later produced an improved model, in his *Ars Demon-
strativa*, with metal circles superimposed upon the figures, and he
declared that those who used it regularly would find themselves
constructing syllogisms in their sleep. Lull acquired the posthumous reputation of an alchemist, and there was a period when
his *Art* enjoyed immense popularity; but even if it deserves
Hegel's description of it as a thinking-machine, there seems to be
no evidence that it enabled Saracens to think on more Christian
lines.

None the less he continued writing, with unimpaired fertility,
throughout the entire course of a long life. His best work,
Blanquerna, is one of the earliest religious novels in European
literature; in true Franciscan spirit it tells the romantic adventures
of a saintly hermit, who eventually becomes Pope, only to renounce his office for the sake of returning to mystic contemplation. The style is simple, with no recondite trivialities, but with
repeated pleas for the conversion of the heathen. Contained within
the novel but really separate from it, there is a little *Book of the
Lover and the Beloved*, so unsectarian in its devotional fervour that
it has appealed to men of many different creeds. "The Lover said
to his Beloved, Thou art all—through all, with all and in all; I
would give Thee my whole self, that I might have Thee wholly
and Thou me. The Beloved answered, Thou canst not have Me,
unless thou art Mine entirely. And the Lover said, Let me be
wholly Thine and Thou be wholly mine." It is possible that Lull
owes a debt here to the Sufi mystics, whom he certainly mentions
in *Blanquerna*. For he was constantly preoccupied with mission,
writing a long poem on *The Hundred Names of God* to prove that
Christianity could go at least one name further than Islam. But as
he pondered missionary problems he became more and more
embarrassed by the divided state of Christendom. There were not
only the two main sections, Greek and Latin, but the Eastern
Church itself was split into a number of separate denominations;
and more than one of his writings shows a well-intentioned
Saracen perplexed and rebuffed by the multitude of competing
Christian sects. Lull himself was convinced in his allegiance to

P

the papacy, but he does not seem to have felt that doctrinal differences were all-important. His *Book of the Holy Spirit* describes a debate between Latin and Greek in the presence of a Saracen, using arguments on either side so fantastic that they read like a satire on disunity. In a later treatise, the *Book of the Five Sages*, a Nestorian and a Jacobite are added to the original trio; here again division among Christians is regarded as a severe handicap to evangelism. But Lull was confident that agreement could be reached by the unimpassioned use of logic, vainly offering his beloved *Art* as the God-given means to unity. At Paris he took up the cudgels against Averroism with its pernicious doctrine of a double truth; but going to the opposite extreme, he identified revelation with reason and dogma with philosophy. In all, Lull wrote at least two hundred and fifty books, if not the thousands with which he was credited by later followers, covering every subject of the curriculum in both prose and verse.

But writing, however voluminous, was always subsidiary to the main objective of his life. While engaged upon his books he pleaded repeatedly for active missionary effort, and no sooner had he completed his *Ars Magna* than the first encouraging response was made. For in 1276 his boyhood playmate succeeded to a part of the dominions of King James I; and among the earliest acts of James II was the foundation of a college at Miramar in Majorca, where thirteen friars might be trained in Arabic. Next year Lull was on his way to Rome, with an appeal for similar missionary colleges to be established elsewhere; he arrived when the papacy was vacant, but in 1278 Nicholas III sent five Franciscans to preach in Persia and China, and seven years later Honorius IV ordered the teaching of Arabic at Paris. On these decisions Lull must have had at least some influence, and although the Dominican Chapter General was not impressed when he spoke to it about his *Art*, the University of Paris gave that treatise a more cordial welcome. Believing that it provided unimpeachable proofs of Christianity, Lull lectured on it at both Paris and Montpellier; in the latter place, discouraged by the chill Dominican attitude, he attended the Franciscan Chapter General of 1287. And a year later, a kindred spirit mounted the papal throne in the person of the first Franciscan Pope, Nicholas IV, who sent his fellow-Franciscan John of Montecorvino on a highly successful mission to China.

With the conscience of the Church at last awakened to its missionary obligations, Lull felt that the time had come for him to put his theories into practice. He was at Genoa in 1291, ready to embark for foreign parts, when a sudden fear of personal

danger overcame him. Having remained ashore when the boat
sailed, he was at once prostrated with remorse, culminating in a
nervous breakdown. To his fevered imagination it seemed that
he could only be saved by joining the Dominicans, but that if he
did so his books would be suppressed; he therefore sought to don
the Franciscan habit, preferring that his person rather than his
books should be condemned. He received communion, believing
that in his present state he did so to the judgment of his own unworthiness, and then by a tremendous effort had himself carried,
ill as he was, down to the port. Friends prevented him from sailing, but a few days later he managed to embark, and as soon as
the ship left harbour his illness vanished. Arrived at Tunis he
challenged a debate with the scholars of Islam, arguing that God
must be a Trinity of Persons, since otherwise He would have been
inactive and unloving in His solitude before the creation of the
world. So penetrating a critique of Unitarianism was considered
by the authorities to constitute a public danger; Lull was denounced to the Caliph and promptly banished. By now the old
fears had left him. As he was dragged to the harbour, his one
thought was of the multitude of doomed souls whom he was
obliged to leave in ignorance; and he stole ashore unnoticed, only
to discover that for the moment his task was without hope. Yet
when he turned his back on Tunis he had the consolation of
knowing that he had produced solid reasons in defence and con-
firmation of the Faith. He had been able to argue publicly that the
Moslem conception of God is inadequate, since it acknowledges
no more than the two attributes of will and wisdom; whereas
Christianity, in his own words, "ascribes the greatest possible
perfection to the Supreme Being." It seems from the remarks of
Jacques de Vitry that Moslems were always ready to discuss
Christian doctrine, only becoming angry when Mohammed was
attacked.

In 1294 Lull addressed to the Pope and Cardinals a detailed
petition, setting out his recommendations for the campaign. He
had come to believe that preaching alone was insufficient, and
that Crusades should be continued, as well as missionary effort,
for the defence of Christendom. He therefore suggested that the
Church should set aside a tenth of her entire wealth for missions
and Crusades, until the world had been won for Christ; that
attempts should be made to reconcile the schismatic Churches of
the East; and that one Cardinal should devote his whole time to
recruiting suitable preachers, who would be trained for their task
in missionary colleges. The Mongols, under Jenghiz Khan and
his successors, had been pushing steadily westward, reaching the

Adriatic for a moment in 1241; with their primitive Shamanism, it was obvious that they must soon adopt some form of higher religion, and they were known to be not unsympathetic to Christianity; Lull therefore urged that the opportunity of evangelism should be seized without delay, before this powerful horde of invaders could be converted to Judaism or Islam. He concluded by requesting that he might himself be sent as a preacher to the Saracens. But Boniface VIII, who became Pope in the same year, was at once embroiled in political quarrels over France and Sicily, and Lull was reduced to writing a disconsolate poem, the *Desconort*, where some inner doubts of his apologetic method make their appearance, together with a determination to continue reasoning with men.

He joined the Franciscan Third Order, probably at Assisi, and certainly in the year 1295; and thus, while remaining a layman, he acquired the habit which in his illness he had so ardently desired. Some four years later, the King of Aragon gave him licence to preach in all the synagogues and mosques of his dominions. It was not unusual for such permission to be given, for although Jews and Moslems were legally tolerated, they were frequently obliged to attend Christian sermons. At all events, Lull does not seem to have regarded it as a pressing opportunity, since in 1301 he sailed for Palestine in the belief that that country had at last been conquered by the Mongols. Finding at Cyprus that the news was false, he devoted some time to promoting reunion with the schismatic Eastern Churches, while he also urged that the crusading Orders of knighthood should be unified under a royal leader, so as to strengthen the military defences of the West.

But these early years of the fourteenth century were a period of mounting disappointment. When death had removed the arrogant Boniface VIII, France began to press for his posthumous condemnation, eventually accepting the Templars' wealth as an alternative; and Pope Clement V, himself a Frenchman, was too preoccupied to listen to Lull's pleadings at an audience which was granted him in Lyons. By 1307 Lull had decided to attempt a second African mission on his own. He chose the town of Bugia, some hundred miles East of Algiers; but the choice proved to be unfortunate, for Bugia was then distracted by a war with Tunis, while its populace was excited by the preaching of a Moslem religious reformer; and when Lull shouted in the market-place that he would prove the truth of Christianity, a furious mob haled him before the chief magistrate or *cadi*. At the hearing of his case, which was at first conducted courteously, he argued against Unitarianism with such vigour that the mob began to insult him, pelt him with stones, and pull his long white beard. Christian traders in the town petitioned for his safety, and for six months he was lodged in a comfortable prison, to be plied with offers of wealth, women and honours if he would apostatize to Islam; to these he replied with the offer of eternal life in Christ, and when his captors found that their arguments made no impression, he was again banished from North Africa. After the strain of imprisonment and violence, he suffered shipwreck during his return voyage to Pisa, but the indomitable old man of seventy-five continued writing, planning and pleading to the end. He attended the Council of Vienne in 1311 to propose his customary suggestions, and the results were entirely gratifying; for the Council decided to found five missionary colleges, at Rome, Paris, Bologna, Oxford and Salamanca, for the teaching of Hebrew, Arabic and Syriac.

Next year, a peace treaty was concluded between the authorities of Bugia and Majorca, which gave Lull an opening for his final mission. Though now over eighty years of age, he sailed for Africa in August 1314; spent a quiet period in Tunis, where he secretly won at least five influential converts; returned to Bugia with a brave lack of caution; and there, at the end of 1315 or the beginning of the following year, was stoned by the indignant people as he preached publicly upon their streets. Two Genoese merchants carried him home, either dead or dying, and he was buried at Palma in St. Francis's Church. Dominican hostility followed him beyond the grave; intent on proving him a heretic, the inquisitor Eymeric even forged a papal bull to that effect. But although an apologetic interest may have led him at some points into error, his life was more important than his books, and he died like his Saviour "in the glow of love."

Though Lull was perhaps more picturesque a figure than the others, he by no means stood alone in the missionary movement of the late thirteenth and early fourteenth centuries. Raymond of Penafort had worked steadily for the same purpose, encouraging the Dominicans to study Arabic and prompting Aquinas to write his *Summa contra Gentiles* as a mission textbook. Produced as they had been by a religious revival, the friars were inevitably concerned with evangelism, either at home or overseas, and in the early years a small but gallant army of martyrs was found in both their Orders. Other organizations also were at work in Moslem countries: notably the Trinitarians and the Order of Our Lady of Mercy, who arranged the ransom of Christian prisoners, pledging their own persons as a guarantee, and are said in course of time to have secured the release of nearly a million and a half captives.

But it was the friars whom both Popes and kings most naturally employed as missionaries or ambassadors. When the Mongols appeared on the horizon, the West made immediate efforts to secure an alliance, both religious and political, in opposition to the forces of Islam. In 1245, Innocent IV sent a Franciscan embassy, under John of Plano Carpini, to the court of the Great Khan at Karakorum; Dominican envoys were also despatched at the same time; and Louis of France, having made a tentative approach from Cyprus to the Mongols, sent them the Franciscan William of Rubruquis in 1253. Little resulted, except that the Khans promised toleration to their Christian subjects; but this renewed contact with the farther East gave currency to the legend of Prester John, an Oriental priest-king supposed to be ready to assist his fellow-Christians of the West. The fact behind the legend is that in the tenth century the Nestorian Church was the largest Christian body in the world, having penetrated as far as China in the year 636; but by now the Nestorians were no more than a small and scattered remnant, suspicious of Europeans, and exerting what little influence they possessed through inter-marriage with the Mongol Khans. One of them became the mother of Khubilai Khan, who was visited by the Polo brothers in the course of their trading expeditions; and in 1269 the Polos arrived back at Acre, with letters from Khubilai to the Pope asking for teachers in European science and religion. Two Dominicans were appointed to travel with the merchants, accompanied this time by their young relative Marco Polo, but the difficulties and dangers of the journey deterred the friars from proceeding. In the year 1280, however, when Khubilai had established himself as Emperor of China, with his capital at Cambaluc or Peking, two Nestorian monks from near the capital went on a pilgrimage westward to the Holy Land. Stopped in Persia by the Moslem barrier, one of them remained at Maragha to become Catholicos or Primate of the Far Eastern Church, while the other was sent by the Mongol Khan of Persia as ambassador to the European courts at Constantinople, Rome, Paris and Bordeaux. At the latter place he was presented to Edward I of England, who asked him to celebrate in his own Syriac rite; and the English King received communion from the Chinese monk, while the bystanders declared that though the words were different the service was the same.

The Mongols, tolerant as they were of Christianity, tended to be too eclectic in their religious outlook, lending an equally ready ear to Moslems and to Buddhists also. But with the advent of Khubilai, the road to China was laid open, and shortly after the great Emperor's death, the Franciscan John of Montecorvino reached Cambaluc in 1294. He had already laboured for some years as a missionary in India and other Eastern lands; once arrived in China he built a church, translated the Psalms and the New Testament, and purchased forty slave-boys whom he baptized and taught to chant. The new Emperor was fortunately fond of music; about six thousand converts were won; and John was soon appointed Archbishop of Peking, seven friars being consecrated in Europe to assist him as his suffragans. Churches were established at Hangchow and other places, while the number of conversions grew; and although John died about 1328, his mission continued until the rise of the Ming dynasty, forty years later, brought it to an end.

Less spectacular but equally determined efforts were made by missionary friars in Prussia, Lithuania and Finland; among the Turkish-speaking Cumans of the Ukraine; in Persia and Mesopotamia; and in the Arab countries of the Mediterranean shore. Work among Moslems was always particularly slow and unrewarding, though the Franciscan Conrad of Ascoli is credited with over six thousand conversions in Libya, and in Palestine the Dominican William of Tripolis baptized at least a thousand. Towards the end of the thirteenth century, the Dominicans began to organize their Society of Pilgrim Brothers, with two and later four convents in the Near East, which acted as missionary centres and were supplied with a fixed quota of members from each province of the Order. The Franciscans also had a society with the same name, organizing their missions in six vicariates, three among the Mongols, one in Morocco and two in the Balkan regions. Between them, the two Orders covered most of the Moslem world, with warm backing from the papacy, which chose several of their members for consecration as missionary bishops. But after the fall of Acre in 1291 had demonstrated the military weakness of the West, the Mongols were less anxious to enter an alliance; several of their Khans adopted the faith of Islam, while the break-up of their huge Empire in the later fourteenth century permitted the Arab powers to reassert themselves; communications between Europe and the Far East were once more closed, and from 1369 Tamerlane, an ardent Moslem, was ruling much of central Asia from his capital at Samarkand. Meanwhile, the Black Death carried off so many of the friars that they lacked the personnel to maintain their widespread missions; and the Church's missionary effort dwindled into insignificance, until it was revived partly by the voyages of discovery to America and Africa, and partly by the religious ferment of the Reformation.

CHAPTER XV

DANTE AND THE DAWN OF A NEW AGE

BY THE BULL "UNAM SANCTAM" OF 1302, BONIFACE VIII asserted papal sovereignty in its most explicit and most sweeping form. "There is one Holy Catholic and Apostolic Church," outside of which "there is neither salvation nor remission of sins;" she is the dove of the Song of Songs, undefiled and unique, the mystical body of Christ her Head, prefigured by the one ark of the one helmsman Noah, the seamless robe which cannot be rent asunder, the single fold of the Great Shepherd, all of whose sheep are committed to the sole government of Peter; and since this Church is entrusted with control of the two swords, both spiritual and temporal, "it is essential for salvation that every human creature be subject to the Roman Pope." Distinguished above contemporaries not only by the greatness of his claims, but also by the completeness of his failure, Boniface had mounted the papal throne in 1294. He succeeded Celestine V, an aged and impractical hermit, who resigned after a pontificate of five months had shown his incapacity for ruling; too much of a visionary, Celestine sought guidance from mystic portents, and it was said that Boniface hastened his abdication by arranging for an angelic voice to address him through a megaphone at midnight.

Once installed in the papacy, Boniface acted with tactless disregard for the sincere and growing sentiments of nationalism by which he was surrounded. Attempting to mediate between France and England over the French possessions of the English Crown, he issued in 1296 the bull *Clericis Laicos*, by which kings were forbidden to tax their clergy without papal consent; the professed purpose of the bull was to protect Church property, and incidentally to bring the two monarchs to heel by cutting off an important source of revenue for the war; but when the English clergy were outlawed by Edward I, and when in France Philip IV prohibited the export of clerical subsidies to Rome, the imperious Pontiff was obliged to moderate his claims. To a papal remonstrance Philip replied that long before clergy existed the King of France had ruled his kingdom, that laymen have their place as well as clerics in the Church of Christ, and that the New Testament commands all alike to pay their tribute to Caesar. Such views were amplified by a group of learned civil lawyers at the French court, Pierre Flotte, William of Nogaret, and above all Pierre Dubois, who seems to have envisaged a universal French Empire based on Philip's succession from Charlemagne. Overwhelmed by the spate of argument and beset by his personal enemies at Rome, Boniface virtually conceded the right of sovereigns to levy taxes on their clergy; and in 1297 he offered a belated olive-branch by canonizing Philip's grandfather Louis. For some years thereafter, polemical pamphlets appeared on either side. Dubois was a caustic critic of both Pope and clergy; he wished to confine the papacy to purely spiritual functions; he pressed for a reform of the monasteries, the adoption of clerical marriage, and the secularization of Church property; and he suggested that clerics should be paid fixed salaries by the State. But Egidius Romanus, writing on behalf of the papacy in his treatise *De Ecclesiastica Potestate*, declared that the Pope is lord paramount of all men, with a dominion which extends to secular as well as spiritual concerns; that only through the Church can a man receive the grace which entitles him to exercise authority or own possessions; and that an excommunicate person has neither civil rights nor lawful status.

These views of Egidius, in the lofty tradition of Hildebrand and Innocent III, coincided entirely with the sentiments of Boniface. But it was now too late for them to arouse anything but opposition, and in small matters no less than great ones the papal pretensions were met with scorn and ridicule. When Boniface attempted to confine monks and nuns more strictly to their cloisters, and when the Bishop of Lincoln read his bull on that subject to the convent of Elstow, we hear that "some of the nuns, in disobedience to these injunctions, hurled the said statute at his back and over his head, and the prioress with all the sisters seemed to agree with those who threw it, following the bishop to the outer gate of the house and declaring unanimously that they would by no means observe that bull." When Edward I asserted his suzerainty over Scotland, and Boniface tried to defend the Scots by claiming that their country was under special protection of the papacy, his claim was indignantly repudiated by the English Parliament in 1301; and although the Scots under Wallace and Bruce continued their gallant war of independence, they on their part were later ready to brave a papal sentence of excommunication, in order to maintain their national liberties, in 1320, by the memorable Declaration of Arbroath. Later still, by the statutes of Provisors in 1351 and of Praemunire in 1353, the Parliament of England denied the papal right of appointment to English benefices, and forbade appeals from the national courts to the alien jurisdiction of the Roman See. Since Henry VIII was to use these statutes in defence of royal supremacy, the Reformation may be regarded as an ultimate reaction to the claims advanced by Boniface.

But for the moment his pontificate acquired an added lustre through the institution of the Holy Year or Jubilee in 1300, when special indulgences were offered to those who visited Rome and paid the appropriate devotion at its shrines. Boniface had intended that the event should take place only once a century, but it proved so rewarding that later Popes shortened the interval between Jubilees to fifty and finally to twenty-five years. A vast crowd of pious pilgrims flocked to Rome from all quarters, so eager to view the relics that many lost their lives in the press; immense money contributions were gathered into the papal treasury; and fortified by this loyal demonstration, Boniface began to measure swords again with France. When his legate was arrested on a charge of treason, he at once revoked his former concessions, and summoned Philip to attend in person or by representative at a Roman synod. His letter was publicly burnt at the French court, but was followed in 1302 by the strongly worded bull *Unam Sanctam*; the French clergy were called to Rome to sit in judgment on the rebellious king; and finally Boniface appointed 8th September, 1303, as the day on which he would depose Philip and lay his kingdom under interdict. To this the French monarch replied by a communication, beginning "Philip by the grace of God King of the French, to Boniface who pretends to be chief Pontiff, little greeting or none at all," and ending with the assertion that those who thought a sovereign subject to anyone else in matters temporal were fools and madmen. Meanwhile the States General of France were induced to urge the convocation of an Ecumenical Council, where the Pope might be deposed for heresy, simony and tyranny. Boniface purged himself on oath from the lurid charges laid against him; attacked the University of Paris, which seemed to be the centre of the learned opposition, by depriving it of the right to grant degrees in theology and law; and to forestall the threatened meeting of a Council, declared that it could only be summoned by a Pope. But Philip had his agents in Italy, William of Nogaret and Sciarra Colonna, who entered Anagni at the head of a band of mercenaries, and there captured Boniface on the day before he had promised to depose their king. He was vilely abused, struck and manhandled, and although rescued three days later, he died within a month from shock. It was a staggering reversal of Canossa that conditions in the four-

teenth century produced. A later wit summed up the career of
Boniface by saying that he "came in like a fox, ruled like a lion
and died like a dog." Dante, who had been among the crowd of
pilgrims at the Roman Jubilee, consigned him, as "chief of the
new Pharisees," to a particularly painful part of hell.

France had now assumed the mantle of the defunct Hohen
staufen as the papacy's chief secular opponent, and for the remainder of the century the Popes were largely obliged to follow
French dictation. Benedict XI, who ruled for less than a year, was
naturally forced to annul the decrees against Philip, but he refused
to join in vilifying the posthumous reputation of his predecessor.
On Benedict's death Philip determined to secure the election of
an outright Francophile. Through the intrigues of the French
cardinals, the Archbishop of Bordeaux was elected and enthroned as Pope Clement V in 1305. Significantly enough the
ceremony took place not at Rome but at Lyons, and it was
attended by King Philip in person; he had extracted a pledge from
the new Pontiff to reconcile France with the Church, to allow a
levy of tithes from the clergy, and to investigate the charges
against Boniface. In 1309 Clement removed his residence to
Avignon, thus inaugurating the so-called Babylonian Captivity of
the papacy, which lasted until 1377; though Avignon was technically within the domains of the Pope's vassal, the King of
Naples, it lay too near the French frontier for independent action
to be possible. Twelve French cardinals were created, to give
their nation a preponderance in the Sacred College, while in 1311
the bull *Rex Gloriae* asserted that France now occupied the place
of Israel as God's chosen people. Meanwhile a legal inquiry into
the life and conduct of Boniface had begun, but Clement was
unwilling to have the papacy still further degraded, and Philip
agreed to drop proceedings in return for the suppression of the
Templars. His exchequer, desperately short of funds, could be
replenished by confiscating the banks of that wealthy Order, and
a convenient pretext was supplied by popular rumours of lewd
and idolatrous practices performed in secret by the knights. Some
individuals may indeed have been contaminated by long residence
in the East, but there can be little doubt that the Order as a whole
was guiltless. However, an apostate Templar called Roffo promised Philip to reveal these dark abominations; he said that at
initiation each novice was compelled to deny Christ and spit upon
the cross, that they worshipped an idol with a cat's head, called
Baphomet, whom they anointed with the fat of a slaughtered
child, that they were encouraged to practise unnatural vice among
themselves, that the officers, though laymen, granted absolution,

that the words of consecration were omitted in the service of the mass, and that the Order had often betrayed Christian armies, especially that of King Louis, to the Moslems. There was a sudden arrest of leading Templars, including the Grand Master Jacques de Molay, who had been beguiled into bringing the Order's movable treasures home with him from Cyprus. Confessions were extracted from some of the victims by savage and prolonged torture; but the statements showed a suspicious similarity of phrasing, and others stoutly maintained their innocence. Clement at first protested at the cruel irregularity of the procedure, deposing the Dominican inquisitor William Imbert from his office; but to stop the process against Boniface he eventually abandoned the Templars to their fate; and although the Council of Vienne in 1311 thought the evidence insufficient for condemnation, the Pope on his own authority dissolved the Order in the following year. Many of its members had already perished at the stake. De Molay, having withdrawn a previous confession, was slowly roasted to death in 1314, and as he expired he is said to have summoned Philip and Clement to meet him within a year at the judgment seat of God. The story may be apocryphal; but the summons was fulfilled.

Though politically impotent, the Avignon Popes were distinguished by a patronage of art and letters which foreshadowed the outward splendour of the Renaissance papacy. Boniface had founded the Roman University of the Sapienza in 1303; Clement prompted the Council of Vienne in 1311 to establish chairs of Oriental languages; Avignon itself was beautified with costly buildings, and the brilliant profligacy of its court was described from personal experience by Petrarch. But such extravagance demanded money, of which Popes were in no less need than kings. Revenues became all the more difficult to collect after 1337, when the Hundred Years' War began between France and England, and by its departure from Rome the papacy had cut itself off from the normal sources of its income. Indeed, Rome became a centre of anti-papal feeling, so that in 1347 Cola di Rienzo there set up a short-lived Republic, with a devotion to the classical Roman heritage which was echoed by Renaissance scholars of the following century. Lacking money the Popes resorted to novel methods of finance. Though simple in his personal tastes and strongly opposed to nepotism, John XXII was the first Pope really to organize the marketing of grace on a sound financial basis. Officials of the Curia, now rewarded with a fixed salary, paid a fixed price to obtain their posts, and simony was thus virtually legalized. Clement V had vainly tried to abolish the custom of giving tips

and fees to the papal entourage, but under John there was a
regular price-list for special favours, ostensibly to remunerate the
secretarial work involved; money could buy a permit for almost
any privilege—exemption from fasts, legitimization of children,
marriage within the prohibited degrees, together with such wholly
secular matters as a change of seal or the right to issue coins.
Crippling taxes were levied from the clergy, particularly in
France since that country was the most readily accessible. Annates,
the first year's income from a benefice, were demanded for the
papal treasury. Procurations, which originally had been expenses
paid to a bishop when he visited his diocese, were now diverted
to the papacy; episcopal visitations naturally ceased, and the
central funds were enriched at the expense of local discipline.
Bureaucracy with its attendant evils grew apace, while Avignon
concerned itself increasingly with centralization and finance. Of
particular importance was the bull *Unigenitus*, published in 1343
by Clement VI and later elaborated with a view to the Jubilee of
1350, which gave official sanction to belief in a Treasury of
Merits, acquired by Christ and the saints, and available for dispensation by the Pope.

These trends of the new age did not however pass without
strong protest. Having antagonized the Franciscans, John XXII
found himself opposed by the Emperor Louis of Bavaria, whose
cause was ably championed by the pens of both Occam and
Marsiglio of Padua. As a spiritual Franciscan, Occam believed
that reform could only come by cutting down the vast wealth of
churchmen; he wished to draw a sharp distinction between Church
and world, thus depriving the Pope of all secular authority; and
he regarded the papacy as a merely human institution, although
he would have been prepared to accept it in a limited and constitutional form. In his view, however, "only Scripture and the
beliefs of the Universal Church are of absolute validity." For
Church government he desired to see large powers given to the
laity and their representatives, amongst whom he was sufficiently
advanced to include women, and in his appeal from Pope to
General Council he anticipated the stand later to be made by
Luther. Views even more radical were advanced in the *Defensor
Pacis*, published by Marsiglio in 1324 with the probable collabora-
tion of John of Jandun, and designed to promote peace by defin-
ing once and for all the disputed jurisdiction of Papacy and
Empire. If any individual deserves to be called the morning star
of the Reformation, Marsiglio has as good a claim as others to
that title, though his works have been strangely neglected in the
modern world. His most revolutionary idea consisted of the

proposition that in human affairs the people is the ultimate
sovereign. The Church comprises, not the hierarchy, but the
universitas fidelium, the whole body of Christian people, whose lay
representatives or rulers have power to excommunicate, to exercise discipline, to appoint and dismiss the clergy. The sole clerical
function is to preach the gospel and administer the sacraments;
bishops and presbyters are fundamentally of equal status; Peter
had no primacy over the other apostles, nor is it certain that he
was ever Bishop of Rome; and the Pope, whose position is that
of a mere president, derives his alleged authority from the grant
made to him by the State in Constantine's Donation. The Church
in fact enjoys no rights or property other than what the State
may be pleased to bestow upon it, and what the State may at any
time withdraw. Marsiglio was naturally condemned by John
XXII; but in answer to his theories the papal apologist Augustus
Triumphus could do little more than repeat the bare assertion
that on earth the Pope's authority is conterminous with that of
God.

By now the lines of debate had been clearly drawn, and the
varied strands of medieval Christianity, catholic, liberal and
evangelical, were to separate still further until the final breach
occurred. The year 1350 marks a turning-point, for by destroying
so many of the population the Black Death brought decisive
changes in society and human life. But there were already pointers
to an altered world. The Renaissance had blossomed into early
spring; the forces of nationalism, even of democracy, were working; in England Thomas Bradwardine had revived the study of
Augustine which was to play so vital a part in the development of
Wycliffe, and Richard Fitzralph spoke of dominion by grace in
terms that might almost have been Lollard. Into this strange
universe of new ideas Dante did not enter fully, for he died in
1321 at the age of fifty-six, and his eyes were fixed less on the
future than on the ancient glories of imperial Rome. Yet his very
timelessness equipped him to act as a link between the old world
and the new. As he wrote his *Divine Comedy* in Peter Damian's
cell at Fonte Avellana, his mind returned to that earlier and perhaps idealized period, before Europe had been troubled by the
thunderbolts of Hildebrand, when the several powers ordained
by God had worked in harmonious co-operation for the peace of
men. And so the establishment of universal peace became the
burden of his labours as poet, politician and philosopher. Into the
chaos of human affairs order must be introduced, an order based
on sharp distinction between the various spheres; the Church must
not seek to rule the Empire, nor must theology dictate to reason;

for the Emperor, fortified by his divine right, is called to promote
the reign of justice, while the Church, purged through acceptance
of Franciscan poverty, should confine itself to the things eternal
and unseen. But as he surveyed the life and times of Boniface, he
saw a Church corrupted by wealth and power, an Empire broken
and humiliated, his own beloved Italy enslaved by foreigners;
pondering the inscrutable certainty of divine judgment, he found
consolation in the Augustan harmonies of Virgil, and for guidance
toward heaven looked to Beatrice as a symbol of hallowed love.

More than once, Dante alludes with obvious pride to the
ancient and supposedly Roman origins of his family. To his
father, who had grown rich through money-lending, he refers
but seldom, and home circumstances seem to have made him a
lonely child; at all events his mother died when he was young,
and nine children were born to a second marriage before his father
also died when Dante was eighteen. A year later he married
Gemma Donati, to whom he had been betrothed at the age of
twelve, but always in the background there was the memory of
Beatrice, whom he had seen from time to time since boyhood and
for whom he conceived a romantic and undying devotion. The
Florence of his youth was a gay city, enlivened by occasional wars
in which Dante was proud to play his part. It was an artistic city,
with Cimabue and later Giotto as its painters; it was a home of
culture, where he could study rhetoric and politics under the
teaching of Brunetto Latini; and above all it sided with the
Guelfs, that strict, sober, middle-class party which tended to
support the Church against the Empire. Though there were many
shades of Guelf opinion, and Florence was itself torn by the
strife between Blacks and Whites, the party may be fairly regarded
as puritan, at least in contrast to the cavalier Ghibellines, and it
was this latent puritanism of the Guelfs in Florence that was later
to welcome the stern preaching of Savonarola. Dante entered
politics in 1295, enrolling himself for that purpose in the guild of
doctors and chemists which, with medieval comprehensiveness,
admitted philosophers to membership. In an Italian city-state it
was natural for a philosophical poet to be also an active politician.
His studies, which had been pursued for a time at Bologna, were
now continued both at the Franciscan Santa Croce and under the
Dominicans of Santa Maria Novella. Philosophically he stood
nearer to Dominican thought, but he regarded Francis as the
ideal saint and towards the end of his life became a Franciscan
tertiary. At the same time, he did not neglect Virgil, the Latin
poets and the Provençal troubadours, with an eclectic delight in
every achievement of human genius which prompted him to scale

new heights in the literature of his native tongue. The power of malignant rhetoric at his command is shown by the tenson in which he engaged with his former friend Forese; but of that he soon repented, turning to a loftier theme.

In 1300 he attended the Roman Jubilee, where he was as much enthralled by the city's classical grandeur as disgusted by its present worldliness. The month of June saw him installed a member of the Priorate or governing body of Florence, in which capacity he came into immediate collision with Pope Boniface. Three Black Guelfs, bankers to the Roman Curia, had been condemned for treason, and despite papal protests their condemnation was confirmed by the new government; three times in a single day Dante blocked a proposal to grant the Pope subsidies for war; and when Boniface in desperation sent Charles of Valois to impose his will on Florence, the White Guelfs fell through their timidity and Dante was exiled with his friends. He spent the remainder of his life as a wanderer in the North Italian courts, probably with a spell at Paris University, and in September 1321, shortly after completing his great poem, he died of malarial fever at Ravenna.

His political convictions are expounded in the treatise *On Monarchy*, so anti-papal in tone that it was put upon the Index, publicly burnt, and finally condemned at Trent. Surveying the whole field of history, he traced God's hand in the destinies of Rome no less than Israel; in other words, he proclaimed Romans equally with Jews to be a chosen people. "Of all things that work to bless mankind," he stated at the outset (I, 4), "peace is best;" and he continued (I, 16), "at no time has the world everywhere been quiet, except under the divine Augustus who ruled alone in the perfection of absolute monarchy." At that single period of universal peace, described by St. Paul as "the fulness of the times," Christ chose to be born, thereby sanctioning the *Pax Augusta* of the Roman Empire; and He likewise sanctioned its justice by suffering death under sentence of a Roman magistrate, who represented the divinely established rule of universal law, since "all mankind was punished in the flesh of Christ, and none could be a proper judge unless he had jurisdiction over all mankind" (II, 13). Hence it follows that Empire no less than Church is directly ordained by God; the two powers are equal and co-ordinate in their separate spheres of authority; and just as the Supreme Pontiff is alone competent "to guide men to eternal life according to the truths of revelation," so the Emperor must be unhindered in his proper task of "providing mankind with happiness in this world by the principles of reason" (III, 16). There are indeed,

Dante at once continues, "certain matters in which the Roman
Prince is subject to the Roman Pontiff, since mortal well-being is
in a sense subordinate to that well-being which is immortal."
But the claims of the papacy to temporal dominion are dismissed
with short and acid syllogisms, and Dante clings to his view that
a strong Empire is essential to human felicity and peace. Sovereignty is by nature inalienable, so that Constantine could not
bestow those rights which the papacy claimed from his Donation;
nor could the Church properly receive them, since she is tied to
the example of Christ's poverty. Religion will not mix with state-
craft, and the one hope for the world is that a Franciscan Pope
should mind his spiritual concerns, while an absolute monarch, as
the embodiment of justice, guides the mundane affairs of men.
Dante seems to have regarded Celestine's resignation as invalid,
with the result that Boniface was no true Pope; at the same time
he thought the Empire to have been vacant since the death of
Frederick II, until the appointment in 1308 of a likely candidate,
Henry of Luxembourg, afforded him a short-lived gleam of hope.

Although he very definitely sought to limit the pretensions of
the papacy, Dante was an orthodox Catholic in his strictly theological ideas. As early as 1556 men were treating him as a precursor
of the Reformation, but in the field of doctrine that is demonstrably untrue; for he accepted the divine origin of the papacy, the
whole round of contemporary beliefs on Church and sacraments,
and it was only practical abuses that he criticized. None the less
his criticisms are always trenchant. He turns purgatory into a
place of expectation, where souls gladly receive the cleansing that
will at last fit them for the sight of God; such a scheme leaves no
room for papal indulgences, and in paradise St. Peter blushes at
the false privileges that are sold under his seal (*Par.* 27, 52-4).
Indeed, heaven itself turns red with shame when Peter catalogues
the corruptions of the papacy, and although Dante finds numerous
Popes in hell and purgatory, there is only one, the unimportant
John XXI, whom he actually sees in heaven. He would have
rejoiced in the salvation of righteous pagans, but here current
dogma was too strong for him except in the single case of Trajan,
where an old legend asserted that that Emperor had been saved
through the prayers of Pope Gregory the Great. But papal sentences are by no means always executed; Manfred, the bastard son
of Frederick II, had died excommunicate and yet is placed in
purgatory, since pontifical curses cannot reach beyond the grave.
In his deep personal allegiance to the Virgin, even more perhaps
than elsewhere, Dante is the typical medieval churchman. He
loves to hear the ringing of the Angelus, a devotion said to have

Q

been introduced by Gregory IX and extended by John XXII. To
Dante's mind Mary is symbol, source and medium of prevenient
grace; here he closely follows Bernard of Clairvaux who, like
himself, had lost his mother at an impressionable age; and it is on
Bernard's lips that he places the great prayer of *Paradiso* 33 to the
"Virgin Mother, daughter of thine own Son." But despite the
exuberance of his Marian devotion, Dante apparently believes that
Christ alone was born into this world without sin (*Inferno* 34, 115),
and in thus rejecting Mary's immaculate conception he seems to
have felt the restraining influence of Aquinas. He has a sincere
love and wide knowledge of the Bible, quoting Augustine to the
effect that "faith will falter if scriptural authority be shaken" (*De
Monarchia* III, 4); and in the same passage he accepts a high doctrine of inspiration, declaring that "though there are many re-
porters of the words of God, yet there is only One who tells them
what to write, even God Himself, who has condescended to
reveal His will to us through the pens of many writers." None
the less, Dante believes that, as well as canonical Scripture, conciliar decrees and patristic writings are inspired; it is only the
decretals of the Popes that he places on a lower and definitely
human level, and here his strict sense of justice made him so
severely critical that he would doubtless have applauded Luther's
attack upon indulgences. It was presumably this puritan severity
that prompted Horace Walpole to describe him as "extravagant,
absurd, disgusting—in short, a Methodist parson in Bedlam;" but
in his own day, Friar Guido Vernani contented himself with
calling Dante an Averroist.

The election of Henry of Luxembourg may well have been the
event that inspired Dante to embark on his *Divine Comedy*. He
had just been reading an apocalyptic book, filled with dreams of
spiritual regeneration, by the Franciscan Ubertino da Casale; and
the major theme of his own poem is the same—regeneration of
human society, portrayed in the regeneration of himself. On Good
Friday, under the Easter moon of the Year of Jubilee, he pictures
himself wandering through a darkened wood, in terror of lion,
leopard and she-wolf, when Virgil appears and offers to guide
him in a better way. There follows a pilgrimage through hell and
purgatory, where Dante experiences a cleansing of his sins; and
then in heaven, closed to the unbaptized Roman, Beatrice is substituted as his guide. Throughout, the poem is studded with the
vivid sights and sounds of ordinary life: the aged tailor peering
to thread his needle, the wet logs sputtering on the hearth, the
darting lizard, the snail drawing in her horns. Science as well as
nature is used in illustration, and discourses on Ptolemaic astron-

omy supplement the beauty of the shooting star. But more in-
teresting and more important are the people, chiefly contemporaries, who throng the pages and by their several fates illustrate the
inexorable justice of the ways of God. Thanks to his alleged sympathy with Monophysites, Pope Anastasius II is in hell for heresy.
Nicholas III, condemned for simony, awaits the imminent arrival
of Boniface VIII and Clement V. In purgatory Hadrian V and
Martin IV expiate their respective sins of greed and gluttony. At
the lowest bottom of the infernal pit Satan eternally chews Judas;
but the devil has three mouths, and the other two are occupied by
Brutus and Cassius who, in attacking Caesar, laid hands upon the
Lord's anointed.

In heaven also there are surprising bedfellows, for Bonaventura
is accompanied by Joachim of Fiore, and Siger of Brabant follows
close beside Aquinas. The Angelic Doctor had fought the arch-
Averroist on earth, but Siger is apparently redeemed for cham-
pioning men's right to think; and if Joachim became extrava-
gantly spiritual he had at least marked out the pathway of Franciscan life. Paradise is in truth a place where earth's misunder-
standings are transcended. It is Bonaventura who comes forward
to praise Dominic, and Aquinas who tells the glory of Francis.
Anselm is there with Chrysostom and Donatus, while Augustine
takes his place with Benedict as the founder of a mighty Order.
The Venerable Bede joins Richard of St. Victor among those who
were afire with contemplation. Bernard stands as faithful liege-
man to the Virgin, Damian still speaks with scorn of prelates
fattening on the Church. Stout soldiers of God are gathered,
Charlemagne along with Roland, and Joshua with Judas Macca-
baeus. In the great assembly of the just, Hebrews and Christians
are united, with saints of either Testament in equal number;
Adam and Eve, their primal sin forgiven, sit beside patriarchs,
prophets and apostles; and while the hymn rises to its climax,
Dante is vouchsafed a fleeting foretaste of the Beatific Vision, as
his soul is drawn into that Love which pulses through the
universe,

L'amor che move il sole e l'altre stelle.

BIBLIOGRAPHY

For studies of the general background, reference should be made to the *Cambridge Medieval History* and the French *Histoire de l'Eglise* edited by A. Fliche and V. Martin; the latter work contains a full account of continental literature on the subject. J. P. Migne's *Patrology* (Latin and Greek), though now superseded in many parts, still provides the most complete collection of original sources up to the time of Innocent III; a selection of the more important source-documents, translated into English, will be found in B. J. Kidd's *Documents illustrative of the History of the Church*, Vol. III (1941), and more briefly in H. Bettenson's *Documents of the Christian Church* (1943). Though not infallible, F. L. Cross's *Oxford Dictionary of the Christian Church* (1958) is a most useful work of ready reference, particularly for its up-to-date bibliographical material. The student should have access to a good atlas, such as *Muir's Historical Atlas Medieval and Modern* (eighth edition, 1952).

I. General Works

Adams, H., *Mont St. Michel and Chartres* (1913): illuminating, but not entirely accurate, on the wider implications of Norman and Gothic architecture.

Baynes, N. H., and Moss, H. St. L. B. (ed.), *Byzantium* (1948).

Brooke, Z. N., *The English Church and the Papacy from the Conquest to the Reign of John* (1931).

Butler, C., *Benedictine Monachism* (second edition, 1924).

Coulton, G. G., *Five Centuries of Religion* (four volumes, 1923–50).

Deanesly, Margaret, *A History of the Medieval Church* (1925, and many times reprinted).

History of Early Medieval Europe 476–911 (second edition, 1960).

Duckett, E. S., *Anglo-Saxon Saints and Scholars* (1947).

Duke, J. A., *History of the Church of Scotland to the Reformation* (1937).

Dvornik, F., *The Photian Schism* (1948).

Flick, A. C., *The Decline of the Medieval Church* (two volumes, 1930): a good general account, sometimes wrong in detail.

Gilson, E., *La Philosophie au Moyen-Age* (1922 and subsequent editions).

The Spirit of Medieval Philosophy (English trans., 1936).

History of Christian Philosophy in the Middle Ages (1954).

Graham, Rose, *English Ecclesiastical Studies* (1929).

Haskins, C. H., *The Renaissance of the Twelfth Century* (1928).

Jones, R. M., *Studies in Mystical Religion* (1909).

Laistner, M. W. L., *Thought and Letters in Western Europe*, 500–900 (second edition, 1957).

Latourette, K. S., *A History of the Expansion of Christianity*, Vol. II (1947).

Lea, H. C., *History of the Inquisition* (three volumes, 1888): highly critical.

Levison, W., *England and the Continent in the Eighth Century* (1946).

McIlwain, C. H., *Growth of Political Thought in the West* (1932).

Maclear, G. F., *History of Christian Missions during the Middle Ages* (1863): an old book, but not yet replaced.

MacNaught, J. C., *The Celtic Church and the See of Peter* (1927).

Moorman, J. R. H., *Church Life in England in the Thirteenth Century* (1945).

   A History of the Church in England (1953).

Pantin, W. A., *The English Church in the Fourteenth Century* (1955).

Poole, R. L., *Illustrations of Medieval Thought and Learning* (second edition, 1920).

Rashdall, H., *Universities of Europe in the Middle Ages* (three volumes, revised edition, 1936).

Runciman, S., *A History of the Crusades* (three volumes, 1951–54)

   The Eastern Schism (1955).

   The Medieval Manichee (1947).

Smalley, Beryl, *The Study of the Bible in the Middle Ages* (second edition, 1952).

Smith, A. L., *Church and State in the Middle Ages* (1913).

Southern, R. W., *The Making of the Middle Ages* (1953).

Stenton, F. M., *Anglo-Saxon England* (1943).

Taylor, H. O., *The Mediaeval Mind* (two volumes 1911).

Turberville, A. S., *Mediaeval Heresy and the Inquisition* (1920).

Ullmann, W., *The Growth of Papal Government in the Middle Ages* (1955).

Waddell, Helen, *The Wandering Scholars* (1927 and subsequent editions).

Whitney, J. P., *Hildebrandine Essays* (1932).

II. BIOGRAPHICAL STUDIES

Abelard: J. G. Sikes (1932), E. Gilson (English trans., 1953).

Alcuin: C. J. B. Gaskoin (1904), E. S. Duckett (1951), L. Wallach (1959).

Anselm: R. W. Church (1870 and subsequent editions), J. McIntyre (1954, an analysis of the *Cur Deus Homo*).

Aquinas: M. C. D'Arcy (1930), A. Walz (English trans., 1951), K. Foster (1959).

Bede: A. H. Thompson, ed. (1935).

Berengarius: A. J. Macdonald (1930).

Bernard: E. Vacandard (French, two volumes, 1895), W. Williams (1935), B. S. James (1957).

Boniface VIII: T. S. R. Boase (1933).

Boniface (Winfrid): G. F. Browne (1910), G. W. Greenaway (1955).

Dante: R. W. Church (1850 and many reprints), E. Moore (Studies, second series, 1899), E. Gilson (English trans., 1948), U. Cosmo (Handbook, English trans., 1950).

Dominic: B. Jarrett (1924), P. Mandonnet (English trans., 1944).

Dunstan: J. A. Robinson (1923).

Erigena: A. Gardner (1900), H. Bett (1925).

Francis: P. Sabatier (English trans. 1894), Father Cuthbert (1914), G. K. Chesterton (1923), J. R. H. Moorman (Sources 1940; short popular life, 1950), L. Sherley-Price (1959).

Gregory the Great: F. H. Dudden (two volumes, 1905), P. Batiffol (English trans., 1929).

Hildebrand: A. Fliche (French, 1920), A. J. Macdonald (1932), J. P. Whitney (1932).

Innocent III: A. Luchaire (French, six volumes, 1904–8), L. E. Binns (1931).

Lanfranc: A. J. Macdonald (1926).

Langton, Stephen: F. M. Powicke (1928).

Louis IX: H. Wallon (French, two volumes, 1875), F. Perry (1901), E. Wedgwood (1906, a translation of Joinville's Memoirs).

Lull, Raymond: E. A. Peers (1929; and short popular life, 1947).

Waldensians: J. A. Wylie (1880, now largely outdated), W. F. Adeney in Hastings's *Encyclopaedia of Religion and Ethics*, Vol. XII (1921), L. Christiani (article, "Vaudois") in *Dictionnaire de Théologie Catholique* XV (1950).

Willibrord: A. Grieve (1923).

INDEX